To activists of the past, present, and future,
especially those I agree with

Contents

Preface • ix
Introduction • xi

I. The problem of guns in America • 1

GUNS ARE KILLING US • 1
What is our alternative?
Peace is a choice
America's ethos of violence
Where is violence a problem?

VIEWING THE PROBLEM CLOSE-UP • 11
Abdul's story
Learning from another death

WHY DO PEOPLE HAVE GUNS? • 16
Alienation leads people to own guns
What's the emotional appeal of guns?
Are sportsmen a different kind of gun owner?
Can we keep dangerous people from having guns?
Guns are a hazard in anyone's hands

THE DEMOGRAPHICS OF GUNS AND VIOLENCE • 34
Guns and gender
Why aren't women drawn to guns?
Are women's voices being heard?
How racism enters the discussion
How race issues intersect with economics and class
How do blacks view gun ownership?
How do other minorities feel about guns?
Does religion enter into the debate?

IS VIOLENCE AN AMERICAN CHARACTERISTIC? • 54
American entertains itself with violence
Violence pervades our speech
How are we raising our children?
What are we doing that allows the violence to continue?
Another shooting hits home
Who is to blame?

II. What can be done to fix the problem • 69

HOW GOVERNMENT CAN HELP • 69
Regulatory solutions
Private lawsuits could hold people accountable
What have other countries done?
How do gun guys envision a gun-free America?

THE CONSTITUTIONAL AMENDMENT OPTION • 79
Our governments' failure to act
Why focus on the Second Amendment?
Is gun ownership a God-given right?
Hiding behind the Second Amendment
How does the Constitution say the Second Amendment can be repealed?
Other amendments that succeeded
Has anyone ever tried to repeal the Second Amendment before?

III. The Constitution and the people • 103

HOW AMERICANS VIEW THEIR CONSTITUTION • 103
The Constitution as sacred text
The many functions the Constitution serves

THE SUPREME COURT'S ROLE IN CHANGING THE CONSTITUTION • 112
The Supreme Court and the Second Amendment
How the Supreme Court avoids changing the Constitution
Why the Supreme Court declines cases
Approaches to constitutional interpretation
The will of the people and the law of the land

THE SUPREME COURT'S RADICAL SHIFT • 124
How was the Supreme Court persuaded to change the Second Amendment?
The dark origins of the Second Amendment
Pro-gun explanations for the Second Amendment
Textual origins of the Second Amendment
The Supreme Court reanimated a dead Second Amendment

THE IRRELEVANCE OF THE SECOND AMENDMENT TODAY • 139
Guns as a right of individuals
Guns for personal defense
Defending our country from tyranny
Will gun owners save America?
What does stop tyranny?
America's wars against tyranny
Will we need guns to fight the next Hitler?

IV. Overcoming fear and moving forward • 161

GUNS AND FEAR • 161
The gun industry thrives on fear
How can we overcome fear?
What *should* we be afraid of?
Distortion and manipulation
Why is the gun industry so successful in making us feel afraid?

Seeking comfort from guns instead of from people
But some of us are not afraid

ALLIES AND OPPONENTS OF REPEAL • 172
What can we learn from the NRA?
Our organizational limitations
What we are doing right
Who is on which side?
Are there any reasonable gun guys?

WHAT'S THE PLAN? • 191
Lessons from previous amendment efforts
What happens if we don't do anything?
How long will it take?
Why repeal is likely to happen
Where can we find inspiration?
But the Constitution is so hard to amend
How repeal will affect gun ownership
The time is now

Appendix • 209
Second Amendment
Proposed Repeal Amendment

Notes • 211

Preface

My daughter and son-in-law threw their bodies over their 11-month-old son to protect him. They had heard gunshots in the neighborhood before, but never this loud. This time they sensed that the shots were so close that the bullets might come right through their window.

The shots were fired from a car two doors down from their home. It's a nice enough neighborhood. The homes are close to each other, and well-kept. Neighbors say hello when they meet. Some people tend gardens or relax on their decks. I visited with my daughter and her family a few months before the shooting and felt safe walking the streets. When she had told me back then that she had heard gunshots in the area, I was disturbed, but not surprised. People in cities all across our country occasionally hear gunshots. So do people in rural areas where there are open-air shooting ranges and where people go hunting.

The police say that it looked like the shooting was gang-related. The people who were the intended targets were inside a car when the shooters drove by and opened fire. One of the victims was taken to the hospital. He had been hit by several bullets. The other victim fled on foot through the neighborhood. It appears he had been wounded, too.

But many shots had been fired. Some of them hit cars that were parked outside my daughter's house. A couple of bullets hit her neighbor's house, and one went through the window. The police responded very quickly, but they must not have been too interested in where all the bullets lodged. They barely looked around. Just another drive-by shooting. Except this time, it was my daughter, my son-in-law, and my grandchild who were within range of the bullets that were flying in their general direction. This time, my daughter and son-in-law used their bodies to shield their baby. None of them was hurt, but they could have been. Just three days before, another mother had been shot dead in front of her children—the victim of a stray bullet from another drive-by shooting—just a few miles from where my daughter lives.

My daughter didn't immediately tell my wife and me about the shooting because she thought we would worry. She knew I was finishing the work on this book when the shooting happened and that I was sensitized to the issue of gun violence. A new mother herself, she has come to understand that all parents worry about their children.

I hope everyone who reads this book is worried—not just about their own loved ones, but about everyone's.

Introduction

We don't need guns in America, and we'd be better off without the Second Amendment.

Almost everyone seems to feel that major changes are needed in our country. Although well-intentioned people have differing ideas on what most urgently needs to be changed, this book is about one important change that must be made if our country is to survive as anything resembling the country we have grown fond of. We must eliminate the violence that is destroying our sense that we live in a safe place.

The conundrum is that the things we most need to fix are those that seem impossible to fix. This is certainly true of violence. Many people throw up their hands when asked what can be done to fix this problem. They know what needs to be done, at least in general terms, but they don't believe that we can do what is needed. They think the situation is beyond anyone's control.

Most people don't own guns and don't want to own them. Most people understand that guns are designed to kill people and that guns actually do kill people. In private, they will say that they would like to get rid of all the guns, and that they would be willing to repeal the Second Amendment. But few people will say so in public. They think it would be impossible to get rid of the guns because the Second Amendment guarantees the right to own guns. And they think that it would be impossible to get rid of the Second Amendment because so many people own guns. The circle of discouragement is complete.

Even the mainstream gun control groups are reluctant to categorically speak out against guns. Their spokespeople are all quick to deny that they want to take away anyone's guns. They pose at rifle ranges, holding guns and shooting at targets, to prove that they are not against guns. Former Congresswoman Gabrielle "Gabby" Giffords, who was shot in the head while talking with constituents, later posed for pictures at a firing range while shooting a handgun.[1]

Is it any wonder that the National Rifle Association (NRA), the preeminent lobbying group for gun manufacturers, wins most of its legislative initiatives to put more guns into the hands of more people? They are virtually unopposed. Many of the organizations that we might expect to be working to reduce the number of Americans who own guns and the number of guns those Americans own disavow that they are working toward these goals.

In these pages we will take a look at gun violence in contemporary America, the reasons why people think they are helpless to fix the problem, and how we can accomplish what needs to be done. My orientation is not academic. Rather, I view these issues in light of my experience as an activist who has more than once taken on challenges that seemed impossible, frequently failed, but occasionally achieved some level of success. These experiences have taught me that seemingly impossible goals are the ones that are most worth pursuing, the ones we learn the most from, and the ones that are most satisfying to achieve. It turns out that Don Quixote was right. As long as there are windmills, we must tilt at them. Sometimes they tumble.

I. The problem of guns in America

GUNS ARE KILLING US

In America, guns are the prevalent lethal expression of personal violence. In other times, people have used all kinds of weapons to kill one another. Spears, rocks, swords, arrows, and bludgeons all do the job. In modern times and in other countries, people generally use guns, too, but on occasion they use machetes, explosives, and other weapons to kill one another. But here, guns are the thing.

Guns kill about 30,000 Americans each year—year in and year out. They wound another 60,000 or so each year, and the injuries are often quite serious. Guns make some people paraplegic or quadriplegic. They can leave their victims in terrible lifelong pain. They render people depressed and subject to violent rages. They may rob them of the ability to talk or to see, hear, smell, taste, and touch. They leave some people unable to use a toilet or unable to make love. Since 1960, more Americans have been murdered by guns than were killed in World War I, World War II, the Korean War, the Vietnam War, the Gulf War, and the wars in Iraq and Afghanistan combined.[2]

Guns are the leading cause of childhood death in some communities.[3] More than 7,000 children are hospitalized for gunshot wounds each year in the US. More than 1,100 of them have traumatic brain and/or spinal cord injuries. About 450 of them die in the hospital. Another 3,000 children die from gunshots before they get to the hospital.[4]

Guns set in motion disabilities that can kill people years after they were shot. Occasionally a news story will report, for example, that someone died from a gunshot wound that was inflicted 20 years or more ago. What they mean is that for years, the person suffered to some degree from depression, restricted mobility, or other problems that eventually led to the person's death. The medical examiner, as a matter of science, not politics, objectively reports that the cause of death was gunshot. In simple terms, if the person hadn't been shot, the person wouldn't have died that way at that time. James Brady, President Ronald Reagan's press secretary, is among the most famous of such victims. He died from gunshot wounds more than 30 years after he was shot during an assassination attempt on the President.[5]

But the damage that guns inflict is not just suffered by the people whose bodies are pierced, torn, ripped, exploded, and shattered by bullets. Guns also injure mothers and fathers of victims who have to care for their injured offspring, or bury them. Guns terrify bystanders who observe shootings and narrowly escape being shot themselves. Guns traumatize children of victims who have to deal with the loss of a parent's companionship and guidance. Guns deprive spouses of their life partners. Guns destroy marriages when spouses can't reconcile the different ways they cope with a loss due to gun violence.

Guns also destroy communities, when shopkeepers are slain or forced out of business by shootings, and when people are afraid to attend church services because they perceive that the neighborhood has gotten too dangerous to be in or travel to. Guns destroy communities when school programs are canceled because students' safety cannot be assured, and when police, fire, and ambulance services are reluctant to respond to emergencies in neighborhoods where they don't feel they will be safe.

Violence can destroy entire countries. In our times, violence has led to the complete collapse of civil order in a number of parts of the world. Within neighborhoods and among nations, gun violence is a daily destroyer of all that people hold dear.

What is our alternative?

In order to appreciate the need to take action against violence, it is helpful to think about the alternative. In simple terms, the absence of violence is peace. People who study peace would say that peace is much, much more. But to get a start on thinking about peace, let's look at what a peaceful world would look like.

Peace is being able to walk through any neighborhood without worrying that someone will shoot you. It is knowing that you need not be concerned that where you park your car could endanger your life. It is knowing that you don't have to be afraid that a parent or partner might beat you. Peace is seeing a police officer and not thinking you might be chased if you turned and walked the other way.

Peace is going to school without needing to act tough to keep other kids from pushing you around. Peace is being able to stay late to talk with a teacher who isn't afraid to be in your neighborhood after school.

Peace is getting off the bus or subway at any stop without fear that you are in a "bad neighborhood." It is being able to attend any street fair or club you want. It is being able to wear any hat without worrying that its color might signal that you belong to the wrong gang.

Peace is being able to buy gasoline without paying in advance. It is shopping at convenience stores where the cashiers don't hide behind bullet-proof glass. It is being able to walk through a forest without wearing bright orange clothing so you won't be mistaken for a game animal. It is listening to the evening news without hearing a body count.

Peace is this, and more. But it is not everything.

Peace is not utopia. Peace can exist, temporarily, in very unpleasant conditions. If people are hungry, they can be at peace for a while, though impending starvation may push them over the precipice into violence. If people are discouraged, they can have peace, unless their desperation leads them to become violent. If people are repressed, peace can prevail, until the repression becomes intolerable.

For peace to prevail long-term, a community or larger society must provide a minimal level of sustenance for people. The people must feel that they are being treated with some measure of fairness. They must believe that mechanisms exist for resolving disputes without violence. They must have a degree of respect for the people they interact with and for the institutions that are in place.

For peace to exist, people must have a commitment to peace. They must understand what peace is and what it can do. They must understand what violence is and what its consequences are. They must have hope and faith. They must see peace as being preferable to violence, and they must believe that peaceful resolutions of conflicts can be as effective as violent resolutions. Many people do not share this belief. I recall sitting in a man's living room trying to persuade him that a peaceful solution could be found to a dispute he was having with his neighbor. While his young daughter listened, he scornfully and angrily said to me, "I suppose you believe in that harmony crap, too?" To him, living in harmony with his neighbors was inconceivable and not even desirable, and my contrary belief marked me as a fool.

Perhaps most of all, for peace to exist, people must respect life—something that America has a very questionable history of.

Peace is a choice

Whenever violence is one response we could choose in a situation, we should remember that peace is also an option. A good example took place in a school in Decatur, Georgia in August, 2013. A 20-year-old man who was armed with an assault rifle entered an elementary school and told the office clerk that he was going to kill himself and other people. He fired off at least one round inside the school and several outside. Eventually he surrendered to the police. No one was hurt, because instead of trying to attack the man, the clerk talked to him. She sympathized with the difficulties he told her he was having with his life. She told him that she had had tough times, too, but that everything turned out OK for her, and that it could for him as well. She used something much more powerful than any gun to help the man and protect the school children. She used her humanity.[6]

After the massacre at Sandy Hook Elementary School less than a year earlier, the NRA had launched a nationwide campaign to take advantage of the tragedy. The NRA's message was that people should carry guns so that if they ever had to deal with a gunman, they could simply shoot him and prevent him from injuring anyone. If the school clerk in Georgia had followed the NRA's advice, she might have been able to stop the gunman with her own gun. Or she might have gotten herself and a whole lot of other people killed. Instead, she talked to the man, and no one was hurt.

It must be conceded that the Georgia situation might not have turned out so well. The gunman might have rebuffed the clerk's attempt to pacify him and proceeded with his original plan to use his gun. So there is room for the pro-gun folks to argue that the clerk was being careless by taking a moment to attempt to resolve the situation peacefully. They might think that the more prudent course of action for the clerk to have taken would have been to try violence first and not bother to give peace a chance.

The pro-gun folks made exactly that argument after a gunman shot up a movie theater at Aurora, Colorado in July 2012, killing 12 people and injuring 70 others. They said that if everyone in the theater had been armed, someone could have stopped the shooter sooner. What they overlook is that armed theater patrons probably wouldn't have helped the situation at all and might have left a lot more people dead from all the crossfire. This was demonstrated after another mass shooting occurred in France. Shooters attacked the offices of Charlie Hebdo, a magazine that had published cartoons the shooters found offensive. Trying to prove that the massacre could have been prevented if the office workers had guns, a pro-gun group in Texas reenacted the shooting, giving the pretend office workers paint-ball guns. In the first reenactment, the armed office workers were shot while trying to defend themselves. The group then re-ran the simulation with the same result. They tried again and again, and each time the armed office workers were unable to prevent the massacre. In all but one of the re-enactments, the armed office workers themselves became targets of the attackers and were killed. The only armed office worker who survived in the simulations was one who ran away.[7]

A similar result was reached a few years earlier and recorded for public broadcast. After the mass-shooting at Northern Illinois University, ABC News simulated an attack on a class of college students. First, they taught college students how to carry concealed weapons and use them in an emergency. Then they staged the attack. As with the Texas simulations, the students who were carrying concealed handguns ended up getting shot and were unable to stop the attack.[8]

Gun advocates profess a belief that the violent solution is always the most prudent one, even though there are plenty of examples, like the Georgia instance, where the non-violent solution turned out to be optimal. Because we cannot know how any situation will turn out, the choice of violence must be based not on demonstrable fact, but on belief. The gun folks willingly choose violence, although they could, with equal justification, choose non-violence.

The choice between violence and non-violence is also made by our nation. Far too often, we hastily choose violence without giving non-violence serious consideration. In 2003, when faced with the possibility that Saddam Hussein might harm some of the Iraqi people, we invaded his country and overthrew his regime. We moved in quickly, because it was becoming clear that much of the case against him was based on unreliable and even fabricated evidence. Our government wanted to act violently, so it truncated inspections that had started to cast doubt on claims that Hussein had weapons of mass destruction. We set a deadline for negotiations, and we made those negotiations difficult. We used violence to assure that we would never be able to know whether non-violence might have worked.

In 2013, the US was faced with a similar choice—violence or non-violence in the buildup to our proposed attack on the Syrian government. There were allegations but almost no evidence that the Syrian government had used chemical weapons to attack the rebels who were trying to overthrow the government. There was also some evidence that the Syrian rebels had used chemical weapons, which raised the question of our own CIA's role, since we had become involved in support of the rebels in the Syrian civil war, which was by then two years old.

This put the US in the difficult position of deciding which side to attack. Logically, the stated purpose of our proposed attack was to show that we would not tolerate anyone using chemical weapons, but that logic could lead us to attack either side, both sides, or even ourselves. Such an attack would seem bizarre to most people, but it would serve our stated purpose. It would also serve our broader purpose of demonstrating our power and willingness to use violence to perpetuate our influence around the world.

Not long after the issue over chemical weapons arose, we announced our decision not to attack. The Syrian chemical weapons stockpile was scheduled for destruction voluntarily and by international agreement. We chose the non-violent alternative of a negotiated resolution of the issue of chemical weapons, and it worked. The fact that the insurgency in Syria continued does not argue against the soundness of the decision regarding chemical weapons. Whether the U.S. should involve itself militarily in Syria was a much broader question which depended upon more than just the question of those weapons. As of this writing, the U.S. has bombed and sent troops to attack some rebels, but not the ones we were initially going to side with. We are now attacking the group known as ISIS or ISIL, which we view as more threatening than the original rebels and worse than the Syrian government.

In international affairs, the option of talking things out as we initially did with Syria is always an option. This option even has a name: diplomacy. Our government has members of the diplomatic corps stationed all over the world. Their mission is in large part to pursue non-violent solutions to problems. They are led by our Secretary of State, who is one of our highest ranking and most visible government officials.

Our ambassadors and other members of the diplomatic corps serve in times of peace and in times of war, in safe areas and in areas that are so hazardous that they get additional pay just for being there. They are recognized by foreign governments as the official representatives of our government. They are given immunity from arrest under local laws, so that the governments that host them will not interfere with their important missions. If they commit transgressions, they can cause international incidents that embarrass us and for which our government may feel compelled to issue official apologies and make restitution. If they are attacked, it is considered an act of war against our entire nation. Everything about the work of our ambassadors and diplomatic corps indicates that they are important and that their mission of seeking peace is important. We also pay a large part of the expense of maintaining the bureaucracy of the United Nations so that our diplomats at the UN will be able to talk with diplomats from around the world and seek peace.

But when given the choice between allowing our diplomats to solve problems and using our military to solve problems violently, all too regularly we order our diplomats to abandon their posts so that they will not be hurt when our bombs start dropping. Sometimes, as happened in Iraq several years after Saddam Hussein was ousted, we leave our diplomats in place and instigate violence under the pretext that the violence is intended to protect the diplomats.[9] All too frequently, we suppress the advice our diplomats give us and hide the analytical reports they write, so that the peaceful solution will not even appear to be a possibility. All too often, we act as if the judgments of the generals were superior to that of anyone who might even entertain the possibility that killing is not the only thing our country knows how to do.

The question of whether to choose violence or peace, whether it is in the international realm or in our personal lives, is guided by the same principles. It should therefore not be surprising when people who live without guns in their lives also oppose the use of guns by our government. Companies that sell guns to our government know this, and they can be expected to oppose the reorientation of our domestic policy not only because it will affect domestic gun sales, but also because it will jeopardize their highly lucrative military weapons business.

America's ethos of violence

We have always claimed that people have the right to "life, liberty, and the pursuit of happiness," but we have always recognized exceptions to the right to live. We killed to conquer this continent. We have resisted the modern trend among nations to abolish the death penalty for committing crimes.[10] We readily deploy our military. Our laws permit people to kill in self-defense and even in the defense of property.

There have always been economic and political reasons we acted in these ways, but we would not have been able to condone such violence if killing was contrary to our fundamental moral convictions. Throughout our history, it was not. The prevailing view of life in America has always been that life is not sacred. It can be taken by individuals and by the government under certain circumstances, without either violating the law or offending God.

In addition to drawing distinctions between circumstances where killing is prohibited and those where killing is allowed, we have also distinguished between lives that were deserving of protection and lives that we were not concerned about. Too often we have been concerned only with the lives of people who were like us. That aspect of our violent history, often rooted in racism, finds analogs in the way we view violence today.

It used to be OK to shoot escaping slaves. White Americans did not identify with slaves and did not believe that the slaves' lives were as sacred as white lives. Black slaves were not viewed as being as human as whites were.

Today it is still OK for police to shoot fleeing suspects, even if they have not been proven guilty of anything. Even though longstanding legal doctrine assures us that people are presumed innocent unless and until they are proven guilty in court, we accept this violence against people who have not even been charged with a crime. Our assumption is that anyone who the police chase is probably guilty, especially if the person flees. It is easy to view a fleeing suspect that way because most people don't imagine that they will ever be running away from the police. People who flee are not like "us." They are different. They are the "other."

Because the shooting of suspects is accepted, there may also be little or no condemnation or punishment of police who shoot at fleeing suspects and hit and even kill innocent bystanders. Although we may say that the killing of bystanders is regrettable, we view the bystanders as expendable, just as we view the lives of non-combatants who are killed in war-torn areas as acceptable "collateral damage."

In some states, the law also allows private citizens to kill people if they believe those people are threatening them, even if the gun-wielding private citizens are wrong. Like police, they may also get away with shooting bystanders.[11] Bystanders become expendable not because of anything they are or do, but instead because of what someone else did whose life was expendable. Momentary proximity to expendable people determines a bystander's value.

It used to be OK in parts of the US for a man who caught his wife having sex with another man to kill the man. That's not allowed anymore, but those circumstances could still result in a reduction of the offense from murder to manslaughter. A man who violates the marital bed, even with the willing consent of the woman, is thought to have forfeited his right to be treated with the full measure of respect that we normally extend to visitors to our homes.

It used to be OK to kill Native Americans who got in the way of our expansionism. As the westward expansion was accelerating in the days leading up to the American Revolution, our government not only allowed the killing, but at least one colony encouraged killing of native people by offering bounties for their scalps.[12] We had a

Manifest Destiny. According to our government, it is still OK for our government to kill people all around the world who threaten what our government calls "American interests," even if those interests are the profit-making property of private corporations.

Notwithstanding our violent history, there appears to be a long-term trend away from violence, and a great many people in the US have views concerning killing and the sacredness of life that are not always reflected in the way our government acts. Some people believe that life should be protected in all circumstances. Some oppose the death penalty. Some conscientiously object to military service. Some say our country shouldn't torture people to get them to confess, regardless of whether the confessions are reliable. Some people are vegetarians because of the violence that is inherent in the slaughter of animals for food and in the conditions that many of our food animals are raised in. Some people object to hunting and boxing as sports. Some people object to capturing wild animals for display in zoos and aquariums because that capture is traumatic and the cages or habitats where the animals are exhibited are restrictive.

The question facing America today is to what extent it will continue its historic ambivalence about the sanctity of life and to what extent will it move towards a greater commitment to peace. The way we answer this question will affect how we live our lives on American soil and how our government behaves around the world.

Where is violence a problem?

Major newspapers and other media report on violence that occurs in the larger cities, where they have their offices and reporters. This leaves people with a distorted impression of where violence occurs. But violence, including gun violence, is a problem everywhere.

There are more guns in the US than anywhere else, and more shootings. Most of the shootings in America occur in places that have the highest concentrations of guns.[13] This only makes sense. No one gets shot where there are no guns.

Where are the guns? They are everywhere. They are in high-rise condominiums, houses, apartments, trailer parks, and hotel rooms. They are in cars, pickup trucks, boats, buses, taxis, and trains. They are in restaurants, bowling alleys, and bars. Guns are in nightstands, desk drawers, and under beds. They are on kitchen counters, in holsters, and under cash registers. Guns are in purses,[14] pockets, paper bags, and diaper bags.[15] And wherever the guns are, people get shot.

But guns are not distributed in proportion to the population. They tend to be more prevalent in some places than in others. They are mostly in states and rural areas where people go hunting, in homes of active and retired military and police, and in the waistbands of people who think they need guns to defend themselves from whatever frightens them. Guns are where people grew up with guns and where people think guns are safe, even though that's where the shootings are. Guns are where guns are socially acceptable.

The problem of guns is found wherever the guns are. People who take guns with them take the problem with them. When people go hunting, some of them accidentally shoot themselves and other hunters, whether they are hunting squirrels[16] or deer,[17] or even Bigfoot.[18] When they come home, they store their guns at home, and the guns are sometimes used in domestic violence. When military and police come home, they use their guns to kill themselves at much higher rates than their civilian counterparts, because they have guns and have accepted guns as a solution to problems.[19] When people carry guns, they use them in response to imagined threats, and they escalate small insults into deadly assaults.[20]

Despite the often-repeated claims that guns prevent violence, they cause violence and death. People who try to kill themselves usually fail, unless they use guns, in which case they almost always succeed.[21] People who run away from fights usually survive, but people who stand their ground and try to shoot their way out of situations are much more likely to get shot themselves. In theory, you can kill someone without using a gun. In reality, it's hard to do and doesn't happen very often.

People who live with guns live with the problem of gun violence. People who banish guns from their homes, workplaces, schools, and communities live longer, safer, and healthier lives.

VIEWING THE PROBLEM CLOSE-UP

I thought I had a pretty good understanding of the effects of gun violence. I had come to know Jennifer, whose pregnant sister Nancy was shot 25 years ago. Both Nancy and her unborn baby died, as did Nancy's husband. Jennifer's life has never been the same. Neither has her mother's or her other sister's. They will never forget, and there is no indication after all these years that their pain and sense of loss will disappear.

I had come to know Bill, whose 16-year-old son William was shot to death on his second day on the job at a fast food restaurant. I had come to know Steve, whose 19-year-old son Andrew was shot to death while sitting in a car at a stop light, and Annette and Ron, whose son Blair was shot and killed while coming home from school on a bus, and Pam, whose son Terrell was killed by gunfire as he was going into church for choir practice. I had met many more people who have lost sons, daughters, siblings, and other relations to guns, all right here in America.

I had also known two people who had themselves been shot. Dick was working in the southern US to help African Americans secure their civil rights during the 1960s. While protesting, he was shot in the back by a white sheriff. When I met him in the late 1970s, he still walked with a limp because of the shooting.

Jim was shot in the hand by someone who was trying to rob him. He told me the pain was intense and that getting shot was not like on TV or in the movies, where heroes struggle on and overcome their adversaries despite having been wounded. He described the pain as the most intense thing he had ever felt.

I had met a few people who said they had shot other people, either during combat or while high on drugs. They didn't talk much about the shootings.

All of those shootings were in the past by the time I learned about them. But while writing this book, a friend of mine lost two sons to gun violence. Adding to what I already thought or felt about guns, this incident gave me a real-time view that has added a dimension to my understanding.

Abdul's story

My friend's name is Abdul. He came to the US several decades ago. Trained as a chemist, he got a job in the medical examiner's office. In some cities, medical examiners are called coroners. It is their job, among other things, to perform autopsies to determine the cause and method of death when someone dies unexpectedly.

Abdul and his wife were raising two sons and a daughter. When I met him in the 1980s, he had left his job as a chemist and was the proprietor of the sort of tiny store that used to be more common before chain convenience stores sprouted up everywhere. He sold candy, cigarettes, cigars, soft drinks, snacks, and assorted other merchandise. My wife, our small child, and I lived in an apartment across the street from Abdul's store, and we bought countless gallons of milk from him. I have no idea what his store was called, or if it even had a sign. We just knew it as Abdul's.

Abdul was almost always in the store, ready to greet us with a smile. We still have a little stuffed animal that he gave our daughter when she was born. Our daughter tells us that one of her earliest memories is of standing in Abdul's shop, looking at merchandise in a glass display counter that was at her eye level. She was about 2 or 3 years old.

On occasion, when Abdul was in the store, one or both of his sons would be there with him. When they grew older, they would tend the store when Abdul was away. A handful of times, we saw Abdul's wife or another relative there. Abdul always introduced us, in the way proprietors did before the days of chain convenience stores. As his customers, we were important and respected people, even though our purchases usually cost just a couple of dollars.

Abdul later had another store in the downtown area of our small city. That store mostly sold tobacco products. Every so often, after we had a second child and had moved out of our tiny apartment and into a house in a nearby town, I would visit Abdul if I happened to be in the neighborhood. He never seemed to change. He was always gentle, and he always greeted me warmly.

In 2013, I read in the morning news that two men were found shot dead in their downtown tobacco store. They were Abdul's sons, then aged 34 and 38. They had been just a few years older than our daughter. Accompanying the story was a family photo of Abdul and his two sons, who by then were running the store. Abdul was in his eighties.

The news reported that Abdul's wife had phoned the store because her sons had not come home for dinner. When they didn't answer the phone, she drove there from their home about a mile away. She arrived to find the store locked, but the "Open" sign in the window was on. Unable to get inside, she summoned a nearby police officer who, with her permission, broke the door open. In the basement, the officer found the two brothers—dead.

I have tried to imagine how a police officer tells a woman that he has found two bodies that might be her sons. Police must get some sort of training about what to do in such a situation. Do the police come right out and say what they know? Do they try to soften the news?

Doctors, nurses, lawyers, and soldiers have all told how their training helps them remain detached during stressful situations so that they can do their jobs. They also talk about the emotions they may experience after the crisis has passed. What did the officer feel when he went home that day? Did he look at his wife and kids differently? Will he hesitate the next time he starts down the stairs into a friend's basement? Will he always remember the look on Abdul's wife's face?

I visited Abdul at his home three days after the shooting. He was surrounded by relatives, but his wife and daughter were not there. They were at the medical examiner's office—where Abdul once worked—arranging for the bodies to be released for burial following the autopsies.

Abdul's brother-in-law explained that Abdul's wife had been distraught since the shooting. Abdul was obviously in similar shape. He welcomed my wife and me as always, "Hello, Mr. and Mrs. Goodman." Almost immediately he said, "I cannot cry. I have no more tears. Who would do this? Everyone loves us."

Abdul was right. Everyone loved them. Such a gentle man, with gentle sons. Yet, for reasons unknown to any of us, someone had shot and killed his two boys. It didn't really matter who had done it, or why. All that mattered was that a man, his wife, his daughter, and their extended family had suffered a huge, unanticipated loss. They were grieving. I was privileged to be there, to share their pain, to show them that the world had not abandoned them, and to learn about the effects of violence.

When my daughter next phoned home I could barely choke out the words to tell her what had happened. Several times over the next few days I found myself contemplating the shootings and their aftermath. I kept thinking how awful it must be for Abdul, an immigrant to a country that promises so much. How can he bear to have lost his sons? I'm sure the tobacco store will never reopen.

Not long after the shooting, I ran into a friend who works at the same department store where Abdul's wife has worked as a sales clerk for the past ten years. He told me that everyone in the store was upset when they learned the news. Many of them had met the two sons when they visited their mother at the store. The shooting deaths of two men had touched not just the victims' family members and their friends, but also dozens of other people—whether they knew the family or not.

The newspapers ran stories reporting that shopkeepers near Abdul's tobacco store were feeling unnerved. The shooter was still on the loose and could kill again. For a while, the police said they didn't have any suspects. A couple of months later, the police announced that they had shot and killed a bank robber who they believed was also responsible for shooting Abdul's sons. The police said they didn't have any idea what the motive for the shootings had been. Within a year, Abdul and his wife had moved out-of-state, where they now reside with their daughter.

Learning from another death

Getting to know some of the victims of gun violence does not make me an authority on the issue. But it has allowed me to learn about the personal anguish and pain that survivors experience. The day after visiting with Abdul, I attended a funeral of a man who died at age 64. He was a college professor. His death was not caused by gunshots but by cancer. There was no one to blame. The survivors did not feel angry, just terribly sad. They were shaken by the death of someone relatively young, but they had had several years to prepare for the eventuality as he endured rounds of chemotherapy. Their loss, of course, was felt as deeply as was the loss of Abdul's sons.

Abdul's grief at losing his sons to gunfire was in most respects no different from the grief the professor's family felt upon losing their loved one to cancer. But there were a couple of big differences. One was the type of questions that each set of mourners was left to ponder. No one in the cancer victim's family was asking "Who would do such a thing?"

Another difference was that although both families' faiths taught them that they should look to their God in their time of need, only Abdul's family found itself also looking to the police to answer unanswered questions.

And most painful of all, only Abdul's family would learn in coming days that people were speculating, based on absolutely no evidence, that their sons may have been involved in some sort of foul play that resulted in their being shot. It is not unusual that families of people who are shot have to deal with the stigma that is placed on them by people who are willing to invent explanations for unexplained violence. Victims are often blamed for their own victimhood.

WHY DO PEOPLE HAVE GUNS?

Gun owners give many explanations for why they share their lives with lethal weapons, but they rarely admit to the real reasons they have guns. They may not even know what has led them to become enamored with instruments of violence. On the other hand, they may know but not be willing to acknowledge their motivations to themselves because their reasons for owning guns conflict with the self-image they maintain. Or they may not want to let other people know, for fear that people will not approve. Our society has norms, and ideas that are not considered politically correct can lead to rejection.

To understand why people turn to guns, it is best to look for something other than reasons. Gun ownership is not a logical response to an intellectual problem. It is an emotional response to a life situation. People have guns because of the way they feel, and they don't feel good.

Alienation leads people to own guns

There is no single emotion leading people to have guns, but a lot of people have guns because they are angry. Their lives have not gone as they wanted them to. They may not have gotten jobs or promotions they wanted. They may have been fired. They may have been ordered to pay child support or alimony. They may have lost their homes to foreclosure. They may have lost their savings in the stock market, or they may have lost their health insurance or pensions when their companies went bankrupt. Our capitalist system encourages people to envy one another's material possessions and wealth, in theory so that people will work hard to be able to accumulate the things they covet. That envy can lead to much unhappiness.[22]

People's anger can also come from non-economic sources. They may have lost their driver's licenses because they drove drunk. They may feel resentful toward people who are more educated and have advanced further in life, or they may imagine that the government prefers minorities and women over them. They may have seen their children unable to succeed in life because they did not get college educations, or because they were just unable to get jobs in a depressed economy.

In addition to being angry, gun owners are often resentful and frustrated. The world may seem to them to have changed, and they haven't been able to keep up. They may feel that promises that were made to them were not kept. They may feel that the American Dream, however they understand it, has been unfairly denied to them. They may not be competent with technology. They may resent foreign workers and students taking jobs and school positions that they think should go to Americans.

They may feel that the movement towards diversity comes at the expense of their position as members of the privileged class they were born into.[23] Gun owners may or may not see themselves as racist or misogynistic, but they tend to glorify a past that was not very pleasant for a lot of people they would like to feel superior to.[24]

There are countless reasons why people get angry, resentful, and frustrated. It's surprising that more people aren't feeling these emotions. We live in challenging times. Massive technological innovations occurred early in our country's history and shifted our population and much of the world from overwhelmingly agricultural to primarily industrial. Disruptions occurred in society as a result. Those changes and disruptions have continued in our time, moving American workers out of factories and into offices, then out of jobs into independent contractor status, and then onto the streets.

We have failed to adjust our economy to keep pace with

technology, so we now have a surplus of labor that has left millions of Americans permanently or sporadically unemployed or underemployed. Our corporations have embraced the ethic of maximizing profits by minimizing the number of people they employ. In America we refer to people as being "laid off," but the English expression, that people are made "redundant," is more descriptive. Mergers and acquisitions are entered into specifically so that fewer people are needed to do the work. Computers and robots are seen as superior to humans because they never take coffee breaks or ask for raises. The notion that work has "dignity" seems outmoded.

There are defensible reasons for these changes. Much work has been mechanized not only to save labor costs but also because the work itself was boring and hazardous. Take, for example, the US Postal Service. The task of sorting millions of pieces of mail was time-consuming, led to repetitive motion injuries, and was prone to error. Machines were developed that can now inexpensively sort mail at incredible speeds. Thousands of workers have been replaced. But they were not re-deployed. They were dumped. The same thing has happened industry by industry. Good for the business owners and consumers. Bad for the workers. Ultimately, bad for everyone.

A while back I saw a surveyor outside my house and asked what project he was working on. I looked around for the other guy who typically works with a surveyor—the guy who holds the stick so that the surveyor can sight it with his transit. Not seeing anyone, I asked and was told that the type of surveying he was doing could now be done with only one worker using a GPS-based system. Great, but what happens to the guys who used to hold the sticks? Half of the jobs on a survey crew don't exist anymore because of the new technology.

At the same time that we have been eliminating jobs, we have subjected the people who are still working to an accelerated pace of work—the modern day analog to what happened when the early industrialists would speed up the assembly line in order to get more productivity out of workers. It looks funny when Charlie Chaplin gets caught in giant gears as he races to get his work done in the classic silent comedy *Modern Times*. It's not so funny when you are the one risking life and limb for a paycheck.

Some of these changes have taken place during the working lives of people today, such as when companies like FedEx first introduced overnight delivery services into the workplace. Previously, during the few days that it took for proposals, reports, or other work-products to get from one office to another, workers had time to step back from their projects and relax or work on something else. When overnight delivery became commonplace, workers suddenly had to resume work on the projects the next day when their packages were received. It wasn't unusual that workers found themselves rushing to meet the pickup deadline that same evening. This cycle could be repeated each day.

That change took place not that long ago, but workers back then didn't realize how easy they had things. Within just a few more years, electronic communications sped things up even more. With email, workers no longer had the luxury of knowing that the delivery service's pickup schedule set their deadlines. Work products could suddenly be sent anywhere in the world instantly at any hour. The recipient could likewise respond instantly. Workers found themselves on-call 24 hours a day, seven days a week.

Those were the good old days, too, before handheld electronic devices and cell phones meant workers could be reached not only anytime, but anywhere, even while driving their cars or commuting to and from work, when walking the dog or even on vacation. The science fiction fantasy that robots would work for us while we slept turned into the modern reality that machines could summon us to work from our sleep and could thrust our assignments at us at any time on screens we carry with us.

The factory speed-up used to lead to workers walking off the line or staging slowdowns to protect good working conditions. Today, lacking unions to protect them, workers respond to the stress that their jobs create in ways that do nothing to improve conditions at the workplace. Massive numbers of workers simply take their stress home with them in the form of stress-induced high blood pressure and other diseases. They erupt in rage when cut off in traffic. They figuratively (and sometimes literally) "kick the dog."

While technology has increased worker productivity, there is little evidence that it has increased workers' satisfaction with their jobs. Nor have wages increased to compensate people for the larger share of their lives they must devote to their jobs. To the contrary, wages for almost all workers have declined due to inflation, increased costs of living, and an increasingly large percentage of wages going to a tiny portion of workers at the highest levels of companies.[25]

Technology was supposed to make our lives easier when we were not at work. In some ways it has. For example, not so many years ago, the high cost of long-distance phone calls made them a luxury. Today they are affordable to a much broader segment of the population. At the same time, however, technology has degraded our lives. When portable transistor radios and earphones were introduced in the late 1950s, the stereotypical parent was shown in cartoons as yelling to get the attention of the stereotypical teenager who was listening to music and oblivious to the world. Today on streets all around America, you can see mothers talking on cell phones while ignoring the children they are pushing in strollers, people crashing their cars because they are paying more attention to their phones than to traffic, and people sitting at cafes ignoring their companions while communicating electronically with someone in another town.

We have simultaneously become more connected and less in touch. Our interpersonal relationships have been impacted, as have our family dynamics. We are living in a pressure-cooker world with relief valves that are prone to fail. No wonder people are upset. Guns are one response to these and many other problems we haven't been able to fix. The Executive Vice President and CEO of the NRA, Wayne LaPierre, summed it up:

> "We're worried about the economic crisis choking our budgets and shrinking our retirement. We're worried about providing decent health care and a college education for our children. We fear for the safety of our families—it's why neighborhood streets that were once filled with bicycles and skateboards, laughter in the air, now sit empty and silent.
>
> In virtually every way, for the things we care about most, we feel profound loss. We are sad not because we fear something IS going wrong, but because we know something already HAS gone wrong.
>
> It's why more and more Americans are buying firearms and ammunition—not to cause trouble, but because we sense that America is already IN trouble."[26]

What's the emotional appeal of guns?

People can be angry, frustrated, and resentful without turning to guns. Most people never take up arms. We manage to cope. Why, then, have so many people sought relief from the difficulties of their lives by picking up deadly weapons? There are many reasons.

One major reason guns are so attractive to people who are dissatisfied with their lives is that guns create a cultural alternative. Strange as it seems to people who remember the hippie counterculture of the 1960s, with its ethos of love and peace, guns are the counterculture for a lot of people today, but they reflect an ethos of bitterness and violence. Gun owners join the NRA, go to the shooting range, and attend gun shows for the same reasons model railroaders join clubs and go to swap meets. They like being with people who will affirm them. Gun owners know that when they're with other gun owners, they won't have to justify themselves or be compared to people who don't own guns. Some gun owners use their gun ownership to isolate themselves from a world in which they feel inadequate and uncomfortable. When they're with other gun owners, everyone is a friend, and anyone who doesn't like guns is viewed as a gun-grabbing enemy. It's a simple, comfortable world.

Guns can also let people feel competent. In today's fast-changing world, competence can be very attractive. Although hitting a target with a bullet can be difficult, with practice most people can learn to do it, especially if they attach enough laser sights and other assist devices on their guns. Target shooting gives instant, tangible feedback of success. If you can put out of your mind that guns are made for killing people, many people find that shooting can be fun. The gun industry has become very adept at bolstering people's desire to feel competent. It sponsors contests and gives away trophies and prizes. Step right up, anyone can do it, everyone wins a prize. Often, the prize is a gun.

The government unintentionally makes gun owners feel competent by giving them licenses. Although gun licenses are issued to anyone who meets minimal requirements and in some states can be obtained through the mail without even demonstrating that you aren't blind, having gun licenses in their wallets is taken by many gun owners as a seal of approval by their government. Some gun owners see themselves as practically being deputized when they get their licenses, especially if their licenses entitle them to carry their guns around with them in public. They talk as if the government had certified them as responsible and important members of society.

Of course, other pastimes can also give people the sense of satisfaction that comes from associating with like-minded people and being competent. But guns have an attraction that very few other hobbies can offer: guns intimidate people. If someone is bothering you, just pick up a gun and that person will probably shut up and go away rather than risk being shot. Most rational people will back off if they are threatened with a gun.

Even more important than actually scaring people who are actually bothering you, if you have a gun, you can imagine that if anyone did bother you, you could shut them up and make them go away.[27] You can sit in your den, clean your gun, and say to yourself, "Just let one of them come in here, and I'll show them who's inferior!" If you have a gun, you can walk down the street thinking that you have the respect of everyone because you can kill them or give them something to remember you by if they don't treat you the way you think you deserve. Every time someone walks past you on the street without hitting you on the head and stealing your wallet, you can puff up your chest and think, "He must have been frightened by my gun."

That delusional thinking is what is behind the gun lobby's claim that people in the US successfully use guns to defend themselves hundreds of thousands of times each year. The FBI statistics say it is more like a few hundred times, but the gun folks insist that if they imagined someone might have hurt them, then their guns are what protected them.[28] They live in their own fantasy world and see every non-confrontation as a vindication of their theory that guns make people safer, and of their self-centered view that the world owes them more respect than it has been giving them.

A couple generations ago, Danny Kaye portrayed the fictional title character in the 1947 movie, *The Secret Life of Walter Mitty* (reprised by Ben Stiller in the 2013 remake). The Internet Movie Database says Walter is "a daydreaming pulp-fiction proofreader with an overprotective mother" who "likes to imagine that he is a hero who experiences fantastic adventures." Today's gun owners are a bit like Walter Mitty, but with a dark side. They also bear a resemblance to Barney Fife, the not very bright and even less competent deputy sheriff on the *Andy Griffith Show*, who was only allowed to carry one bullet for his gun, and he had to keep the bullet in his shirt pocket so that he wouldn't hurt anyone. Barney had a limited role in law enforcement, except in his own imagination. Today's Walters and Barneys carry their guns to the grocery store and dream of getting a chance to do something heroic to prove their worth to a society that has somehow failed to give them the adulation they feel they deserve. But their fantasies aren't harmless. They can have deadly consequences.

If you have a gun, you can also secretly indulge in more graphic and sadistic fantasies of actually shooting people and watching them crumple, run, scream, bleed, or whatever else gives you a thrill. We don't know what goes through people's minds most of the time, but we can infer their thoughts from what they say and how they act. The popularity of violence in movies, on TV, and in gaming is a pretty good indicator of just how prevalent these fantasies are.

Gun lovers love to talk about guns. They talk about the guns they own and the guns they want to buy. They talk about how much fun they have shooting things. They retell with relish every news story about suspected criminals being shot by "law abiding" gun owners. They say they have guns merely to protect themselves, as if they got no thrill from their guns. If that was the case, they probably wouldn't talk about their guns so much. People wear underpants to protect themselves, but they don't talk about them a lot.

The fantasies that gun owners lose themselves in are harmless to others, as long as they remain fantasies. But unlike little boys tying capes around their necks and pretending to be super-heroes, gun owners are arming themselves with the most lethal technology they can find, turning their personal fantasy life into a public menace.

In addition to the sense of physical power that guns provide, the right to own a gun is itself a very powerful attraction. Because the Supreme Court has interpreted the Second Amendment to the US Constitution as saying that people have a fundamental right to have guns, many gun owners feel empowered that no one will be able to take their guns away. Anyone could point to the First Amendment right to free speech and feel the same way about being able to stand tall in the face of threatened government oppression, whether or not they have a gun. But by owning a gun, a person can align himself with the obstinate and proclaim, as former NRA president Charlton Heston did, that no one can take his gun until they pry it from his "cold, dead, hands."[29]

Any gun owner, no matter how puny and pathetic, no matter how inept a marksman, no matter how inarticulate, can feel like an immovable force when he has a gun. The women may be able to take away his position in society, the blacks may be able to get his job, the Arabs may control oil, the Jews may control everything else, the intellectuals may try to make him look foolish, the government may be able to make him buy insurance and keep him from smoking inside buildings, but, by God, no one can take away his gun. If the Constitution guaranteed the right to own red licorice, he might fixate on that and proclaim that no one can have his Twizzlers and Whips until they pry them from his cold, sticky hands.

Are sportsmen a different kind of gun owner?

Whenever there is a discussion about eliminating the dangers that guns pose to people, gun advocates object that they should be allowed to keep their guns so that they can go hunting. This argument quickly becomes absurd when the pro-gun folks try to justify their ownership of handguns. No one hunts deer, ducks, or any legitimate game with a handgun.

Nor do real hunters have a plausible claim that they need military assault weapons with high capacity magazines to hunt. As any hunter will tell you, if you need more than one or two shots to kill your prey, you shouldn't be hunting. If your first shot misses, it will startle any game in the area into immediate flight, making it nearly impossible for you to hit anything with a second shot. If your first shot merely wounds your target, the animal may flee, also making it unlikely that you'll get a second shot. If your target cannot successfully flee, you will be in the unsportsmanlike and unglamorous position of tracking the wounded animal and shooting it until it succumbs. If a wounded target animal is able to escape, it will live out whatever remains of its severely shortened life crippled and in pain.

There are, or course, hunters who use appropriate rifles and shotguns to hunt their prey, and who are skilled enough to kill without first maiming. They claim that they kill in order to eat what they shoot, and many do. These claims have generally been accepted by the public as legitimate reasons why people should be allowed to have guns. Even many people who favor gun control concede the debate when hunting is brought up. But this should not be seen as the end of the discussion. It should be the beginning.

Why should we accept the maiming and violent killing of wild animals? Certainly there is no need for hunting in the US. Our farms raise more than enough cattle and other animals to supply not only domestic demand but to export around the globe. No one who wants a steak or a hamburger or even some venison stew needs to shoot their own dinner. Whether or not the killing of farm animals is acceptable is certainly worthy of discussion. There is plenty of evidence that even cattle slaughtered in the most humane way still suffer before they die. Most cattle, raised and fattened in massive commercial operations, are forced to live lives that are anything but natural. And they do, let's not forget, die.

We have laws against torturing and abusing animals. Anyone who is caught starving or beating a pet dog faces not only criminal prosecution but also condemnation from nearly everyone in society. In most places, it is illegal to set dogs to fight for sport. As a country, we expect humane treatment of animals. Why, then, do we accept that if the label "hunting" is placed on an activity, it then becomes acceptable to terrorize, maim, and even kill animals that present no threat to people, just so that the person with the gun can have a good time? Someone who kills people for thrills is considered demented. Why is someone who enjoys killing defenseless animals considered to be different?

Hunters don't usually talk about the thrill they get from watching an animal die. They talk about the thrill of the hunt. They take pride in their trophies, and they go on at length telling tales of their hunting experiences. But the kill is a thrill. There are television shows and online videos where you can watch people lie in wait or stalk the animals they want to kill, and then you can actually watch the kill. The narration becomes hushed, similar to a golf tournament. The hunters pose with the warm bodies of their prey, cradling their dead heads, smiling as if showing off their grandchildren.

The dead animals don't seem to have died smiling. If they were chased by dogs, their last minutes were spent in terror. If they were flushed out of the grass, they were in panic mode. Some may die nearly instantly, but many die more slowly, perhaps falling out of the sky aware of their doom, perhaps crashing through a forest, unable to fully use their legs, feeling their lifeblood spurting from their wounds. Some see their offspring running away from them. Like the dogs and cats we surround ourselves with for companionship and refer to as our best friends, these are animals, capable of feeling pain and fear, capable of communicating with one another, capable of so much, until some hunter kills them for fun.

These are the facts, and yet they are rarely voiced in the debates on gun control. They find voice mostly among vegetarians and animal rights advocates, both of whom are small but growing minorities among our population.[30] But in the halls of Congress, in state capitals, and in newspapers, the violence that hunters commit for their own enjoyment is rarely questioned.

It should be questioned. If we are to make progress in reducing violence against people, we should be looking closely at violence committed by people against animals. What loss would there be to our country if we decided to no longer allow people to kill for their own amusement? I can't think of a thing we would lose by this action. What would we gain, other than knowing that we have taken a stand against cruelty? We would eliminate an excuse that people have for owning guns, which would allow us to regulate guns more fully and thereby to reduce the danger that guns create for people. Protecting animals would allow us to protect people.

The same benefit would result from eliminating target shooting, which is usually thought of as a perfectly harmless avocation. Most people tend to assume that if someone is merely blasting holes in paper or clay targets in a controlled environment such as a shooting range, no one is being hurt. But the reality is that the mere existence of guns, for whatever reason they exist, increases the danger to people.[31] Guns that are purchased for target shooting are also used to commit robberies, suicides, and murders, and they also cause accidental gun injuries. Regardless of the purpose for which guns are purchased, they are dangerous and in too many cases, they will cause harm.

Target shooters have a lot of trouble understanding this concern for public safety. They see their hobby as benign and can't imagine why anyone would want to keep them from enjoying it. They think of themselves as the prototypical responsible gun owners who aren't bothering anyone. They think that people who would limit their pursuit of their hobby are just plain nuts. They might agree that criminals shouldn't be able to get guns, but they fail to recognize that their guns might fall into the hands of criminals. Law enforcement officials, on the other hand, have no hesitation in pointing out that one of the first things burglars take in a burglary are guns, for their own use and for sale,[32] and that gun shops are frequent targets of burglaries, not for the cash that might be in the register but for the guns that are on display.

In today's world, people have plenty of challenges. If target shooting were just a harmless pastime, we might want to not only allow it but encourage it as a way for people to amuse themselves and relieve stress. But the sport of target shooting cannot be evaluated from a public policy perspective without taking into account the extent to which it increases the hazard of violence.

We may or may not want to go all the way and eliminate guns entirely, just to make our world safer—even if the guns are ostensibly only used for target practice or hunting. But we should be allowed to have that discussion. The only way we can have it is to repeal the Second Amendment.

Can we keep dangerous people from having guns?

Guns are lethal machines that are designed and manufactured to kill animals, usually human ones. When they are in the hands of angry, frustrated people, we all have a problem. If we could figure out a way to help people get over their anger and work through the difficulties in their lives, guns might not be such a problem. Unfortunately, we haven't made much progress along these lines.

Instead of working with people so that they can become more comfortable with their lives and be less angry and frustrated, far too often we show little concern for them and offer them little help. We treat those with more serious anger issues as mental patients, and the major mode of therapy that is made available to them is prescriptions for pills. Sometimes the pills help people who are upset, but in many cases, medicating people doesn't provide a complete solution. They are still angry, and compounding the problem, they are now dependent upon medications. They don't always take their medications on schedule, and the meds are not always effective. Some medications have been shown to make people more prone to violent outbursts. The science and practice of mental health has not advanced to the point where we can count on it as a solution to gun violence. We have no way of knowing whether it ever will.

One solution that has some support among the gun control activists is that if we can't keep people from becoming violent, we should keep people who are likely to become violent from having guns. The NRA from time to time even says it supports this idea. Usually, the NRA gets behind this idea after someone has gone on a rampage. It is convenient for the NRA to label someone who kills a bunch of innocent people as a lunatic who should not have had a gun. It is not so easy, though, for the NRA or anyone else to tell us in advance who those people are.

Psychologists have been unable to come up with reliable tests to predict which people are likely to use guns to commit violence or to become violent in any manner.[33] Once a person is in psychiatric care for a serious mental disturbance, mental health professionals don't have too much trouble advising that that individual should not have guns. They know, for instance, that someone who says he is thinking about killing a bunch of people might do just that. Mental health professionals can't be sure what their patients will do, but they can be cautious. We are left, therefore, operating on the assumption that everyone is as mentally fit to have a gun as anyone else, although we know this isn't true.

The broadest attempt we make to keep guns out of the wrong hands is to keep people who have committed certain crimes from having guns. We do this not necessarily because we assume that these people are violent. We know that isn't the case. We just do it because we can, and it kind of looks like it might make sense.

It doesn't, really. The federal Gun Control Act of 1968 says that people who have been convicted of felonies cannot own guns. It doesn't make any distinction, however, between people who used guns when committing their crimes and people who didn't. It doesn't even distinguish between violent crimes—murder, armed robbery, rape, etc.—and non-violent crimes such as drug possession, except that it says that people who commit certain white-collar crimes such as anti-trust violations are not prohibited from having guns.

The federal law also doesn't keep people who have actually been convicted of violent crimes from having guns if their crimes were misdemeanors, unless they were convicted of domestic violence. People who have been repeatedly convicted of battery, for example, are allowed to buy guns so long as they beat up people who they don't live with. It is obvious that this law, like so many other laws, was written to satisfy political objectives and mollify discreet constituencies, but not necessarily to keep people who have been violent in the past from getting guns.

This shortcoming of the law is also found in the provisions that prohibit people who are mentally ill from getting guns. The Gun Control Act states that only a person who has been "adjudicated as a mental defective or has been committed to any mental institution" is barred from owning guns. People who only receive voluntary outpatient treatment for mental health problems are allowed to have guns, no matter how serious those problems are. One notorious example is James Eagan Holmes, who shot and killed 12 people and wounded 70 more inside an Aurora, Colorado, movie theater in 2012. He had been under psychiatric care prior to the shooting but had not been committed.[34] People who merely checked themselves into mental hospitals voluntarily can have all the guns they want, no matter how violent they might be.

There are many, many examples of individuals who obtained guns and committed atrocious crimes despite existing laws, one of the more spectacular being Aaron Alexis, the 34-year-old former Navy reservist who shot and killed a dozen people and injured three more where he worked as a civilian at the Washington Navy Yard in Washington, D.C., in September 2013. The shooter had passed multiple background and security checks over a period of years and was still able to get a gun and use it on a secure military base, even though he had several arrests in his background, had a history of violence, and had been treated with antidepressants for mental illness.[35]

Not only doesn't the federal law do a very good job of keeping guns away from people who become violent, it also keeps some people who wouldn't become violent from having guns. For example, a person convicted of shoplifting twice is labeled a felon in some jurisdictions and would be prohibited from owning a gun. Surprisingly, this doesn't seem to upset the NRA, which otherwise is quite vocal about protecting people's rights to have guns. It could be that the NRA has made a political calculation that it doesn't want to be seen as being on the side of convicts. It could also be that the NRA realizes that disproportionately, convicts are minorities, and the NRA just doesn't care about minorities.

It is a problem for the gun lobby that we don't know how to keep people from using guns to commit mayhem. Rather than face up to this problem, the gun lobby tries to distract us from it. Among the tactics the gun lobby uses is to point out that some people—gun collectors—have guns without any intention of ever using them for violence. They try to legitimize gun ownership by emphasizing that collecting guns is no more dangerous than collecting teacups or Barbie Dolls.

The gun lobby tells us that gun collectors appreciate the craftsmanship that goes into historic guns, and that they like to study the history of the development of weapons. That's fine in theory. Some old guns have a bit of engraving, though they are nothing compared to the average silver tea service of the same era. But not many people buy modern guns just to admire their craftsmanship. Modern guns are turned out in factories with no more craftsmanship than the faucet on a kitchen sink. The dominant aesthetic of guns these days is to look sleek, industrial, and functional. They have about as much decorative detail as a food processor. There are also gun collectors who claim to be intrigued by the mechanisms of guns, which is also fine. But anyone who is really interested in mechanical wizardry and artistry would find a lot more to marvel at in a vintage sewing machine, antique typewriter, or old-fashioned film camera.

If the gun lobby really thought that gun collectors' only interest in guns was as collectors, they wouldn't object to regulations that would make sure those collections were maintained under conditions that rendered them harmless. Any museum that has a gun collection follows well-established protocols to make sure than no visitor, curator, or exhibit duster ever gets shot. There are no such rules to keep residents, visitors, neighbors, or passersby safe from guns that are kept in the homes of private collectors.

You will also find collectors at the gun range or walking around their neighborhoods with pistols in their pockets. Despite the claims of the gun lobby, most gun owners don't really collect guns; they just have a bunch of guns, and they are just as dangerous as anyone else with guns.

There have been plenty of attempts to improve the federal gun laws so that they do a better job of keeping dangerous people from getting guns. One such proposal would require that every individual undergo a background check before buying a gun, to keep guns out of the hands of those who, by law, are deemed unfit for gun ownership. This proposal has the support of about 90 percent of Americans, according to all the major polls.[36] A recent study concludes that requiring background checks actually reduces the number of murders with guns.[37] The proposal to expand background checks probably has more support than any other law that been proposed in modern history. Santa Claus probably wouldn't do that well in the polls. And yet, the gun lobby opposes the law.

As the law now stands, certain people are not allowed to buy guns. Experience has shown that the most effective way to keep those people from buying guns is to require people who sell guns to check to make sure that each potential customer is allowed to buy a gun. People who are licensed by the federal government to sell guns are already required to check. If they are caught not checking, they can lose their licenses and be exposed to liability for injuries caused by illegal purchasers.

But almost anyone is allowed to sell guns without having a federal license. Unlicensed individuals can sell guns at gun shows, through the Internet, or from the backs of their cars. They do not have to check their customers' backgrounds to make sure the sales are legal. So if someone who is not allowed to buy a gun—a felon, for example—buys a gun from an unlicensed seller, the purchaser is guilty of a crime, but the unlicensed seller is not. This provision of the law is known as the "gun show loophole," and it has spawned a huge gun show industry that exists primarily to facilitate the sale of guns without anyone having to verify the legality of the purchases.

It isn't just that a few guns here and there are sold by people who aren't licensed. Although precise figures are impossible to obtain for sales by unlicensed sellers, those sales probably make up more than 40 percent of all gun sales.[38]

It is peculiar that unlicensed persons are allowed to sell guns at all. This sharply contrasts with just about every other licensing law. For example, it is a crime for an unlicensed pharmacist, lawyer, doctor, nurse, real estate agent, bank, stock broker, veterinarian, barber, beautician, or plumber to ply their trades. Allowing them to do business without licenses would prevent the licensing laws from accomplishing their purpose, which is to protect the public.

The NRA does not object to background checks at gun stores. Because background checks can be performed instantly online by accessing a computerized database that the FBI has set up just for that purpose, they don't interfere with legitimate sales to legal buyers.[39]

Background checks could also easily be performed at guns shows, but the NRA says they shouldn't be required. Why would the NRA object to the same checks at gun shows that are required at gun shops? Could it be that they know that a lot of sales at the shows are to people who would fail the checks, and the missed sales would cut into the gun industry's profits?[40] A revealing study suggests that this is exactly what is happening. Investigators found that felons and other people who would not pass background checks were regularly buying their guns at gun shows and online, where the loophole allows their purchases to proceed unimpeded.[41]

Guns are a hazard in anyone's hands

Not every gun owner is a menace, but every gun is a hazard. Every gun owner can be mistaken and think that something is a threat when it really isn't. There are plenty of instances in which people are shot in their own homes because they were mistaken for burglars, as happened when a 12-year-old who was shot by his 16-year-old brother in Florida, [42] and when a middle-aged man was shot by his father in Chicago,[43] and when a 16-year-old girl was shot by her father in Virginia.[44] Every gun owner can become depressed and maybe even suicidal, homicidal, or both, like the "doting father" who shot his wife and two disabled children to death before killing himself.[45] Every gun owner can accidentally drop a loaded gun and shoot himself or someone else, as did the retired cop who dropped his gun while attending his grandson's Boy Scout troop meeting.[46] There have even been accidents at shooting ranges[47] and instances of people being shot during class by their gun safety instructors.[48]

Every gun owner, no matter how well trained, can miss and shoot the wrong target. In August 2012, nine bystanders were shot by police who were attempting to shoot a suspect outside the Empire State Building.[49] In September 2013, New York cops in Times Square accidentally shot two bystanders.[50] These stories got national attention, but they should not be seen as criticism of any particular police department. Shooters often miss, even under the best of controlled circumstances. In highly emotional situations, most shooters miss their targets most of the time.[51]

Every gun owner can get angry or jealous. Some of them will seek revenge themselves rather than relying on the police and courts, but there is no way to predict which ones they are.

In addition to the risks that guns present when in the hands of their owners, guns also present risks when in the hands of other people. For this reason, law enforcement experts caution people not to carry guns to defend themselves. Assailants all too often take guns away from their gun-carrying victims and use them against their victims. For this same reason, prison guards don't carry guns, since the guns could be wrestled away by prisoners. Even the gun industry encourages parents to lock up their guns to keep them from being found by children.[52] Some gun ranges have stopped renting guns to people because of the number of people who have rented guns just so that they could shoot themselves. The cost of cleaning up the range after the suicides has made renting guns unprofitable.[53]

The undeniable fact is that just like explosives, guns are inherently dangerous. Almost no one has explosives for their personal, non-industrial use, because we all recognize the danger that explosives present, even when handled by trained and experienced people. And yet almost anyone can have a gun.

The mistake we have made is to look at guns and gun owners separately. We have accepted the division the NRA makes when it says, "Guns don't kill people, people kill people." What we should be doing is looking at the combination of people with guns, because it cannot be denied that "People with guns kill people."

THE DEMOGRAPHICS OF GUNS AND VIOLENCE

News outlets try not to appear biased in their reporting, so the demographics of the people involved in shootings are often not mentioned in stories that are printed and broadcast to the public. Criminologists and other social scientists do, however, pay careful attention. They know and have documented that there are aspects to gun violence that involve gender, race, and class. But it's not a simple picture.

When looking at who the victims are, several patterns emerge. One of the clearest distinctions between victims is racial. Nationally, on a per-capita basis, African Americans are twice as likely to be victims of fatal shootings as whites. The disparity is not uniform across the country. The rate of victimization for African Americans is as low as 2.93 deaths per 100,000 African Americans in Hawaii, but the rate of African-American deaths is ten times as high—30.12 per 100,000 in Missouri. Similarly, the victimization rate for whites is as low as 2.57 gun deaths per 100,000 in Massachusetts, but 15.91 per 100,000 in New Mexico. The rate of victimization also varies by race within states. African Americans in New Jersey are 4.5 times as likely to die from gun violence as are whites in that state.

In addition, racial groups suffer from different types of gun violence at different rates. Whites are five times as likely to commit suicide by shooting than they are to be shot by someone else. Conversely, African Americans are five times as likely to be shot and killed by someone else as they are to shoot themselves to death.[54]

Some types of gun violence, such as drive-by shootings, occur mostly in poor urban ghettos, where the victims and the shooters are usually minorities. The victims can be of either gender. Other types of gun violence, such as suicide, span all income groups. In domestic violence, the shooters and their victims are usually in the same socio/economic group, and the victims are most often female. Mass-shooters who attack people in schools and shopping centers are almost all white.

In all of these situations, the shooters are usually male. Interestingly, the most vocal advocates for guns are also male.

Guns and gender

Despite years of efforts by the gun industry to sell guns to women, very few women own or use guns.[55] It's probably not because women are less angry or frustrated than men. It's probably not because women are smarter than men, although that will be a topic for debate for some time to come. Women don't own guns mostly because women weren't taught to love guns and weren't encouraged to let their guns define their femininity.

Men, on the other hand, are constantly bombarded with images of gun-toting masculinity. Through the ages, manly men have been portrayed in literature, movies, television, and comic books as using guns to kill Indians, fight wars, shoot maniacs, enforce the law, defend against terrorists, protect helpless women, and even destroy giant mutant animals and invaders from outer space. With few exceptions, women have not been given these roles. They have been victims needing rescue, behind-the-lines nurses, and nurturing, worrying, and waiting mothers, wives, and girlfriends. If a woman was shown firing a gun, she was either target-shooting, Annie Oakley-style, or it was a comic interlude; either way, everyone was astonished if she actually hit anything. Guns have always been a man's province in America.

Recent changes in the US military's acceptance of women in combat may have some future impact on women's interest in guns, but so far little change is apparent. Nor has the entrance of women into domestic police ranks made much of a difference. Women may be just as competent with guns as men are, but the average woman isn't showing anywhere near the interest in guns that men do.[56]

There is, in fact, a very noticeable resistance to guns by women. Not only do polls show that women have less interest in and tolerance for guns than men, but the ranks of anti-gun organizations are filled by women. The women don't want guns, they don't like them, and they are willing to work to get rid of them.

Why aren't women drawn to guns?

Certainly women are facing the same issues as men in terms of the economy. Due to lingering discrimination and the effects of past discrimination, women continue to have an even harder time than men, despite all of the progress that has been made assuring women equal access to education and jobs. Even though they now outscore men in certain educational endeavors and outnumber them in admissions to many university level programs, they also still bear more of the burden of child rearing, especially those women who are young when they have babies, and when the fathers of those babies do not contribute time, effort, or money to help raise those children.

Without doubt, plenty of women have at least as much to be angry about as men. So why aren't women showing up at pro-gun rallies in more than token numbers when the guys strut their stuff? In part, it is because they sense that the guys don't really want them there. The gun guys tend to idolize very stereotypical male behaviors. They love to talk about having guns to protect their women, as if women are helpless and as if women were their belongings. What are they protecting the women from? Listening to the gun guys, it seems they are mostly concerned with keeping women from being raped, as if women's sexuality was their most important attribute. When they talk about women having guns, they tend to talk about giving women the guns, teaching them how to use them, and picking out guns for them, as if women are ignorant. When women exhibit good marksmanship, they lavish praise on them, as if they were astonished that women were capable of such feats.

A big part of the reason that women aren't interested in guns is that they see the dimensions of gun violence that the men somehow manage to put out of their minds. You could spend an entire day with a bunch of guys who love their guns and never hear a word about anyone suffering from gunfire. If they talk about someone being shot, they might allow that it was unfortunate, or that the guy was stupid and careless, and you might hear that "the guy's number was just up." You'll never hear them say what the women frequently say, that "I wish we could just get rid of all the guns." These days, it is quite likely that you will hear guys respond to a report of someone getting shot with the refrain, "If everyone had a gun, there wouldn't be so many shootings."

But women know about the ways that guns really impact people. Women are not fooled by the gun industry's claims that the guns make them safe. They know that when guys bring their guns home, the guns are sometimes used to terrorize their women, their children, and their neighbors. They know that women are much more likely than men to be the victims of domestic violence and that guns are very common and well-recognized implements of that violence. Women have figured out that like rabbits and deer, they find themselves on the wrong end of gun sights too often. Women know that the guns tend to get the guys in trouble with the law, or get them shot by other gun guys. The guns the guys bring home have a way of falling into the hands of children, who shoot other children by accident. And the guns the guys bring home are very conveniently there when the guys get a little drunk and want to show off. The guns are there when the guys fly into road rage while driving home from being chummy with other gun guys, and when they get home and get mad at their gals for not being perfectly whatever they imagine their gals should be. Women believe the studies that show that the more access people have to guns, the more likely they are to be shot and killed.[57]

The gun guys talk as if guns were always under control and never had any unintended consequences, but women know that this isn't true, especially women who live in places where guns and shootings are commonplace. They know about other women who have lost boyfriends, husbands, and children to gun violence. They set the tables at churches for the repasts after funerals of gunshot victims. They sit by the bedsides of victims in hospitals. They nurse the victims who survive, sometimes for years, giving up whatever lives they might otherwise have had. Women's views of guns are not clouded by love of guns. Their views are sharpened by what they have seen guns do.

Are women's voices being heard?

More than half of the people (and voters) in this country are women. So why don't the women have more influence on our national gun policy? Historically, women in this country have been underrepresented in politics–both as voters and as elected officials–and those who were involved were sometimes kept out of the debate on guns. A lot of guys who tolerated women as elected officials did so only so long as women concerned themselves with very traditionally constrained subjects that were thought to be appropriate for women to discuss. Those subjects did not include guns.

Because women tend not to use guns, they often don't know as much about the mechanics of guns, and they can be intimidated by guys who know more than they do. More than once I have heard a woman talk about bullets when the correct term would have been shotgun shells, and there has always been some gun guy who was quick to point out that she didn't know what she was talking about. I recall hearing a nationally recognized advocate for gunshot victims belittled by some gun guys because she didn't know some technical point about military rifles. Gun guys love to put women in their places when the discussion is about weaponry.

Unfortunately, women politicians who did not want to draw the ire of retrograde men or of women with conservative outlooks sometimes ceded the gun debate to men. This phenomenon is clearly seen in the topics that First Ladies concern themselves with. They are on safe ground talking about children, school lunches, or roadside litter. Not since Eleanor Roosevelt has a First Lady even come close to addressing the full range of national concerns, including matters usually seen as the province of men, such as guns.

We needn't look solely at the highest levels of government to see how women have been censored and have censored themselves. The same dynamic can be seen at the local PTA, which in most schools is either exclusively run by women or nearly so. It has happened, though it has been rare, that the issue of gun safety has been raised in these most local of all forums, but when it has been discussed, it was virtually always raised as a matter of safety for the children. Gun safety for the sake of parents and neighbors is seen as something more appropriately addressed elsewhere, which usually means nowhere.

Women have had more of a voice in discussions that focus on the effects of gun violence than on the question of gun control. In fact, panels on the topic of gun violence are often dominated by women. They know.

Women have had a very significant voice in the struggle to reduce domestic violence. But even there, the successes have been won when women could portray abused women as victims needing the compassionate protection of courts and police, both of which are almost always male-dominated institutions. (Incidentally, men have gained some protection from dangerous women by these same measures.) The form these protections generally take is the adoption of protocols for dealing with emergency situations and for judicial orders of protection, which may take away a man's guns temporarily in individual cases. These are approaches that assume that offenders are exceptions who can be dealt with on an individual basis, and that the problem is not the guns, but aberrant men who do not use their guns in an acceptable way.

Contrast that with the approach that society takes with other threats to public safety, which tend to look for more systemic and permanent solutions to a problem. We build sewage treatment plants to keep our waterways clean. We require inoculation against communicable diseases. We ban explosives and radioactive materials in residential neighborhoods. We try to prevent problems by altering the conditions that could give rise to injuries. We ban toys that contain lead paint or have sharp corners. We don't just wait for someone or something to be revealed as an individual imminent threat, as we do when we address domestic violence.

Contrast that also (although it will infuriate many) with the way large numbers of politicians have for years been urging us to deal with what they perceive to be problems caused by women simply being women. There has been an onslaught of proposals to regulate women's reproductive capabilities, ranging from requiring women to undergo ultrasounds to ever-stricter limits on the availability of abortions. The men (and it is almost always men) who seek to clamp down on women's rights to control their own bodies are taking a much more aggressive approach than women have taken to control men's ability to shoot whomever they encounter. Some men appreciate that they are on thin ice when they try to legislate women's behavior, but a surprising number of men in power tread on this ground with no hesitation. Women have been much more demure when dealing with "men's issues."

Gun guys shouldn't feel overly confident that they will continue to be able to dominate the political debate on guns. The historical parallels to the Prohibition movement are striking. Although the Prohibition amendment was ultimately repealed, passing it was an enormous victory that signaled the rise of women's political power—a power that has been increasing ever since, notwithstanding the repeal of Prohibition. The Prohibition movement was driven to a great extent by women who had the same concerns about alcohol that women today have about guns. Men who drank excessively were beating their wives, losing their jobs, squandering their money, neglecting and abusing their children, and generally screwing up, all to the detriment of society in general. The women got fed up and spoke out for temperance. Their efforts grew into an organized movement that ultimately resulted in the passage of the 18th Amendment, which banned the production, transport, and sale of alcohol. At the same time that they were working for Prohibition, the same women went on to obtain voting rights by passing the 19th Amendment. One of the main reasons they wanted the right to vote was so that they could fix the problems drunken men were causing. Prohibition is gone, but women still have the vote, and they are a key component of the movement against gun violence.

Although things are rapidly changing as women gain more prominent public positions, there is still a considerable remnant of the thinking that women are qualified to act on some issues but not on others, such as guns. Perhaps now that we have a few women on the Supreme Court and have had a female Speaker of the House and Secretary of State dealing with global issues of security, things will change more rapidly.

How racism enters the discussion

So the majority of gun owners are male, and as noted earlier, gun owners tend to be angry. In addition, most gun owners are white. How do these factors all fit together? Why is it that the anger that stems from the challenges of modern life seem to lead white men in particular to want to own guns?

White folks haven't had to endure the race-based discrimination that can lead blacks to anger. They haven't been steered into buying houses and renting apartments in sub-standard neighborhoods where people have to protect their families by putting bars on the doors and windows. They haven't experienced racial profiling and harassment by police. They haven't been denied educations and jobs simply because of the color of their skin. They haven't carried the burden of racism that has endured since their ancestors were clapped in irons and shipped to this country to be slaves.

But if you listen to these angry white guys talk, you are bound to hear a version of history that makes it sound like they have been suffering under racial oppression while the blacks, Latinos, and occasionally other minorities have been getting all the advantages.[58] They'll tell you that blacks get all the college scholarships, jobs, free public housing, food stamps, and welfare. Of course, none of this is true. It's just the same racist trash we've been hearing for years, even before Ronald Reagan popularized the myth of the "welfare queen" who drives a Cadillac to the store where she shops with food stamps. These tales of imagined unfair treatment are ever present among the grievances of the angry white men.[59]

Scientists who have studied angry white men use the term "symbolic racism" to describe the way these men express their resentment towards minorities. The scientists point out that angry white guys don't want to appear to be racist, so they use code words that seem to be more socially acceptable. The scientists have demonstrated that there is a direct correlation between racism and gun ownership. The more racist people are, the more likely they are to own guns, assert their rights to have guns, and support the idea that people should be allowed to carry guns.[60]

Ask the angry guys what they need guns for, and they'll say that it is to protect themselves and their families from gangbangers, robbers, rapists, and burglars. In their imaginations, their nemeses may live in ghettos or undesirable neighborhoods across town. They'll avoid describing all these criminals as minorities, but it's obvious who they are talking about.

It's not fair to disparage all gun owners as racists, but the non-racist gun owners don't seem to make much of an effort to keep the racists from speaking for them at all levels of the debate on guns. Apparently, if racist arguments will safeguard their right to bear arms, racist arguments aren't objectionable to people who claim not to be racist.

Before we explore why there is so much racism among proponents of guns, we should look at the larger issue of racism in America. It has been 50 years since this country passed the Civil Rights Act and officially renounced racism as acceptable public policy, and 150 years since the Civil War decided the fundamental issue of racial equality. By many measures, with this passage of time we should have become a more tolerant, multi-racial, integrated society. We have, to a large extent. But not completely.

After the Civil War and again after the passage of the landmark civil rights legislation, much of the nation celebrated, assuming that enacting laws would assure that people would follow those laws. That was not the case, either in the South, where segregation was the expression of entrenched social norms, or in the North, where segregation was officially banned but carried out through private instead of public practices.

To erase the effects of racism, more was needed than just proclamations and laws. Programs to implement the laws were needed, but we retreated from the effort before the task was completed. After the Civil War, racism was permitted to reestablish itself with Jim Crow practices and laws. In the 1960s, money was diverted from domestic social programs to fund the war on Vietnam. America let itself believe that everything would take care of itself with time, so we did not fully fund programs that would erase the effects of slavery and racism. Dr. Martin Luther King Jr. spoke out against this lack of commitment to domestic programs. He understood that it would make hollow victories of the advances that the civil rights movement had worked for. He knew that implementing racial reform in America would disrupt the lives and institutions of white people in this country and that many of them would resist change.[61]

As a result of our failure to fulfill our commitment to change, the US is still burdened with the legacy of racism. In recognizing the racism that is found among gun owners, we should not be blind to the racism that can be found to a greater or lesser extent everywhere in this country. But why is there such a pronounced expression of racism among gun owners in particular? Do racists become gun owners? Do gun owners become racists? Is the current gun-owning milieu one that encourages or tolerates racism?

Racism gives a group of people who are afraid of unseen forces a target to focus their fear on. The angry white guys aren't suffering because of anything blacks have done or gotten, and at some level they know this. They know that, as a group, blacks remain at a disadvantage in our country. They know that blacks have less money and power than they, the white majority, have. But the gun owners also know that although they are white, their position within white society has been slipping.

For decades, wealth has been concentrating into fewer and fewer hands, and it has been slipping through the fingers of the angry white guys. They are the losers in the game of wealth re-distribution. They are not the rich, who are getting richer; they are the middle class, which is getting poorer. They are scared to death that soon they will be treated the same as blacks, who they always could feel superior to and who they unconvincingly blame for their problems. Even though they talk about blacks living easy on the dole with their cell phones, big cars, and flat screen TVs, they sure as hell don't want to trade places with them.

The angry white guys feel helpless. They don't know how to reverse the trends that are pushing them lower and lower in our society. All they have been able to figure out to do is try to look and sound scary, as if they could bully their way out of a situation that threatens their entitlement to remain among the privileged class.

How race issues intersect with economics and class

Setting aside for a moment the response these angry white guys have chosen and focusing instead on the situation they find themselves in, I can see why they are angry. Their plight is real. They are falling by the economic wayside as just more surplus labor. There isn't much reason to think things will get better in their lifetimes. They aren't able to live up to the promises they made to their wives. Whatever sacrifices they made to save for retirement haven't assured them a secure future. They can't ease the way for their children, and they can't be sure that their children will be able to provide for themselves. Even worse, they fear that they will become dependent upon their children when they get old and that their children may not have the resources to help them. The present is disappointing. The future is bleak. Being angry feels better than feeling hopeless. Being angry feels alive and in control. And there is nothing like having a gun to make a fella feel like he is in control.

As the economic condition of the country has declined in recent decades, plenty of liberal theorists have become exasperated that these angry white guys choose to blame minorities for the problems that the minorities couldn't possibly have caused. These liberals have tried to convince the angry white guys to join them in working against the international financial interests that they believe are the real cause of the economic collapse of America's middle class. The angry white guys went along with this part way, but no further. Along with the liberals, they blame financial interests. But they refuse to make common cause with the liberals and minorities. Why?

I don't know that anyone has a complete answer to that question. Plenty of political analysts have noted that in the past several decades, many voters have supported candidates who promote policies that are contrary to those voters' economic interests. These voters have been convinced that it is more important for them to vote for what are loosely called "values" than for anything else.[62] They have been educated to view politics primarily from the viewpoint of religion, lifestyle, and morality rather than looking at the economic consequences of political choices. From Richard Nixon's "southern strategy," which took advantage of a racist backlash against liberalism of the 1960s, through the emergence of the wedge politics of "God, guns, and gays," which the Republican party promoted, to the "Contract for America" and the Moral Majority, up to the present Tea Party, people who used to identify as being part of the "silent majority" have let themselves be led in directions that have contributed to their own misery.

For some time now, certain conservative commentators have been promoting the idea that liberals are fundamentally different from conservatives. They use the same stereotypes that Vice President Spiro Agnew used and others have used for a long time, depicting liberals as effete, ungodly, citified, pointy-headed, college-educated intellectuals who have different values and different ways of looking at the world than ordinary folks, i.e., pro-gun folks. This criticism is meant not only to convince the angry white guys that liberals are wrong in their assessment of what this country needs. It is also meant to depict the liberals as inferior because they only have book-learning and that they lack the common sense that comes from working among ordinary people.

The roots of these class distinctions go back at least as far as the very founding of our country. In the time of the American Revolution, Thomas Jefferson and others popularized the notion that people who worked the land had an innate honesty and ability that was lacking among the upper class political elite.[63] This revolutionary egalitarian ethos also found expression in the French, Russian,

Chinese, and other popular revolutions. It served the purpose of giving the mass of Americans, who were farmers of moderate means, the feeling that they were valued in the revolutionary struggle. That was important for many reasons, not the least of which was that those farmers were needed in the revolutionary army. It probably was also an honest expression of Jefferson's enlightenment views, which were widely shared at the time.

When the war was over and the Constitution was submitted to the states for ratification in 1788, people continued to identify themselves and others by class, just as they do today, despite the unifying power of wartime populist patriotism. In some regions, class differences were a significant basis for the struggle between those people who wanted to ratify the Constitution and those who did not. As today, those who saw themselves as being the disrespected underclass resented the attempts of the powerful upper class to control the course that the country was poised to take, which led many members of the underclass to oppose ratification. One observer at the time explained in a letter to James Madison that the resentment the underclass was feeling was more of an impediment to ratification than any disagreement the underclass had with the provisions of the Constitution. The opponents of ratification felt that the upper class "plotted against them" and that ratification would result in "the establishment of two Orders in the Society, one comprehending the Opulent & Great, the other the poor and illiterate."[64] Even though opposition to ratification was largely an underclass movement, its leaders were mostly members of the upper class. They took advantage of the resentment the underclass was feeling, just as the political elite among today's conservative movement takes advantage of the resentment "ordinary people" are feeling.

Immediately after the Constitution was ratified, the new federal government had to deal with class identifications that were dividing the country. Among the most well-known is the Whiskey Rebellion, which arose during the presidency of George Washington. Farmers in what was then our western frontier resisted paying a tax that the first Congress imposed on distilled spirits. The tax was needed so that the new country could pay its war debts, but the farmers knew that much of the debt was owed to eastern speculators who had bought up the war bonds at deep discounts. They also knew that wealthy financiers were amassing large landholdings in the west, where ordinary farmers were struggling just to get by. The farmers also knew that large distillers in the east were allowed to pay their taxes at a lower rate than what the farmers had to pay. The farmers resented these powerful financial interests and viewed them as being allied with the distant federal government which they felt had been insensitive to their need for protection from Indians during the revolution. The farmers' tax resistance became an all-out rebellion with complaints of taxation without representation and of tyranny, accompanied by calls for secession. The farmers' revolt was only quashed by a show of overwhelming federal military force.[65]

The NRA is promoting exactly the same division and resentment in America today, portraying its members as patriotic "good guys" and opponents of gun violence as un-American. As stated by the NRA's president:

> "We are the good guys—good, decent, honest men and women—who look at the world around us, shake our heads in sad disbelief, and can't help but wonder, 'What in the world has gone wrong with our country?'
>
> Everywhere you look, something has gone wrong. You feel it in your heart, something is just not right. The core values we believe in, the things we care about most, are slipping away. Our entire national character is changing. As if the values we've always lived by and counted on no longer matter, no longer make a difference." [66]

Although today's pro-gun leaders have had some success in taking advantage of modern class distinctions, their decision to portray anti-gun folks as being intellectuals has caused some problems for the pro-gun people they are trying to appeal to. In a culture that still values education and intelligence, even angry guys have a hard time convincing themselves that people who they accuse of being annoyingly smart are actually stupid. Some of the angry guys no doubt feel intellectually inferior to the liberals, and they don't feel like the liberals would accept them as equals if they were to work together for economic reforms. That feeling of inferiority could be what is keeping them from cooperating with liberals. It's not very different from the way underperforming school children tease and attack kids who are doing better than they are for being "teachers' pets."

I recall speaking to a large roomful of angry white gun lovers—nearly 200 of them. They kept interrupting and heckling me and the other speakers. I did not yell back at them. I ignored their taunts and name calling and waited for them to quiet down so that I could continue my remarks and answer their questions. Instead of recognizing that I was showing respect for those among them who were behaving well, they accused me of being arrogant because I did not respond in kind to their belligerence. Tellingly, in their blogs and discussions after the event, they referred to me as a "professor," which I am not. Recognizing themselves as playing the role of disrespectful students, they projected me into the role of their superior, and then they reveled in their resentment of me, assuming that I viewed them as inferiors.

Many times since that day, I have encountered similar behavior directed not just at me but at others who remained calm in the face of their provocation. Lacking confidence that their arguments match those made by people whose views differ from theirs, they abandon debate altogether, deny that scientific and scholarly studies are valid, ignore well-established facts, and seek comfort as part of a mob of angry guys.

This kind of behavior is not just seen in the debate over guns. It was seen among people who fought against school integration in the 1960s, and among the goons who threatened Florida election officials in the 2000 presidential election. It was engaged in by Hitler's Storm Troopers and Mussolini's Blackshirts. They were all angry white guys who felt their economic and social positions were on the decline.

What angry white guys fail to see is the similarities between their behavior and that of the young black gangbangers whom they despise. Just like angry white guys, gangbangers know that their future is bleak.[67] They feel abused, betrayed, and neglected. One of the reasons most commonly given for why gangbangers engage in drive-by shootings is that someone disrespected someone else. They feel that their value as human beings has been denied. In the ghetto, violence and threats of violence are reactions to a hostile world. Ghetto violence is repugnant to most of America, but for those living within the ghetto, it isn't irrational, and it may seem prudent, although in the long run, it will bring bad results. [68]

Gangbangers and angry white guys really have a great deal in common. Both groups are standing on the same train platform, resisting being sent further down the line. Liberal theorists may want them to come together, but each group has its own reasons rooted in history for not seeing themselves as similar, let alone as equals. Imagine the conversation:

> "Why are you blaming me for taking your job? I don't have a job."
>
> "Yeah, well, why are you blaming me for keeping you down? I'm down, too."

Now ask yourself which speaker was white and which was black. Then imagine where this conversation could go, if it were to play out:

> "Must be the Jews." (Or the Arabs, or the Mexicans.)
>
> "You got that right."

All too often, the response to hardship in this country and in many other countries has been to blame some group that is not the cause of the problem and has little power to defend itself. So while it is important that we be honest about the problems the pro-gun forces are causing and understand what is driving them, we shouldn't stereotype them. Some of them are nice people who just haven't woken up yet.

How do blacks view gun ownership?

Many black leaders have been highly vocal and involved in the struggle against gun violence. Black clergy are there at the funerals of black gun victims. They comfort the families. They hear the women wailing. They help pay families' expenses from church-sponsored charitable funds. They are expected to help people transition from grief to coping and hopefully back to living. They are asked to make sense of an irrational world that robs people of what they hold most dear, and to give hope to people who have plenty of reason to despair.

Black politicians are also called upon when constituents are shot, and many of them have shown leadership on shaping public policies that seek to reduce the violence.

Blacks have been at least as involved in efforts to reduce gun violence as whites have. There isn't really any reason why it should be otherwise. Despite the stereotypes, shootings are an equal-opportunity hazard, although most shootings take place within the white community, because there are more whites than minorities and they have more guns.

Some types of shootings do occur with more frequency in some poor minority neighborhoods. All indications are that this is not due to the race of the people in these neighborhoods but because the people there live in poverty. In this country, poverty is correlated to a lack of political power, so the voices we hear speaking out against violence in these communities may not get the results or the attention that they should.

We must be cautious about making generalizations, but for quite some time, blacks as a group have tended to align themselves with the anti-gun movement.[69] They have also tended to have lower rates of firearm ownership than whites.[70] History is probably the main reason. During the era of slavery, blacks were prohibited from owning guns in the regions where most blacks lived. After slavery was abolished, the prohibitions were continued in many areas through laws that became known as the Black Codes. Blacks, therefore, did not grow up in the gun culture to the same extent as whites who lived in rural areas.

The gun culture didn't exist in urban areas the way that it did in rural locales, so when blacks migrated north, they were still not living among gun lovers. As the civil rights movement of the 1960s evolved, coalitions of liberal whites and blacks embraced non-violence and hence non-gun ownership, not only as a tactic to be used in political struggles but also as a philosophy to guide daily life.[71]

There are certainly pro-gun blacks. Some feel that it may not be a good idea to disarm people of color before all of the angry white guys are disarmed. They believe that trying to disarm the angry white guys is not only unlikely to succeed but could be dangerous and is a task that must be undertaken by the white community itself. There are also some who still either don't trust the police to protect them or who don't think the police have adequate resources to protect them,[72] so they want to have their own guns.

Plenty of blacks, having served in the military or on police forces, also tend to view guns in positive ways, similar to the ways that white veterans view guns. And importantly, having struggled for years to be treated on an equal footing with whites in the military and on police forces, they aren't likely to want to be seen as having different views from their white comrades.

It shouldn't be surprising that most black men don't seem to be as angry as white gun owners are. A tiny number of blacks who are gangbangers are angry, for sure. But the far greater number of blacks and other minorities reject anger and seek only to live their lives by working and relating to people as people, just as the vast majority of whites do. I have been at plenty of meetings and rallies held by the angry pro-gun folks. There are practically never any blacks among them.

Maybe the majority of blacks have learned from long years of racial struggle that anger is not productive. Maybe they realize that when they appear angry, some whites, drawing on a history of white racism in this country, feel frightened and are prone to react violently. Maybe they have learned from a history of relative powerlessness that guns are not really going to be much use to them in defending themselves either against a tyrannical government or against armed individuals. Maybe they have just known too many of the victims of gun violence.[73]

One pro-gun researcher has recently written about the history of gun ownership by blacks in America, from slavery to the modern day. Lacking adequate contemporaneous records, he has not been able to quantify how many blacks owned guns. His accounts draw largely from news stories and other non-empirical sources. Nonetheless, he has demonstrated that at various times throughout American history, some blacks owned and used guns for reasons including political activism, hunting, and defense from lynching. Although he posits that there is a "tradition of arms" among African Americans, the accounts he cites of blacks owning guns occurred almost entirely in the rural South, and mainly during a relatively short time frame. He concludes that although gun ownership was sometimes promoted by inflammatory rhetoric, it was generally not viewed among the black community as the most desirable route, in large part because blacks with guns were likely to be "outnumbered and finally outgunned."[74] Even during Reconstruction, when blacks in the South were beset by massive violence by whites and may have seemed to have both a need and a justification for using guns for personal defense, he concludes that "Urging blacks to get guns, or more guns, seems like a fruitless recipe for escalating violence. The prescription seems desperate, reflexive, not fully rational." [75]

Blacks have experienced the ultimate tyranny in the US, both from the government and from violent individuals and organizations like the Ku Klux Klan. They may have learned that it was not Nat Turner's armed rebellion that freed them, but rather it was non-violent resistance, organizing, and political empowerment that lifted them up. They appear to believe that more guns will not solve the problem of too many guns, and that acting in anger gives them no advantage over other angry people. The anger may be there. It may be repressed, or maybe blacks are rising above it. But it is not finding expression in a culture of guns.

How do other minorities feel about guns?

Other minorities in the US are identified mostly by national origin and/or race. Hispanics are the largest group that might be expected to have concerns about guns, not only because there are so many Hispanics here, but also because they are disproportionately among the lower income strata of our country and tend to live in less desirable urban areas where they might experience gun violence. But, like most blacks, most Hispanics have no use for guns,[76] in large part because they come from countries where gun ownership is not commonplace, if it is even allowed. In fact, there is hardly anywhere in the world that has gun policies that are as lax as in the US.

When people come to this country from places where they don't have guns, it doesn't generally occur to them that they should have guns. They don't grow up thinking of guns as important or even desirable, and they don't generally mingle with the angry white guys whose attitudes about guns they might adopt. The angry white guys are angry about the minorities being here, so they don't encourage them to come to their gun meetings, gun shows, gun rallies, or firing ranges. The fact that the angry white guys might laugh about shooting at targets with the images of Arabs or Mexicans on them probably doesn't win them many converts to their views, either.

Does religion enter into the debate?

America includes people of many religions, and many sects and divisions within those religions. It is also made up of an increasing number of people who feel no connection to any religion.[77] For some time now, the participation in religious rituals, worship service attendance, and other aspects of congregational life—even among people who claim a religious affiliation—has been declining.

Among people who do claim a religious identity, there are those who believe that their religion guides the way they should view violence and guns. It is not surprising, therefore, that some people claim the sanction of their religion for their views on these matters.

Because there is such a diversity of religious beliefs and practices, it is difficult to generalize about how any particular religion views guns. It is clear, however, that there are delineations of religious orientation between people on the two sides of the gun debate. The pro-gun side tends to profess a religion that takes a more positive view of violence, just as they themselves are more violent by nature.

Christianity is the religious identity the majority of Americans profess—both those who favor guns and those who do not.[78] But when religion is raised in discussions among Christian gun owners, the tone and message are very different from that heard in discussions among those Christians who are not gun owners.

Non-gun Christians tend to speak of peace as a Christian value. Their view of Christ centers on his teachings about turning the other cheek, loving one's neighbor, and feeding the hungry. They emphasize the Good News that Jesus brought and his message of hope, forgiveness, and grace. They also quote from verses in the Jewish Bible that refer to turning swords into plowshares and the commandment to not kill.

Gun-loving people who call themselves Christian tend to focus on the more violent portions of the Old Testament, pointing out depictions of battles that were fought. They interpret the passage that talks about "an eye for an eye" as condoning violent retribution, not as a limitation on ancient practices that allowed disproportionate retaliation. They see Christ not as advocating non-violence on Earth, but as someone who endorsed violence,[79] as told in the Gospel of

Matthew, where Jesus violently overturned the tables of the moneychangers in the temple,[80] and in the Gospel of Luke, where Jesus advised his disciples to get swords.[81] They see Jesus as the son of a God who is subject to fits of rage and who facilitated the slaughter of entire peoples when they displeased him. They view peace as something that exists once you have vanquished your enemies. They obsess over the darkness and fail to see the light.

In its long and diverse history, church leaders and adherents of Christianity have professed a broad range of views on violence. There have even been instances of church-sponsored violence, some of it quite remarkable. But in modern times, many branches of Christianity have clearly been oriented towards peace.

There are comparable differences among non-Christians in the pro- and anti-gun groups. Many Jews, for example, believe that passages in the Bible that say that man was created in God's image teach that people are expected to behave peacefully towards one another because all people were created by the same God in the same image. There are also numerous non-biblical rabbinic Jewish teachings and prayers that make it clear that peace is a central tenet of that faith. On the other hand, particularly since the founding of the State of Israel in modern times, violence has crept into some schools of Jewish thought. Much of this discussion arises in the context of self-defense, either as a matter of personal safety or as a matter of defense of Israel.[82] Some Jews refer to ancient rabbinic teachings that say that a person has the right to kill another in self-defense, because the commandment to love others as you love yourself means you must first love yourself. Others believe that the teachings say that all life is of equal value and that even killing in self-defense is objectionable.

The way people feel about killing finds expression in their views about arming themselves. People who believe that killing is morally acceptable are more likely to believe that they should have guns so that they will be prepared to kill other people. People who believe that killing is to be avoided are less likely to want to carry killing tools with them wherever they go. Catholics tend to be more anti-gun than Protestant Christians are.[83] And compared to mainline Protestants, Evangelical Christians tend to be more in favor of guns.[84]

IS VIOLENCE AN AMERICAN CHARACTERISTIC?

In a nation as diverse as the United States, it is difficult to generalize about whether we are a violent country. In theory, there are two ways this can be viewed. One would be to look at how individual Americans think and act. The other would be to look at how our government acts. In reality, it is difficult to separate the thoughts and actions of Americans from the actions of America. The country consists of the people and is a reflection the people.

Americans like to think of their country and of themselves as being champions of peace. And yet, we frequently act violently. This is not simply because we have been unable to control our violent impulses. It is also because we don't try to reduce violence, due to our lack of a firm belief that violent behavior is inherently bad. We tend to think of it as sometimes being good and sometimes necessary under the circumstances. In particular, people who believe that America is exceptional and has a special role to play in the world readily accept our wars and our violence.

One of the ways to judge America's level of violence is to compare America to other countries. Although it's not a simple comparison to make, certainly the progress we have made in some areas, such as the reduction of domestic violence and spousal abuse, is more than the progress made in some other countries. But by other measures, our country is lagging behind much of the rest of the world, which has been more successful in finding ways to live peacefully.

We certainly put more of our national resources than anyone else into our military, which is institutionalized violence aimed at the rest of the world. We spend more on our military than the countries that are the next fifteen largest spenders. Our military spending makes up more than 40 percent of all military spending in the world.[85] We have an arms industry that not only supplies our needs but also supplies many countries that are friendly to us and some that are not very friendly. We are so prolific with our arms that whenever a world conflict arises, we can have a hard time deciding which faction to support, because they are all good customers.

At the visitor's center at Pearl Harbor in Hawaii, a label in the exhibit gallery *Road to War* explains that the Japanese invasion was due in part to that country viewing violence as a legitimate tool of foreign policy. It reads: "The military used its power to dominate government agencies and citizens. Perhaps the most important factor that enabled the military dominance, however, was grassroots militarism. The glorifying of war dead and promotion of selfless sacrifice, coupled with fear of social ostracism, served as powerful motives for otherwise unwilling people to support the war effort." Couldn't the exact same thing be said of the US today? Is there a town anywhere in the U.S. that does not have at least one monument glorifying our military veterans? Haven't we demonstrated repeatedly that we view war not as the last option to exercise, but as the first and best?

Our belief in the utility and legitimacy of violence is also apparent in the way we run our country's domestic affairs. We put more of our people in jail, per capita, than any other country.[86] Prisoners in the US are often subjected to violence on a daily basis—both by other inmates and by prison guards—and barely anyone outside the prison walls complains. Even before they arrive in prison, many inmates are subjected to physical violence by the police. Again, there is little concern about how they are treated. Add to this the much larger number of people who are rousted by the police but remain at large, and the scope of our government-inflicted violence starts to become clear.

Our police like to say they "serve and protect" us. They like to be called "peacemakers" or "peace officers." But they present themselves as anything but a peaceful presence. Out of a legitimate desire to protect themselves, police in many cities wear bullet-proof vests every day. Not so long ago, the vests were only used when an unusually threatening situation arose. The police carry guns, clubs, handcuffs, chemical weapons, and electric shock devices, none of which are implements of peace. They equip themselves as armored warriors because they are afraid that they will be attacked. Often, they are equipped with exactly the same hardware that our military uses, because the military donates their surplus to police forces within the U.S.[87] They project themselves aggressively to discourage resistance, even though this approach tends to alienate people and can prompt resentment and an escalation of violence. This dynamic came to the attention of mainstream America in Ferguson, Missouri in 2014.

Following the shooting by a police officer of an unarmed citizen, the community protested. The police response to the demonstrations was so out-of-proportion that it was blamed for inflaming the citizenry to the point where the National Guard was brought in to restore order.[88] Police across this country bring the specter of deadly violence to every street they patrol and every situation they respond to. Private security guards in many places are similarly equipped, as they carry out their duties of preventing shoplifting at suburban malls.

Then there is the matter of violence by parents against children. Many people not only tolerate physical punishment unless it becomes lethal, but they actually condone it as a parent's prerogative, or even advocate it as a parental obligation.[89] Some people still extend the option of treating children violently to private school teachers—and, in some places, public school teachers as well—who take the place of parents during the school day. "Spare the rod, spoil the child" is still a widespread theory of child-rearing.

Equally disturbing is the violence against the elderly that takes place in nursing homes. In many cases, it is hard for families to monitor how nursing home patients are treated. Sometimes there are no nearby relatives who can keep an eye on things. Sometimes patients' complaints are given little credence. But sometimes it is just convenient not to look too closely into how old people are treated in their declining days.

Americans may or may not think they are violent, but the rest of the world thinks we are. They see our violent movies, which are one of our major exports. They read of the shootings in our streets. They are warned by their governments to be careful when visiting the US so that they don't get shot.[90]

America entertains itself with violence

Americans don't find violence repulsive. We find it downright entertaining. Our movies, which are one of our most widely viewed forms of entertainment for people of all ages, have always contained a certain level of violence. But they are getting more violent. Since 1950, the number of violent scenes in the most popular American movies has more than doubled. More than 94 percent of our recent movies contain at least one violent scene. Movies that are rated as appropriate for people 13 years old and older (PG-13) now have as much or more gun violence than movies that are rated as appropriate for people aged 17 and older (R). The number of times that gun violence is contained in PG-13 movies more than tripled between 1985 and 2013.[91]

Violence is as American as, well, football. And let's not forget professional wrestling, boxing, and the biggest, newest, and most violent entertainment of all, video games, which are viewed by children on a daily basis throughout America on devices that were given to them as gifts by adults.

There is an ongoing controversy about the effects that video game violence and other fictional violence has on children and adults. Video game violence is not real, and while it appears realistic in a graphic sense, it isn't realistic in a life-and-death sense. Bad guys get gunned down around every corner, but they don't really die. They just disappear from the screen. The good guy never slips on the blood he has spilled. He never hears the moaning of victims he wounded. He never sees their relatives wailing as they crouch over their loved ones' bodies. The ambulance never comes to pick up bodies. The bodies don't get buried. No one puts flowers on their graves. It's all a game—and a powerful teaching tool. The violence is antiseptic and without consequence. No gamer ever needs to feel remorse.

The violence that we teach kids and that we were taught by our parents may not appear at first glance to be violence at all, and even if it seems violent, it may seem harmless. Thumb through a Superman comic book and you will see the Man of Steel crash through walls and toss bad guys around, all without giving them any injuries that required more than a Band-Aid to fix. In real life, they would have had concussions and broken bones. But in the comics, violence doesn't hurt.

And yet, there is definitely a connection between the comic book, action movie, or video game and reality. That connection is routed through the viewer, who responds emotionally and viscerally, just as gamblers respond to video poker and slot machines. Studies have shown that people who play violent video games exhibit increased levels of aggressive behavior and decreased levels of helping behavior and feelings of empathy for others.[92] There is a demonstrated link between violent games and actual behavior. It isn't just speculation that these games are altering the way players relate to people in the world around them. The proof is in.

There is plenty of reason to think that fictional and simulated violence numbs people to violence and may lead them to act violently. Both children and adults pattern their behavior on the behavior of others. You can see "monkey see, monkey do" in operation not just at the zoo but also at day-care centers, at schools, and at home. Mimicry is a powerful mode of learning. But in order for it to be a positive influence, the role model has to teach the child what is correct behavior and what is not. Putting the raisin in your mouth is good. Putting it in your ear isn't.

When kids see violence, they mimic it. Lots of parents have seen their kids playing shoot-'em-up games that reflect what they see on TV, just like the games the parents played themselves, based on the TV shows and movies about cops and robbers or cowboys and Indians. If there is no toy gun at hand, a kid will use whatever is available as a pretend gun; a few Legos or a plastic chicken leg will do. If parents plop their kids down in front of a game console or TV and let them amuse themselves with violence without any countervailing peaceful influence, there isn't any reason to think that the kids won't become acclimated to violence.

Some people believe that children who are exposed to this violent imagery are not affected by it. They even claim that children who view fictional violence are repulsed by it and learn to live peacefully. They say that the fictional violence is a substitute for real violence. They have all sorts of theories, none of which has been substantiated.

The apologists for play-violence point out that of the millions of kids who play violent games and watch violent movies, very few actually go on to shoot up their high schools. That's undeniable, but it hardly proves that the kids are not affected by the violent imagery. Some of the young men who have gone on killing rampages were indeed aficionados of violent video games. Among the games played by Adam Lanza—the 20-year-old who shot to death 20 young children and six adults at Sandy Hook Elementary School—was *School Shooting*. According to the police, a player of that video game "controls a character who enters a school and shoots at students."[93] Do we think the games Adam Lanza and others played before they became famous as mass shooters had nothing to do with the killings?

Some critics of violent video games worry that the games isolate kids from more social activities. This might be a factor in how games adversely affect players. We have seen plenty of instances where the perpetrator of a horrendous shooting was described as a "loner" who "kept to himself." Social isolation can lead people to do things they might not do if they were more engaged with and felt accepted by other people.

There is also reason to be concerned about players who aren't isolated but who play these games along with other people. This concern isn't just about kids, since a lot of gamers are adults who play with other adults. People of all ages tend to act in ways that they believe are normal and socially acceptable. Mob violence is an obvious example of people taking their cues from those around them. When people who play shooting games don't just play by themselves but play against each other in friendly, competitive online gaming environments, each player gives the other player(s) the feeling that what they are doing is socially acceptable. When the competitors are good sports, they affirm each other's violence. "Good shot, old boy!" sounds charming if the players are playing cricket. But if they playing games that involve the simulated shooting of people, any affirmation becomes troublesome.

It is also likely that fictional violence is affecting our broader society. In the aftermath of recent mass shootings, our lawmakers have done almost nothing to reduce the likelihood that there will be similar atrocities in the future. Could it be that they and their constituents don't perceive the difference between a television news report of a shooting and the fictional shootings they watch every day on TV? Isn't it plausible that we have become so accustomed to entertainment violence that we no longer react to real violence, which looks pretty much the same?

The biggest institutional proponent of violence in our country—the military—is clearly convinced that there is a connection between fictional and real violence. They have exploited the connection for years by subsidizing pro-military movies. They know that motion pictures and television shows that depict war as heroic improve the public's view of war and violence. One motion picture, *Top Gun*, starring then-heartthrob Tom Cruise, is credited with not only a major boost in people volunteering to join the military but also with helping shift public opinion about US wars in general.[94] The movies make the military look appealing, and the military can easily exploit that appeal by sponsoring recruitment ads that appear on the screen along with coming attractions. They also sponsor ads on video games and even sponsor games that include recruitment messages.

The military also benefits from violent video games in another way. Video game consoles, military training simulators, and consoles that launch and control actual missiles, drones, and other weapons are all very similar in appearance and layout, making for a smooth transition from childhood violent games to adult violent activity. It's not clear whether the military hardware is designed to resemble video games, or the video games are designed to resemble the real consoles with their joystick controllers. Or maybe both. Either way, the military gets soldiers who feel comfortable with their hardware.

Having soldiers feel comfortable with weapon consoles is just as important to the military as having soldiers who feel comfortable with guns. It has been well documented in actual battles that some soldiers avoid firing their weapons, or they deliberately aim them so that they won't hurt anyone. Soldiers, after all, are people, with the same reluctance that other people have to deliberately hurting others. Others soldiers who do shoot may be traumatized by the experience and suffer from the now well-known post-traumatic stress disorder—PTSD. The more normal that killing feels, the easier it is to do without hesitation, regret, or trauma. What could be better for the military than to have people feel as comfortable when they are operating killing machines as they are when they are playing games at home in their living rooms?

Removing soldiers from the battlefield by allowing them to remotely operate drones and other such weapons reduces the stress they would feel on the battlefield, where they would feel vulnerable. This technology also allows our troops to avoid facing the reality of their violence. Although drone operators experience emotional stress by killing from afar, they never come face to face with their victims, and they never have to carry wounded comrades off the field of battle.

Our military maximizes soldiers' effectiveness by training them not to have the revulsion to killing that they otherwise would. They depersonalize the enemy so that our soldiers don't feel they are killing actual human beings. The training desensitizes them to the violence and dehumanizes the enemy. What a boon it has been to the military that this process of grooming people has now been undertaken by parents when children are highly impressionable.

The civilian gun industry gets the same benefit from these violent games. What kid who grows up playing shooting games doesn't want to go out and shoot actual guns? Some of the pro-gun folks are, perhaps surprisingly, honest enough to admit that they want kids to watch violent videos so that the kids will get interested in guns. In their view, there is no reason why kids shouldn't want to shoot guns, because guns are good. They condemn attempts to restrict kids' access to violent video games as a "surrogate" for keeping adults from having real guns.[95]

Violence pervades our speech

Americans tend to describe the world in very violent terms. The violent imagery and language are so commonplace that we use them unconsciously.

Whenever we set goals, we are likely to talk about setting "targets," whether our objective is higher sales in a business or higher test scores in our schools. We "target" political opponents for defeat. Sometimes we try to stay on task, but often we try to stay "on target." A nationwide chain of retail stores is even called Target, and their logo is a concentric red and white circles—instantly recognizable as a shooting target. Even when my fellow anti-gun activists talk about reducing violence, they are apt to refer to what they are trying to accomplish as their "target."

Another way we talk about goals is to say what we are "aiming for." We try to have good "aim" when we go after the objectives we have "targeted." If we try to accomplish something, we "shoot for it" or we "take a shot at it." If we want something, we "fight" for it. If it looks like our objective will be hard to achieve, we anticipate a tough "battle." When we challenge opponents, we say "hit me with your best shot." If we don't think someone is ready, we advise them to "hold their fire."

If we think we have identified a weakness we can exploit in our opposition's argument, we try to keep it "in our sights" or even "in the crosshairs." We "zero in" on things. We want to be ready to "pull the trigger" and take action when the time comes. If we identify a characteristic in ourselves that we are dissatisfied with, such as a tendency to be too argumentative, we "combat" it.

If we succeed in defeating our adversaries, we may "blow them out of the water" or simply "blow them up." When we surprise someone with unexpected information, we "drop a bomb" on them and "let them have it"—either "with both barrels" or "right between the eyes."

At work, someone who sacrifices for the sake of the company "takes a bullet" for their team. If the company is lucky and avoids a catastrophe, it "dodges a bullet."

We use phrases like, "make my day," and "I'll be back" that are lifted from movie depictions of violent characters like Dirty Harry Callahan and The Terminator. If we pursue an opponent vigorously, we justify it as "strictly business," using the Godfather's signature phrase.

People who do really well in business "make a killing." In show business, we say, "knock 'em dead" or "knock 'em out." Years back, a woman might be described as a "knock out." Today she might have "killer looks." Someone with good judgment has "killer instincts." If someone is making us laugh, they might be "killing us."

A bad career move can be the "kiss of death." If we put pressure on someone, we might "put the squeeze" on them, or "hold their feet to the fire." If we get help from someone with influence, we are calling in the "big guns." If we want more persuasive data to present, we ask for "more ammunition."

If something is big, it is a "blockbuster." If we employ our most extreme tactic, we are exercising our "nuclear option."

Our use of violent language and imagery is an implicit acceptance of the violence it refers to. The violent language we use can move us to act violently. George Carlin and your grammar school teacher were right; words matter, and they are powerful.

How are we raising our children?

People everywhere tend to instill their values and outlooks in their children. Kids can end up being different from their parents, but it isn't usually because the parents set out to raise kids who see the world differently from the way they view it. Almost all of us believe that our world view is fundamentally correct and that we have the right and maybe even the duty to pass it along to our progeny. So, pro-gun people are much more likely than anti-gun folks to teach their kids how to shoot, to take them on hunting trips, and to give them rifles as presents. It shouldn't surprise anyone that attitudes about guns are passed from one generation to the next.

The gun industry certainly understands the role that parents play in perpetuating attitudes about guns. To encourage pro-gun families to raise pro-gun children, they sell rifles that are child-sized. One manufacturer of such rifles also sells a line of children's books that includes the title, *Little Jake and the Three Bears,* with a picture on the cover of a child hunting in the woods. Jake decides he needs a bearskin to keep himself warm in the winter, so he sets out to find a bear to shoot that is not too big, not to small, but just right.[96] And who wants to pass up the chance to enjoy kids' birthday parties at the local rifle range, where any child who is at least eight years old and tall enough to see over the counter can shoot real guns?[97] On family vacations, even kids who are too young to ride roller coasters at amusement parks can go to gun ranges where Mom and Dad can rent them fully-automatic machine guns to shoot for entertainment.[98] We all know that a family celebration of Easter, the Christian observance of the resurrection of Jesus after his crucifixion, just wouldn't seem complete without going to the range with the kids to shoot Easter Eggs.[99] You can't make this stuff up. It's real.

However, there are also some similarities between the way pro-gun and anti-gun parents raise their children. There is no strong indication, for example, that anti-gun parents are any less likely than pro-gun parents to let their kids play with video games that feature shooting or to watch television and movies or listen to music that has violent content. Our culture is so imbued with violence and guns that all but the most peace-oriented parents have largely given up on eliminating violent imagery and entertainment from their children's environment. Anti-gun parents may complain about the violent messages more, but they don't seem to be able to turn their disapproval into parenting.

Anti-gun parents acceding to a level of guns and violence in their children's upbringing might tend to indicate that anti-violence messages will be slow to take hold in our society. But there is also a countervailing influence that is acting upon children. Schools are actively encouraging peaceful dispute resolution by children, and they are adopting policies that very strictly punish violence by students. It is not clear, however, how much headway schools can make in their anti-bullying initiatives when children arrive home and are told to stick up for themselves, violently if necessary.

Efforts to reduce violence are also being made in the broader society that may impact how parents raise their children. Lawsuits complaining of harassment and hostile workplace environments have pressured companies nationwide to train their employees to treat each other non-violently and with respect. Fear of liability has led these companies to adopt and enforce zero tolerance policies regarding violence. Even our military is showing some progress in addressing the violence within its ranks, as a result of exposés of brutality at military academies and among active duty personnel.

What are we doing that allows violence to continue?

People often talk about the violence that we commit. The other thing we should be looking at is the violence we permit. By saying that police, courts, and prosecutors are part of a “law enforcement” effort, we are choosing to look at what we intend to do, which is to enforce our laws. We should also look at what we fail to do, which is also to enforce our laws. In some neighborhoods, where residents aren’t satisfied with the efforts being made to keep them safe, police departments are viewed both as the agencies that stop people from breaking the law and that let people break the law.

Career criminals know a little secret that many law-abiding people are ignorant of, which is that almost all crimes go unsolved and unpunished, including violent crimes. No arrest is made in most cases. If an arrest is made, the charges are frequently dismissed. The system simply doesn’t have the capacity to give every crime serious attention, so it triages and ignores most crimes.

Television has distorted our understanding of what the criminal justice system does. In real life, the police in a lot of jurisdictions don’t have the time to investigate most crimes nearly as thoroughly as they do on TV. They just hope that if a person who commits a crime is really a threat to society, sooner or later he will get caught doing something else. The police mostly wait to stumble upon criminals who screw up, and then the police try to pin a lot of earlier crimes on them, using fingerprints and other forensics.

You've probably seen TV news reports with evidence technicians dusting for fingerprints and taking photos of numbered markers where bullet casings were found. Those prints and photos might be useful when it comes time to prosecute an alleged criminal, but all that evidence seldom actually points to the identity of the shooter. It just gets filed away. The way we deal with crime is pretty much the same way we deal with potholes. We keep track of them and fix some of them when we get around to it and can afford to. This isn't a criticism of the police. They do what they can with the resources we give them.

Realizing that at present we are accepting a certain level of criminality and violence, the question we as a society should ask is whether we want that level to continue to be considered acceptable. If we don't, we will have to decide what we are willing to do to reduce the level of violence. Do we want to spend more money on policing, courts, rehabilitation to help fix the problem, and improving conditions so that people won't fall into violent ways? Or are we ready to ask ourselves if our society is violent because we have designed it to be violent and whether a new design to prevent violence is possible?

As a society, we may say we don't want people to be violent, but we let them get away with violence more than we punish them for it. It isn't just that it would be costly to increase police and court resources in order to reduce the violence. It isn't just that we limit police effectiveness because we are hesitant to expand police power to surveil us and otherwise intrude into our lives and impinge on our privacy. And it isn't just that we think we couldn't succeed in reducing violence. We just don't care that much if people hurt other people, and we are all too ready to disregard the violence. Recall that I said that people were speculating that Abdul's sons may have been killed because they were involved in something improper or illegal? That was a reflection of our need to make sense out of confusion but also our urge to find excuses to not be concerned about violence. Similarly, when an elderly man shot his wife who was coping with arthritis, his two sons who had developmental disabilities, and finally himself, his neighbors did not react with horror. Instead, they said that they were sure the man had committed the crimes out of love and concern.[100] If we can see it as somehow called for or explained as a consequence of a victim's behavior or condition, we can put it out of our minds.

Every day about eighty people are shot to death in this country. Our local papers and media may report on the ones in their area, but they rarely report on deaths far away, unless they are particularly newsworthy. I have been posting some of these stories online nearly every day for quite some time, and I get electronic statistical reports on how many people view the stories. I have found that the most outrageous stories are the ones that get read the most. The old newsman's adage, "If it bleeds, it leads," seems to be true. Unless a headline about a shooting is entertaining, people don't pay much attention. Just another shooting. There will be more tomorrow. We really don't care. Our society is producing an acceptable level of violence.

Another shooting hits home

Periodically, as part of my work to reduce gun violence, I send emails to people who have asked to be kept advised on this issue. Barb, a retired minister who I had met several years earlier, replied to one such email.

Over the years, Barb and I had run into each other at a number of events. She is one of those people who puts her beliefs into action both on the public and the private level. She shows up at demonstrations against violence, she signs petitions, and she even raises chickens in her backyard as part of her commitment to healthy food and a sustainable environment. There was nothing about her that would have led me to suspect that she was a minister if she hadn't told me. But when I learned that fact about her, her quiet yet forceful demeanor seemed entirely consistent with her calling. She is one of those people who I am always glad to be with at any political action. She can be counted on to do and say the right thing and to move the cause forward.

Barb emailed that she supported the effort to repeal the Second Amendment. She went on to tell me that a few months earlier, her adult son had shot himself to death. He had been going through a difficult divorce. There was a legal dispute over custody and visitation of his children, ages 8 and 12. Apparently in a moment of despair, he picked up a gun and shot himself in the head.

Barb hadn't known that her son had a gun. After his death, she found he had more than one. She also found his NRA membership card.

I am sure that during her career in ministry she had counseled many people who had experienced deaths in their families. Suicides are so common that I imagine she has also counseled people whose loved ones had taken their own lives. But, of course, her experience with others did not diminish her grief. It seeped out of her email, that most emotionless form of communication. It was obvious in her voice when I phoned her. She was hurt in the way that all parents dread most: she had lost a child. And the instrument of her loss was gun violence, which was one of the many evils she had worked to reduce, probably without even thinking that it could some day visit her own family.

Who is to blame?

Gun lovers are quick to deny responsibility for any part of gun violence. What should be acknowledged is that in one sense, no individual gun owner is to blame for the more than 90,000 shootings in the US each year. But it should also be equally acknowledged that they are all to blame as a group and as individuals for all of the shootings. Every shooting is someone's fault, and all shootings are the result of what gun manufacturers, sellers, and users have been doing. They have been relentlessly and aggressively promoting an increase in the use and ownership of guns, with full knowledge of the devastation that guns are inflicting upon our world.

At the risk of offending readers of this book who are upset about gun violence and want to blame someone else for the problem, I must also raise the question that preachers raise all the time. Do we all share some of the blame? Have we stood by and watched rather than acted? Have we devoted as much effort to this problem as it deserves? If not, is it because we benefit in some way from the status quo?

For many decades, Americans have enjoyed a standard of living that is the envy of much of the world. Things have slipped a bit, but life is still pretty good here. The comforts enjoyed by the fortunate among us have come at a price, and often other people—both in our own country and abroad—have paid that price. American prosperity and influence has been built not just upon ingenuity and determination, but also upon imperialism, environmental exploitation, racism, and, yes, gun violence.

It is not necessarily easy to see how violence has brought advantages to some people at the expense of others. Even those who are the victims of violence are not always aware that their suffering is part of a system that allows others not to suffer. But violence is a dynamic that shapes our society, and our society does not allocate either violence or peace equally. In talking about war, Deepak Chopra, said, "There can be no excuse for living our comfortable lives embedded in a culture of mechanized death and violence. You and I are not innocent bystanders to war. We depend upon it politically, economically, and socially."[101] He could just as well have been talking about all violence.

None of us lives outside of our society. Everything that we do impacts every other person. If any of us could help to reduce someone else's suffering, withholding our efforts in effect increases that person's suffering. If we are comfortable while someone else is not, it is because we did not discomfort ourselves in order that that other person could be comfortable.

II. What can be done to fix the problem

HOW GOVERNMENT CAN HELP

We could fix the problem of gun violence if everyone would simply get rid of their guns. We are headed in this direction. For decades, gun ownership has declined as fewer people live in areas where hunting is allowed and as there are fewer animals left to hunt. There has also been a decline in gun ownership as people's awareness of the hazards of guns has increased. But we will probably never get to the point where everyone will voluntarily choose to live peaceably. The pro-gun folks are determined to cling to their ways, no matter how society changes around them.

Fortunately, we don't have to just wait for people to give up their guns. We can work together to insure domestic tranquility and promote the general welfare.[102] We even have a government that we established just for this purpose.

Regulatory solutions

Our government has an impressive record of helping to eradicate public health hazards. Government warnings about lung cancer and emphysema on cigarette packages and in advertising have helped educate people about the risks of smoking. Government bans on advertising cigarettes on billboards and television have helped reduce the demand for cigarettes. Government-sponsored public education campaigns have helped reduce injuries to children by encouraging their parents to put them in automobile child-safety seats. The government helped convince people to wear seat belts. Why not let the government help reduce the dangers that guns present?

Teddy bears, children's cribs, pop bottles, window blinds, and virtually every consumer product is more regulated than guns are, even though these other products are not inherently dangerous but only present a hazard if designed, manufactured, or used improperly.[103] Products that are inherently dangerous, such as hand grenades, mortars, rockets, machine guns, and sawed-off shotguns, are so tightly regulated that consumers are virtually prohibited from owning them.[104] Products that are inherently toxic, like tobacco and heroin, are subject to multiple layers of regulation, and extensive public education programs attempt to protect people from them.

Government regulations have resulted in dramatic decreases in deaths and injuries in factories, construction sites, and other workplaces. Since 1970, when the Occupational Safety and Health Administration came into existence, workplace deaths have been reduced by 65 percent, and occupational injury and illness rates have declined by 67 percent. Taking into account that the number of people employed during that same period nearly doubled, the improvements in workplace safety due to government regulations is even more impressive that it might first appear.[105]

Deaths from lung cancer have declined due to campaigns that have discouraged people from smoking cigarettes.[106] Deaths caused by automobile accidents have steadily decreased because cars are safer, drivers are better trained, emergency responders are more capable, and the enforcement of traffic laws is more vigorous.[107] From 1982 to 2010, deaths caused by drunk drivers decreased by more than 50 percent.[108] But there has been no significant improvement in public safety related to guns, because we haven't even tried.

Guns are inherently dangerous. Other products that we use in our lives are also inherently dangerous. But when these products are things that we need, we find ways to compensate for their dangerous nature.

For example, gasoline for our cars is inherently dangerous. It is flammable and has a propensity to explode, and its fumes are toxic to breathe. Because we need gasoline, public safety officials haven't banned it. Instead, they have helped us find safer ways to store, dispense, and use gasoline—through regulations and also through public education. Gas stations have tanks, pumps, and hoses that are all situated, designed, fabricated, and inspected to minimize the risks that are inherent in gasoline. Warning signs on gas pumps tell us to turn off the car's engine, not to smoke or use cell phones while pumping gas, and not to pump gas into unapproved containers. Gas tanks on cars are designed so that they will not spill or create conditions that would lead to explosions. We are also instructed not to store gasoline inside our homes. Instead, we keep it in garages where the risk of fire is reduced. Modern building codes require that the floors of those garages are built so that if gasoline spills, it will not flow into an attached house.[109]

There is a broad range of policies and practices the government could implement that would reduce the number of people who get shot and injured and could also reduce the severity of their injuries. The least intrusive of these would be to require that guns, like gasoline, be stored safely, so that children wouldn't get hold of them and shoot themselves and others, as they do every year. Many gun owners already store their guns in gun safes, so this wouldn't seem to be a proposal that would offend anyone, but it does. Lots of vocal gun owners argue against safe storage laws. They say that they need to be able to reach for their guns and start shooting any time of day or night, without taking a moment to retrieve a gun from a safe place. What do they say about the children who stumble upon the guns that they leave lying around? Not much. Just too bad, goodbye, rest in peace. Thank you for sacrificing your brief life for the cause of unrestrained gun ownership.

In other countries, there are restrictions on who can own a gun and how it must be stored, but there are almost no similar laws in the US. Our lawmakers have seldom even considered the myriad steps that could be taken to reduce the hazard of guns in private hands, and even when they have considered them, they have rarely gone the next step to implement any measures that would protect the public safety.

To get an idea of the absurdity of government regulations when it comes to firearms, consider that the US government has safety regulations governing the design and construction of tree stands that hunters climb onto to await passing prey. These regulations are intended to minimize the chance that hunters will fall and injure themselves.[110] But the government does just about nothing to reduce the risk that those same hunters and other gun owners will shoot themselves or other people.

Gun design is another area where government policies could

make a big difference. We let our government do almost nothing about the danger that is inherent in guns. In some other countries, guns have to be designed so that they will not fire if accidentally dropped, but such features are only required by a few states in the US.[111] Other minimal changes that could be implemented to make guns safer would be to require that they not fire unless they are being used by an authorized person. Laptop computers and smart phones come equipped with finger-scan devices and other biometric features that prevent unauthorized persons from using them. There are similar devices that could be built into guns.

Again, you might expect that the NRA, which claims that "the only defense against a bad guy with a gun is a good guy with a gun," would support technology that would render guns inoperative in the hands of unauthorized bad guys. But again you would be wrong. The NRA strongly opposes all technological innovations that would make guns safer.

A perfect example happened in New Jersey in 2002. The state legislature passed a law that stated that if technology ever developed to the point where a "smart" gun could be made that could only be fired by its registered owner, then after three years from the date of that development, the only new guns that New Jersey gun dealers would be able to sell would be guns that had the new safety features. This is a pretty standard approach that lawmakers take when trying to encourage the adoption of new safety measures. They only require the new features on new products, but they still allow older products without safety features to be sold for a period of time.

At the time the law was passed in 2002, such safe guns only existed in people's imaginations. Ten years later, fictional guns of this type were seen in the 2012 James Bond spy movie *Skyfall*. But by 2013, gun manufacturers had perfected the technology and were poised to introduce guns onto the market that had this safety feature. Did the gun lovers rejoice that someone had finally found a way to make guns safer? Hardly. They were resistant to letting the law be enforced.[112] When a gun store in California began selling the smart gun, it was immediately hit with a boycott by gun owners, who view any efforts to make guns safer as a threat to their rights. They fear that the availability of safer guns will lead to regulations requiring safer guns, and they are against any regulation, no matter how sensible it is.[113] Similarly, a few years earlier, the major gun manufacturer Smith & Wesson had entered into an agreement with the federal government to develop safe gun technology. Gun owners organized a boycott of that company. The company renounced the agreement with the government a few years later.[114]

The gun manufacturers have also fought against regulations that would reduce the flow of guns into the hands of criminals and mentally unstable people who shouldn't have them. A very large percentage of guns that are used in crimes are illegally obtained either through theft, the black market, or straw purchases that are technically legal but are effected in order to avoid legal restrictions on who can buy guns. Traditional law enforcement methods could be used to reduce easy availability of guns to gang members, other criminals, and people with mental problems. But the NRA opposes these measures, allegedly because such regulations might also make it a teeny bit harder for "law abiding" citizens to get guns as easily as they buy candy bars. Bowing to pressure from the gun lobby, little or nothing has been done by state, local, or federal governments to stem the flow of guns that result in so much preventable violence.

Why do we let the gun lobby imperil public safety? This gets us back to the angry, frustrated gun owners. They don't want government to help, and they just happen to be among a larger group of angry, frustrated voters who have been encouraged to distrust their government and reject the very notion that government can help them. An earlier generation cheered government help when the government built bridges, roads, public parks, dams, monuments, post offices, courthouses, hospitals, clinics, canals, airports, and countless other buildings and structures for people all across the country. But this generation, quoting former President Ronald Reagan, who said that "government is not the solution to our problem, government is the problem," refuses to let the government act to protect people from being shot.

Private lawsuits could hold people accountable

Although the current political climate in the US does not favor government regulation as a solution to problems, there is another way we could reduce gun violence that has been very successfully employed in the campaign to get safer automobiles, workplaces, and consumer products. All we have to do is to let the people who are injured sue the people and companies who injure them. The only thing the government would have to do is to make its courts available, just like it does for all other injury suits. When manufacturers have to pay for the injuries they cause, they very reliably respond by making their products safer.

A single automobile accident can result in millions of dollars of medical bills, lost work time, and other expenses. So can a single gunshot injury. The average hospital cost of a treating a gunshot victim was $40,000 in 2012.[115] That's for your run-of-the-mill gunshot victim who is brought into the emergency room. Obviously the costs of treating victims with serious injuries and long-term deficits are much higher.

It's worth noting that gunshots are inherently among the most serious and costly of all traumas that send people for emergency medical care. For example, although only 1 percent of children who go to hospital emergency rooms are gunshot victims, they account for 21 percent of the children who die as a result of their injuries, and they account for 23 percent of major surgeries. The average cost for their acute treatment is nearly twice that of treatment for automobile accident injuries.[116] Therefore, just as automobile manufacturers have strong incentives to avoid the costs for injuries that their products cause, so should gun manufacturers. Unfortunately, gun makers have avoided the costs, not by making safer guns, but by getting laws passed that exempt them from liability for the damage they cause.[117] You can sue the manufacturer of a toy gun if it puts out your kid's eye. But if a real gun causes the same damage, you and your kid are out of luck.

Exempting gun manufacturers from liability and leaving the expenses of gun injuries for the victims to pay does not make those expenses go away. To the extent that gunshot victims have insurance, the expenses are distributed among other insured people. The premiums that everyone pays for health insurance go up every time an insured person is shot. But a lot of gunshot victims don't have health insurance. In fact, in some urban areas, hardly any of the people who get shot have health insurance. Who pays for these people's medical care?

In most cases, county hospitals get stuck with the bills. They may be able to get at least partial reimbursement from the state or federal government. Or if the victim is on Medicare or Medicaid or receives medical assistance from the Veterans Administration, the federal government may pay the medical bills directly. In any event, the taxpayers ultimately pay what the gun makers aren't paying. This costs taxpayers hundreds of millions each year. It is an indirect subsidy of the gun industry. It also makes gun ownership more affordable than it would be if gun owners had to pay more for their guns as a result of gun makers having to pay for the costs of gun violence.

But wait, there's more. Medical bills are only part of the total cost of gun violence. Gun victims will typically be unable to work for some period of time while they are recovering from their injuries. If the injuries are serious, the period of disability can be very lengthy—even permanent. When calculating what guns cost society, this lost time must also be included. It is rarely reimbursed by insurance. It might seem that this cost would be borne by the victim, but in many cases it also is covered by the government, because victims who cannot work become dependent upon government-supplied benefits such as food subsidies and income assistance, also known as welfare programs. Yes, some of the victims are already on these programs, but their injuries can make it more difficult for them to become self-sufficient. In some cases, they become permanently dependent on Social Security, the same program that the gun owners look to for benefits when they retire. Every person who collects Social Security disability because of a gunshot injury depletes benefits that the rest of us, including gun owners, might otherwise collect. This depletion increases the cost of the entire program.

Every person who is killed by guns is also unable to support their dependents. Insurance companies are able to calculate the extent of this loss. As of 2005, life insurance premiums alone were increased by $2 billion a year to provide for payments to beneficiaries of people who were shot. At that time, they estimated that on average, white males lived 151 fewer days because of guns, and black males lived 362 fewer days.[118] Most people don't have life insurance, so the loss is borne by the survivors and by society at large.

Other costs arising out of gunshot injuries and killings are imposed directly upon society, including the cost of police investigation, prosecutors' salaries, judicial resources, incarceration, and probation and parole monitoring. These costs can be substantial. In 2013, the cost of incarceration of an average convict exceeded $50,000 a year in some states, comparable to the cost of tuition, room, and board at an exclusive private university.[119]

There are other costs of gun injuries that if the gun manufacturers were liable, they would have to pay, such as compensation for pain and suffering, loss of enjoyment of life, loss of companionship and consortium, and other intangibles. These costs become burdens on the victims and their families.

Some costs are left for the community and society to suffer as a result of the violence that disrupts everyday life. For example, in some areas of the country, the increased use of weapons by street gangs has led to increases not only in the number of shooting victims, but also an increase in the number of shots suffered by each victim. These cases put a strain on emergency rooms and other medical facilities and their staffs. As a result, medical resources become less available to the rest of the community, and people end up having to wait for medical care.[120]

These costs that result in the degradation of the medical system and patients' quality of life are difficult to calculate, but they are real. They are not normally recovered by injured plaintiffs in civil lawsuits, but they can be recovered in lawsuits that are brought on behalf of the people in a society. We see these sorts of suits brought by state attorneys general and by the federal government against oil companies and other polluters. The suits are brought both to shift the hardship from the victims to the companies that caused the harm, and to encourage companies to guard against causing harm in the future. Because gun makers can't be sued in this manner, they leave the public uncompensated for the messes they make.

In 2000, the total cost of gunshot injuries and deaths in the US was estimated to be more than $100 billion dollars a year.[121] The cost has undoubtedly increased since then due to inflation and soaring medical costs. As a policy matter, the question we should be taking another look at is whether it makes more sense to impose these costs on the people and companies that enjoy the benefits of having and selling guns, or on their victims and society at large. The gun industry is the only industry I know of that has managed to protect its profits by making everyone else pay for the problems it causes.

What have other countries done?

Other countries have found that the best way to protect people was to get rid of or reduce the number of guns people have. Following a mass shooting, Australia enacted laws in 1996 that have led to massive reduction in the private ownership of guns. They followed up with a nationwide mandatory gun turn-in law. The result was an instant, enormous reduction in the number of shootings, including homicides and suicides. Decades later, the reduction in gun violence has proved enduring. Australia decided that the best way to stop gun violence was to get rid of their guns, and it worked.[122]

Many other countries have also reduced and prevented gun violence by severely restricting gun ownership. In 2003, Brazil passed laws requiring registration of guns, banning the carrying of guns, and requiring background checks for gun purchasers. It followed up with a national voluntary disarmament program. The next year, the number of homicides using firearms, which had been increasing for a decade, fell 9 percent with no simultaneous increase in homicides by other methods. Accidental and self-inflicted firearm hospitalizations also declined. In the first full year the new gun controls were in effect, as many as 5,000 Brazilians are estimated to have survived who would otherwise have been gunned down.[123]

The US has the highest level of private gun ownership in the world. US rates for shootings are also among the highest in the world.[124] The magnitude of the difference between the ownership and use of guns in the US as compared to the rest of the world is striking. In neighboring Canada, for example, there are 30.8 guns in private hands per 100 people, and 2.44 firearms deaths per 100,000 people annually. In the United Kingdom, from which much of US law and culture is derived, there are 6.2 guns per 100 people and 0.25 firearm deaths per 100,000 every year. In the US, there are 88.8 guns per 100 people and 10.2 firearm deaths per 100,000 per year.[125] Considering the geographic similarities we have with Canada, the cultural and legal similarities we have with the U.K., and myriad other similarities we have with other countries whose gun ownership and gun violence rates are strikingly lower than ours, it seems obvious that the real cause of our gun problems is our guns, and an obvious solution would be to get rid of them.

How much of a difference would it make in our lives if our gun ownership and shooting rates were lower? Most Americans live in towns that have fewer than 25,000 people. If the shootings in the US were equally distributed across the country and you lived in an average-sized town, at the present rate of shootings, every year you could expect that between two and three people in your town would be killed with a gun. If our rate were the same as in the UK, there would only be one gun death in your town about every 16 years. Instead of having more than 30,000 shooting deaths in the US each year, we would have about 750. That's a big difference.

How do gun guys envision a gun-free America?

The most extreme gun owners will tell you that if people didn't have guns, the US government would instantly turn into a militarized totalitarian dictatorship, and everyone would lose their freedom. Really, that's what they say. Gestapo-inspired units would search everyone's houses for guns. There would be no free speech, no freedom of religion, no free press, no freedom of assembly, no freedom to travel, or any other freedom because the government thugs would spontaneously suppress everyone merely because they would know that if people didn't have guns, they would be powerless to resist.

Does this sound like a summertime teenage drive-in horror movie? Now you have an idea of just how goofy the rhetoric has become among gun owners. These are the same folks, by the way, who love to shout "USA" at public meetings to silence their critics, never giving a thought to the fact that their antics are interfering with anyone else's freedom of expression. They are the same people who love to stand and salute the American flag and applaud everyone who ever served in any capacity in our military, whether they volunteered, were drafted, or were dishonorably discharged. They get weepy-eyed at the mention of our brave men in uniform. They regard all policemen, fireman, soldiers, sailors, and marines as true patriots and heroes. And yet, they anticipate that these same defenders of our freedom would strip them of their freedom if they didn't have guns to hold off these government storm troopers.

No, there isn't much sense in what the pro-gun forces say. But there is a lot of emotion. These are angry guys, remember.

According to the pro-gun folks, the other thing that would

happen if the US got rid of its guns is that gangbangers and meth addicts would illegally obtain guns and roam the streets and countryside, raping and pillaging without fear of resistance. It is startling how often and how quickly these folks start talking about rape when they need to come up with a reason to have guns. I have actually been asked—more than once—how I would defend my family if I didn't have a gun when someone came up to us in a parking lot and started raping my wife or daughter. Do they really imagine that is what is in store for us? Yes, they do. They fantasize that the world is filled with people who can barely restrain themselves from raping women and children in public and in broad daylight.

It may seem odd that the NRA has been saying, in the aftermath of spectacular mass-shootings in Colorado, Connecticut, and elsewhere that the government should do more to screen mentally ill people so that they cannot obtain guns. Have they talked with their members lately? They might be surprised to find out how many of them would not be allowed to have guns if their paranoia and delusional detachment from reality was known. Police departments routinely require applicants to undergo psychological testing to detect anti-social attitudes. They don't want people joining the police force who think the world is a bad place, filled with evil people who are out to get them and who will destroy civilization unless a superhero confronts them with deadly force. That isn't Officer Friendly, it's Officer Crazy. There are an awful lot of Officer Crazy wannabe saviors attending NRA rallies these days. Let's recall George Zimmerman. In 2012, he shot 17-year-old Trayvon Martin for no apparent reason other than Trayvon was a young black man wearing a hooded sweatshirt in a neighborhood where there weren't many blacks. Zimmerman was a volunteer in a neighborhood watch program. How did he view Trayvon Martin before he killed him?

THE CONSTITUTIONAL AMENDMENT OPTION

The gun lobby has left Americans with very little choice if we want to reduce gun violence. They have blocked efforts to restrict the availability of guns. They have defeated proposals that would encourage gun makers and sellers to make their products safer. They have blocked efforts to increase enforcement of laws that are intended to protect the public. They have hindered efforts to get people to act more responsibly. If we want to be safe, all we can do now is repeal the Second Amendment so that we can start reducing the number of guns people have.

Some readers may think that I am merely staking out an extreme position in order to bring the debate back to more centrist ground. A few years ago, that might have been a good strategy. Today, it isn't necessary to have such modest goals. Today, the vast majority of Americans are genuinely fed up with the guns and the violence. They are ready for real change, not just cosmetic reform. They are ready for a solution to a problem that they have lived with for too long. They are ready for bold action. They have no interest in appeasing the gun industry, which has proven arrogantly destructive of lives and community. They have read too many news stories of atrocities committed on American soil by Americans. They have thanked their lucky stars and said "There but for the grace of God" so many times that they have come to realize that they can't count on not being a victim the next time tragedy strikes.

Our governments' failure to act

After the mass shooting at a movie theater in Aurora, Colorado, people thought things would change in America. Nothing much did. No new laws to protect people from gun violence were passed at the national level, and hardly any at state or local levels. No large scale shift in the public's attitude towards guns was detected. Gun sales may have actually gone up for a short while.

After the horrific shooting of little children at Sandy Hook Elementary School in Newtown, Connecticut, nothing changed. No big new laws. No new initiatives. President Obama summarized the situation well in a speech following a mass shooting in Washington, D.C.

> "It ought to be a shock to us all as a nation and as a people. It ought to obsess us. It ought to lead to some sort of transformation. That's what happened in other countries when they experienced similar tragedies. In the United Kingdom, in Australia, when just a single mass shooting occurred in those countries, they understood that there was nothing ordinary about this kind of carnage. They endured

great heartbreak, but they also mobilized and they changed, and mass shootings became a great rarity.

And yet, here in the United States, after the round-of-clock coverage on cable news, after the heartbreaking interviews with families, after all the speeches and all the punditry and all the commentary, nothing happens. Alongside the anguish of these American families, alongside the accumulated outrage so many of us feel, sometimes I fear there's a creeping resignation that these tragedies are just somehow the way it is, that this is somehow the new normal."[126]

After Congresswoman Gabby Giffords was shot, there was a public outcry for changes in the gun laws. But Congress did nothing. US lawmakers at the national level and in almost all states and localities have proven time and again that they are uninterested or unwilling in doing anything meaningful to reduce gun violence in America. They know that the majority of people want them to act, but more important to the lawmakers, they know that a well-financed, somewhat organized minority of angry gun owners stands ready to do whatever they can to make sure nothing changes.

I spoke with a legislator who explained the situation. He told me that the people who want to be safe from guns also want a lot of other things. Many would like more school funding, better social services, reductions in drug prosecutions, and so on. Legislators know from experience that if they keep these people happy on one or more of their issues, these voters will still reelect them even if they don't do anything about gun violence.

On the other hand, gun owners are perceived by lawmakers as single-issue voters. Gun owners don't care if we start unnecessary wars, imprison African Americans disproportionate to their numbers, or let Wall Street tycoons rob the country blind. So long as legislators vote for guns, the gun owners will vote for the legislators. But if legislators ever vote for even the tiniest restrictions on guns, they know they can expect gun owners to do everything they can to throw them out of office. So, the legislators do what the gun owners want without worrying about the majority of Americans. The NRA actively promotes this thinking. In 2013, not long after the Colorado legislature made minor changes to strengthen the state's gun laws, the NRA helped organize the first-ever recall of legislators in that state. They succeeded in getting rid of two state senators, including the president of the state Senate, and they did everything they could to make sure that their success was recognized all across the country.[127]

Plenty of people who want to be safe from guns have suggested from time to time that they employ the same single-minded tactics that the gun owners do. The problem is, they aren't as obsessed as gun owners. They really do care about other things, and they have been unwilling and unable to abandon all of their other concerns just to win on the gun issue. God bless them.

Why focus on the Second Amendment?

The Second Amendment is what makes the gun lovers feel they have a legitimate position. They can and do assert that the right to bear arms has exactly the same status as other rights guaranteed by the Constitution. Technically, they are correct, if you accept the peculiar interpretation the US Supreme Court recently gave to the Second Amendment.

The Second Amendment says, "A well regulated Militia, being necessary to the security of a free State, the right of the people to keep and bear Arms, shall not be infringed." For almost the entire history of this country, the Second Amendment was interpreted to mean that the right to bear arms belongs to the states and/or the country, not to individuals. The part of the amendment that talks about establishing well-regulated militias was considered to be in the amendment for a reason. It made clear that the militias were intended to ensure the continued security of the nation as a nation.

But in 2008, for the first time, the Supreme Court decided in the *District of Columbia v. Heller* decision that the part of the Second Amendment that spoke about state militias didn't mean anything at all.[128] The Court turned the amendment upside-down and inside-out, holding that it guaranteed people the right to keep guns in their homes for their own personal protection, even though it was pointed out to the Court that their decision would threaten the public safety and the functioning of state institutions. From the moment that decision was handed down, the gun owners have felt emboldened. They have claimed that because they have a constitutional right to have guns, there is nothing the government can do to limit that right. They overlook the fact that that is not what the Supreme Court said.

What the Court actually said is exactly the opposite of what the gun lovers think it said. The Supreme Court explicitly announced that the government can regulate guns, gun ownership, and gun usage. But the gun lovers ignore that part of the decision. To them, a right is an absolute. In fact, they often claim that the right to bear arms that the Supreme Court said is guaranteed in the Constitution is not just founded on the Constitution. They claim that the right to bear arms is a "natural"[129] or "God given" right that just happens to be mentioned in the Constitution.

Is gun ownership a God-given right?

Gun owners imagine that somewhere in the Bible, God gives them the right to have guns, but they don't say where in the Bible this right is proclaimed. This isn't surprising, since the Jewish and Christian Bibles they refer to were written well over a thousand years before the first rudimentary gun was invented. The gun lovers vaguely refer to the right to own guns as coming from some Biblical acknowledgment of a right to defend one's self and one's family, though they don't cite to where that is in the Bible, either. They conveniently ignore Jesus' advice to turn the other cheek, to love one another, and to build God's kingdom on Earth. They also ignore virtually all modern Jewish, Christian, Muslim, Hindu, and other religious teachings about peacefulness and restraining one's violent impulses.[130] These gun lovers don't let actual religious doctrine get in the way of their claims that God wants them to have guns.

The gun lovers don't see gun ownership as just a right. They see it as a moral obligation. Many times I have been told by them that because I do not own a gun I am not fulfilling the obligation I have to defend my family. They think that everyone should have a gun because there is nothing else anyone can do that will assure their safety.

"What would you do," they ask, "if someone came up to you with a gun and asked for your wallet?" I think the correct answer is pretty obvious, so I usually respond, "I'd give him my wallet. The credit cards can be canceled, the money can be replaced, and I can get a new wallet." Then I ask if they think it would be a better idea to reach for a gun and hope to shoot the wallet thief before he can shoot me or my family. I get a mix of answers to that one, none of which is very persuasive. One guy told me that if it was him, he thought he could win a shootout because he is a pretty good shot. Pretty risky—for the sake of saving your wallet.

Other people have published different answers to the question, "What would you do?"[131] Proponents of violence have been asking the question for a long time, and proponents of peace have a lot of very thoughtful answers. The question tends to suggest that the only possible response to violence is violence. It turns out that in many situations, violence is the least likely way to be effective in eliminating the immediate threat, and it is the most likely to escalate violence and to be destructive of the social fabric.

One problem with the question, "What would you do?" is that it never gives enough information upon which an intelligent answer can be based. The person responding probably doesn't know what has led the offender to take the action he is taking, so he can't know all the options for turning the situation into a peaceful one. If the responder reacts with violence, he also cuts off the possibility that the offender might be frightened off or might chicken out and abandon his attempted robbery before he completes it. Some Christian theologians point out that a lethal response deprives the offender of the opportunity to repent, and that it is a rejection of the notion that God will intervene to protect the potential victim who is threatened with violence. They also remind us that Jesus' message was not just to love thy neighbor, but to love one's enemies as well. Hard to reconcile loving someone and shooting him.

To those who focus more on the emphasis on laws and justice that are found in the Jewish Bible, the lethal response is also a rejection of religious teachings. An individual who kills an offender deprives the community, through its courts and other institutions, both religious and secular, the opportunity to weigh the evidence, apply the laws and teachings, decide guilt, and, if it deems appropriate, counsel, take corrective action, and perhaps impose punishment. At the core of the Jewish Bible is a recognition that people live in society and have obligations both to God and to one another. It does not in any way instruct people to take upon themselves the prerogatives of judgment and punishment.

Although a lot of gun owners claim their right to have guns is given to them by God, I haven't found one yet who could hold up his end of a conversation on religion. Nor have I met a preacher yet who was on their side. I have worked with many religious leaders who are firmly against guns and who can carry on at some length about how their religion doesn't just support but in fact mandates their views against gun violence.

One gun owner walked up to me outside the Illinois State Rifle Association's shooting range where I was silently protesting. He had his little boy with him. He told me he had served in the military and had killed people. He seemed agitated as he started telling me his view that God wants us to carry guns in our civilian lives so we can shoot people who bother us and break the law. I asked him what he thought of the commandment to not kill. He acknowledged that killing is a sin in some circumstances but then went on to remind me that coveting and not keeping the Sabbath are also sins. "When you go to meet your maker," he told me, "He will see you as a sinner, because we all sin," he said. "Perhaps," I replied, "but at least I won't have killed anyone." He didn't have a reply.

Maybe the man felt guilty for having killed people and he wanted to devalue that sin by putting it on an equal footing with stealing penny candy or looking at girly magazines. I really don't know. But he clearly was not at peace. A nearby police officer observed the way the man was confronting me and came over to make sure the man did not harm me. As between me—the peaceful protester—and the upset gun owner, the police officer felt that the one who was more of a public threat was the one who was having trouble controlling his emotions. That guy thought people should carry guns, and he might have been carrying one at the time. That guy might have hurt someone. It was apparent to the cop and to others who were nearby—probably to the guy's little boy, too. The only one who didn't seem to comprehend the threat was the guy who was the threat. Or maybe he did understand, at some level, that he was a walking hazard.

Hiding behind the Second Amendment

If there were no Second Amendment, the pro-gun folks wouldn't be able to win public policy arguments about gun ownership simply by claiming that they have a right to have guns. They would have to demonstrate that it is a good thing for society to allow people to have guns. That would change the conversation dramatically. They would lose.

Let's look at some of the arguments the gun guys would make if there weren't able to hide behind the Second Amendment. The pro-gun folks have a fundamental belief that guns make people safer. According to them, the more people who have guns in their homes, the fewer burglaries there will be, because burglars will be afraid to break in if they think they will get shot. The facts don't support this theory. Plenty of studies show that burglars avoid going into homes that are occupied, whether or not they think anyone inside has a gun. Burglars overwhelmingly just want to get in, get the loot, and get out. They are highly averse to any kind of human interaction during their crimes.[132] Guns don't prevent burglaries, people prevent burglaries. Burglar alarms do, too. So do barking dogs and the sound of a television that is turned on. So do locked doors and barred windows. So do porch lights. These are the things that insurance companies, which end up paying for losses caused by burglaries, advise people to use to keep themselves and their homes safe. [133]

Gun lovers also say that if more people would carry guns with them, there would be less street crime and people would be more civil toward one another, because we would all be afraid of one another. This might sound plausible, but it hasn't proven to be true. Every state in the US now allows people to carry guns, either in the open or concealed, although a couple of states' laws are so restrictive that they shouldn't really be counted among those that allow people to carry. But with more than a decade of experience in almost every part of the country, it is now clear that millions of people carrying guns has not in any way reduced the number of assaults or other violent crimes committed against people. To the contrary, there is a direct correlation between the number of guns in private hands and the number of gun injuries and deaths that will occur.[134] There is also a growing body of statistical evidence that as the number of states allowing people to carry guns has increased, the number of violent crimes using guns, especially aggravated assaults, has increased.[135] More guns, more mayhem.

When Arizona repealed its requirement that people have a permit if they want to carry a concealed gun, injuries and deaths by firearms immediately increased 11 percent among people who were victims of violent crimes or of gun accidents, with deaths increasing 24 percent The total number of violent crimes and accidents had remained stable, but the number of people who might just have been robbed but instead ended up being shot and killed increased dramatically simply because more people were carrying guns.[136]

Although the pro-gun guys vigorously assert that guns are good for us, the gun lobby has succeeded in passing laws that have prohibited the government from funding studies that would have shown us how dangerous guns are. Wouldn't you think that if they really thought guns made us safer, they would want studies to be conducted that would prove they were right? Doesn't it seem likely that they scuttled the studies because they knew that the more guns there are, the more people get shot?[137] Doesn't it seem clear that they knew that the truth wouldn't help their sales, or they at least suspected as much?[138]

Without adequate evidence to support their positions, how do the pro-gun folks claim that more guns means less crime? They cite to misleading statistics. Fortunately, an ever-increasing body of reliable evidence on the other side of the argument undercuts the gun guys' position. For example, most states did not allow people to carry guns until very recently, so it has been easy to see whether the number of crimes that were committed changed when these states started allowing people to carry guns. Sometimes it did, sometimes it didn't. Sometimes crime went up. Sometimes crime went up and then down, and sometimes it went down and then up. But the pro-gun folks pick the figures they like, and they ignore the states where crime went up or remained steady when more people got guns. They point only to the states where criminal behavior went down, even if the decrease was not attributable to guns and was temporary and later went up again.[139]

A clear example of this kind of misrepresentation of reality was seen when Illinois became the last state to allow people to carry concealed guns. Within a month of the first permits being issued, the pro-gun folks were boasting that the number of murders in Chicago had decreased dramatically as a result of people with permits carrying concealed guns.[140] There was absolutely no support for this claim, which was ludicrous on its face. A few weeks later, the murder rate had gone up again. As everyone who lived through that exceptionally cold and snowy winter in Chicago knows, the temporary decline in the murder rate was due not to people having permits to carry guns; it was because everyone, the gang-bangers included, was staying inside to stay warm. As soon as the weather warmed up, the shootings resumed. Nonetheless, the pro-gun folks continue to make their ridiculous claims about the increased availability of guns reducing murders in Chicago.

What we have learned is that the reason for all this fluctuation in the crime statistics is that the frequency of crimes of all kinds, including crimes against people, is influenced by a number of factors. The most important factor is probably the economy. When times are tough, more people tend to resort to desperate measures like committing robberies in order to get by. When people have jobs, they work, get tired, and go home to sleep. Working people don't stop on the way home to stick someone up or rob a bank.

Another factor that has a significant impact on crimes is the age of the population. Crimes such as robberies and burglaries are overwhelmingly committed by young men. When a population in a state or country ages, these sorts of crimes decrease. Weather also influences the frequency of some crimes. If it is too hot or cold, bad guys stay inside, just like the rest of us. The intensity of law enforcement also can make a difference.

Perhaps the biggest flaw in the theory that guns make us safer—particularly that guns in the hands of the "good guys" discourage the "bad guys" from committing crimes—is that a lot of the bad guys are not functioning in a thoughtful frame of mind. They aren't thinking, "I'd better check to see if there's a good guy with a gun around." Drug addicts who stick people up to get money for drugs are not rational. Neither are gangbangers who are out to prove how tough they are and establish their street credentials.[141] They don't wait to see if someone has a gun before committing a drive-by or ambush shooting. They just shoot and run. If they think someone might have a gun, they are more likely to shoot sooner, shoot more bullets, and use more and bigger guns. If these people were thinking, they wouldn't be sticking people up, gunning them down, and committing murder.

It is clear that allowing people to carry guns has had no

significant influence on crime in general. No one should expect that it would, because most crimes are non-violent, such as shoplifting and simple possession of marijuana. Those crimes almost never involve guns, and the frequency with which those crimes are committed has nothing to do with whether anyone—the offender or a bystander—has a gun. The crimes that might be influenced by whether a potential victim is armed—crimes such as burglary and robbery—are the ones which are relevant, and those crimes are not deterred by the widespread carrying of guns.

It's tempting to say that the pro-gun folks simply lie when they talk about guns. Certainly there must be some folks on the pro-gun side who can read and understand the countless studies that demonstrate how dangerous guns are and how they hurt people and society, and yet they still project false information. But a lot of the pro-gun folks, probably most of them, aren't deliberately lying. They are just repeating what the NRA tells them, and they believe it is the truth. The gun industry's distortions of the truth have been pointed out repeatedly, but the gun folks don't care that the information is false, and they believe that any studies they disagree with are the product of biased, liberal gun-grabbers, reported by the biased, liberal media. They repeat the mantra that guns decrease crime because they believe it, reality notwithstanding. They could be accused of being foolish, irrational, uninformed, irresponsible, and gullible, but not necessarily of lying.

When the pro-gun folks can't marshal facts to support their theories, they make up stories. For example, they posit that people don't exhibit road rage as much these days because so many people are carrying guns that everyone is afraid to act aggressively towards anyone else out of fear of getting shot. If their argument was factual, we would have seen a decrease in road-rage. We haven't.

According to the gun industry, gun owners won't beat up their girlfriends, wives, ex-wives, or the girlfriends' or wives' lovers, if they think the women and the other guys might have guns. It turns out that there is still a lot of domestic violence in parts of this country where a lot of people have guns.

The gun industry's stories and arguments are based on a theory of armed deterrence that has been the basis of military planning for eons. They point out that countries arm themselves and show off their weapons to discourage other countries from attacking them, and they try to persuade us that individuals should similarly arm themselves to ward off attacks. The extent to which this works in the sphere of international warfare is debatable, but even if it does, international warfare is not exactly the same as personal violence. Countries do not stumble out of bars at two in the morning and get into tussles, and hotheaded macho-men on street corners don't have to follow a chain of command before using their weapons.

But the facts don't really matter to people who can claim a constitutional right to have guns. They don't need no stinkin' facts, they have their rights! They don't have to convince anyone that they should be allowed to have guns. They don't need to demonstrate that guns are good for society. The Constitution says they can have guns even if guns are bad for everyone. Just like people who exercise their right of free speech, they are protected, no matter what anyone thinks. That's why we have to get rid of the Second Amendment. Because until we do, logic, facts, rational discourse, and the public good are all irrelevant.

How does the Constitution say the Second Amendment can be repealed?

Article V of the US Constitution provides mechanisms for amending the Constitution that have been used many times. It also provides for repealing amendments. The most well-known instance of an amendment being repealed came about when the 21st Amendment repealed the 18th Amendment, which had prohibited the sale of alcoholic beverages. Both amendments were passed the same way, although different mechanisms were used to ratify them.

The Constitution itself specifies two methods by which it can be amended. The first method (which has been used for all 27 amendments) requires Congress to take the initiative to amend. If two thirds of the members of the House and the Senate agree upon an amendment, the amendment then goes to all fifty states to be ratified. If three-quarters of the states ratify the amendment, either by votes in their legislatures (used for 26 amendments) or by special ratifying conventions (used for the 21st Amendment), it becomes part of the Constitution.

The other method for amending the Constitution requires the

states to take the initiative. If the legislatures of two-thirds of the states call for a constitutional convention, Congress is required to convene such a convention for the purpose of considering amendments. This has never been done, perhaps because whenever there has been a strong enough public cry for a constitutional amendment, the Congress has acted first, obviating the need for a convention. But just like amendments that arise out of congressional action, any amendment that arose out of a Constitutional Convention would have to be ratified by the states.

It is not clear which method would be most suitable for considering repealing the Second Amendment. The fact that the non-convention method is the one that has always been used would suggest that it has some advantage. The most obvious advantage is that no one would have to figure out exactly how to run a convention, such as how to select delegates, how many votes each state and/or delegate would get, or whether a simple or two-thirds majority would be required in order to adopt amendments.[142] The Constitution does not specify any of these details on how a convention would be run. It is not even certain that a convention would follow procedures that are similar to those followed in Congress and in state legislatures, wherein proposals are considered in committee, debated on the floor, and voted upon.

The other advantage of considering amendments in Congress rather than in a convention is that it might be difficult to limit the number of topics that could potentially be considered in a convention.[143] Delegates at a convention might not feel constrained to consider only repealing the Second Amendment; they might also consider repealing other amendments or adding new ones. After all, we haven't had a constitutional convention since 1787, and the chance to make history might prove irresistible. Delegates to a convention might not even be office holders and might take a once-in-a-lifetime opportunity to make constitutional changes, since they wouldn't be afraid of being held accountable at the next election.

There are already a few constitutional amendments that could find their way onto the floor of a convention. One is a response to the 2010 US Supreme Court case, *Citizens United v. Federal Election Commission,*[144] which gave corporations the same right of free speech as real people and which threw out the federal law that restricted campaign contributions by corporations. Ever since that decision, people have been calling for an amendment to the Constitution that would reverse it.[145] There is also the Equal Rights Amendment, which Congress passed in 1972 but which was not ratified by the required number of states. It still has many staunch advocates. There have also been calls for amendments to either overturn the 1973 *Roe V. Wade* decision, which recognized a constitutional right of privacy that protected a woman's right to choose whether to abort a pregnancy, or to enshrine that decision in the Constitution as an amendment.

In 2013, right-wing radio personality Mark. R. Levin published a book arguing in favor of a constitutional convention that would propound ten amendments to the Constitution.[146] His proposals have gained some support from Tea Party members and supporters of the American Legislative Exchange Council (ALEC). They include term limits for members of Congress and the Supreme Court, and repealing the 17th Amendment so that US senators would be chosen by state legislatures, as they were prior to 1913, instead of by popular election.[147]

The political process in this country often relies upon coalitions being formed and compromises being made, so if a constitutional convention were called, it is foreseeable that the price asked by one contingent for approving another group's amendment would be the approval of the contingent's own amendment. In the polarized political climate that we have lived with recently, it is unlikely that those who favor repealing the Second Amendment would be eager to approve another group's amendment that would eliminate abortion in the US, and vice versa. A convention could become deadlocked, resulting in no amendments being passed. The opposite could happen, too. A convention might simply pass a number of amendments and throw them to the states to see which ones gained sufficient support to become adopted as part of the Constitution.

Since 1972, Congress has been unable or unwilling to pass any amendments. The history of our country includes only two periods when the Constitution went unamended for a longer time than this latest stretch. No amendments were adopted for 61 years from 1804 to 1865, and for 43 years, from 1870 to 1913. [148]

The big question is whether there is any possibility that the states would call for a convention or that Congress would consider repealing the Second Amendment. Most pundits would quickly say there is no possibility right now. Many would be quick to add that the US will never repeal the Second Amendment.

Other amendments that succeeded

Before we delve further into the Second Amendment, let's take a look at what the chances might have looked like for adopting other amendments. Not too many years before the 13th Amendment was adopted in 1865, it seemed unthinkable to many that the United States would abolish slavery. The institution of slavery was deeply rooted in much of the United States. It was thought to be essential to the economy of the young and growing nation, and it was accepted by many religious people as part of God's scheme. Powerful interests depended upon and protected slavery, and slaves had absolutely no political power to deliver themselves from their situation. Protection of the institution of slavery was one of the reasons America became an independent nation in the first place. Just a few years before the American Revolution began, a court decision in England announced that slavery was not authorized by the common law. Because slavery had also not been authorized by statute, the decision went a long way towards abolishing slavery on the English mainland. Slave owners in the American colonies were extremely agitated by the decision and were worried that in time, the ban would be extended to American soil. In order to preserve slavery, they decided to separate from England and form a new country where slavery could continue to exist.[149] And yet, even though slavery was central to the very existence of the early United States, eventually, due to many converging forces and after a horrific civil war, the US did indeed abolish the "peculiar institution."

Before the 19th Amendment was adopted in 1920, the notion of amending the Constitution to grant women the right to vote seemed extremely unlikely. Women had never voted in most of the states or in many of the countries that sent immigrants here. Women were considered largely to be subject to the control of men and were sometimes likened to possessions. Much contemporary thinking was that women were inherently incapable of making reasonable decisions on who to vote for, because of their emotional and mental composition. Besides, giving women the right to vote was seen as offering little to men, and it threatened to dethrone them from their privileged position. And yet, somehow, public opinion changed sufficiently that men, the only ones allowed to vote on the issue, decided to share their franchise with the other half of the population.

One more example of an unlikely amendment being adopted is the 26th, which in 1971 gave the vote to everyone over the age of 17. What the amendment really did was give the vote to citizens aged 18 to 20, because at the time it was adopted, the voting age was 21. From our perspective, this might not seem like such a radical amendment, but at the time it was adopted, young people were considered not only immature, they were viewed by a large segment of society as a serious threat to everything they thought America stood for.

In 1971, young people were demonstrating for a number of changes, notably civil rights for blacks and an end to the Vietnam War. They were portrayed in popular media as dope-smoking, LSD-crazed hippies who rejected the very notion of working for a living. They were shown romping naked at rock festivals, living communally, and engaging promiscuously in non-marital sex. They dressed funny, too, and listened to wild music. And they didn't get regular haircuts. Middle-class and older Americans feared not only other people's children; they were afraid their own children would turn against them and everything they held sacred. America seemed in no mood to give these young people the right to vote to change the world to suit their unfathomable notions, especially since everyone knew that the young contingent were "baby boomers," who would constitute a large new and enduring voting bloc. And yet, shamed by the fact that these young people were considered old enough to be drafted into the military and ordered to kill people thousands of miles away but too young to vote on whether foreign wars were a good idea, our country gave them the vote.

It is easy to overlook the reality that amendments are usually adopted not only in spite of the fact that they are unpopular, but also *because* they are unpopular. If everyone had readily agreed that 18-year-olds and women should be allowed to vote and that slaves should be freed, amendments accomplishing these changes would not have been needed. States would have simply lowered their own voting ages, let women vote, and freed their slaves. There was nothing in the Constitution preventing any of these changes. Even the infamous provision in Article I Section 2 of the Constitution that counted only three-fifths of non-free men for the purpose of apportionment did not prevent states from freeing their slaves.

The paradox that unpopular amendments get passed can also be seen in the failure of the Equal Rights Amendment to be adopted. When it was passed by Congress in 1972, it was controversial, but to a great extent the reason it was not ratified was because society was changing so rapidly the amendment was not seen as necessary. Many of the goals of the amendment were being accomplished without the need for the amendment. Pay, though still not equal between men and women, was being leveled. Employment by women was skyrocketing. College enrollment was increasing. Women were making great strides, with the assistance of legislation at the state and national levels. Enough of the energy that was needed for adoption was dissipated by a general feeling that the amendment was superfluous. In a society that was already heading in the right direction, and, because of Supreme Court decisions like *Roe v. Wade*, it was felt that the Constitution was already protecting women's rights.

Has anyone ever tried to repeal the Second Amendment before?

Yes, but without much fanfare. There have been lots of proposals to amend the Constitution. According to the US Senate, at least 11,623 amendments have been proposed since 1789.[150] These days, approximately 35 new amendments are proposed each year. There is a lot of overlap in these proposals. For example, at every session of Congress, someone proposes an amendment that would require the President to present a balanced budget to Congress.

But of all those proposals over all those years, only once did anyone try to get the Second Amendment repealed. On March 11, 1992, Representative Major Owens, a Democrat from New York, introduced House Joint Resolution 438, which read: "The second article of amendment to the Constitution of the United States is repealed." There were no cosponsors of the resolution. It was sent to the House Committee on Judiciary, and then to the subcommittee on Civil and Constitutional Rights, where it died. There is no record of any hearings being held on the resolution or of any action being taken. It is not even clear that anyone bothered to oppose it.[151] The sponsor never re-introduced it.

When amendments have been approved by the US Congress, they usually get ratified by the states. But getting an amendment approved by the Congress is the hard part. Thirty-three amendments have been approved by Congress, and 27 of them have been ratified. Only six amendments failed to get ratified. (Technically, four of them could still be ratified.)

Plenty of people outside of Congress have called for repeal of the Second Amendment over the years, often in response to tragic mass shootings or other highly publicized killings. But no serious effort has been mounted.

In 1991, constitutional scholar and *Washington Post* conservative columnist George Will wrote that because court decisions were having difficulty reconciling modern needs for gun control with the world the Founders lived in, it was time to repeal the Second Amendment. "The Bill of Rights should be modified only with extreme reluctance but America has an extreme crisis of gunfire. And impatience to deal with it can cause less than scrupulous readings of the Constitution."[152]

That same year, on the 200th anniversary of the ratification of the Bill of Rights, Warren Burger, a noted conservative and retired Chief Justice of the U.S. Supreme Court said, "If I were writing the Bill of Rights now there wouldn't be any such thing as the Second Amendment." He went on to say that the NRA had misled the American people about the meaning of the Second Amendment, which he believed referred only to service in state militias. "This has been the subject of one of the greatest pieces of fraud, I repeat the word 'fraud,' on the American public by special interest groups that I have ever seen in my lifetime."[153]

In 1993, *Chicago Tribune* syndicated columnist Bob Greene speculated about repealing the Second Amendment. "You're already thinking: This isn't realistic. The right to bear arms is sacred; America can't give up that right. Maybe. Maybe America can't. But America can't continue down the path it's going, either. The murderous gun violence is already beginning to render this country unrecognizable to many people who love it. Guns inside our borders are doing the thing that guns outside our borders never were able to accomplish: They are defeating us and destroying us. We have been invaded, and we are in real danger of losing. Repeal the 2nd Amendment? You say it's unthinkable? Perhaps. But is it any more unthinkable than what this once decent, peaceful and secure nation has become?"[154]

In April 2007, just after a student at Virginia Tech University shot 49 people, killing 32 of them, Walter Shapiro, Washington bureau chief of *Salon.com*, called for repeal of the Second Amendment. He advised people who were fed up with the violence in our country to be bold and begin a campaign that he anticipated would take 15 to 20 years.[155] Writer Zack Beauchamp repeated the call for repeal in 2014 in *The Week*.[156]

In 2007, after a federal court threw out the Washington, D.C., gun ban but before the Supreme Court affirmed the decision, Benjamin Wittes wrote in *The New Republic* that the Second Amendment should be repealed because it was no longer relevant to our modern world. He criticized the Court's decision as a tortured misreading of the language of the Constitution. "The Bill of Rights is sacred, but it is not so sacred that we should prefer lying to ourselves about what it actually says, rather than changing it as our needs shift."[157]

In 2011, political commentator and television host Alex Wagner supported repeal of the Second Amendment. "I'd get rid of the Second Amendment, the right to bear arms. I just think in the grand scheme of the rights that we have, the right of assembly, free speech, I mean, owning a gun does not tally on the same level as those other constitutional rights..."[158]

In 2013, shortly after the mass-killing at Sandy Hook Elementary School in Newtown, Connecticut, Kurt Eichenwald proposed in *Vanity Fair* magazine that the Second Amendment be repealed because it had been interpreted incorrectly by the Supreme Court. He proposed that the amendment be replaced with new wording that would preserve the right of people to have guns, but that the guns would be subject to "reasonable restriction."[159]

Mary Margaret Penrose, a professor at Texas A&M University School of Law, said in November, 2013 that gun violence in the US called for drastic action, including repealing the Second Amendment so that states could regulate guns. "I think the Second Amendment is misunderstood and I think it's time today, in our drastic measures, to repeal and replace that Second Amendment." [160]

In his 2002 Academy Award winning documentary, *Bowling for Columbine,* filmmaker Michael Moore put the massacre of students at a Colorado high school in the context of a culture of violence that included the manufacture of war materiel. In 2012, he tweeted "Let's repeal the 2nd Amendment" after 26 elementary school students and staff were shot at Sandy Hook Elementary School.

The National Catholic Review in 2013 also called for repeal. "In the national imagination, the Constitution is too often thought of as a kind of sacred text. Yet neither our founders nor our forebears held to that view. The Constitution is mere human law. It is excellent law, but it is not divine law; it is not revelation. We should be wary of amending the Bill of Rights. We should also be wary of idolizing it."[161]

Author Timothy Villareal, a contributor to *Tikkun Daily* and other periodicals, proposed repeal of the Second Amendment in 2013, "...to end, once and for all, the fiction that the Second Amendment to the U.S. Constitution is a moral and effective means to deal with the problem of Executive branch tyranny."[162]

In 2014, retired US Supreme Court Justice John Paul Stevens proposed that the Second Amendment be amended so that the right to bear arms would unambiguously only apply to people in connection with their service in a state's militia. His proposal adds five words to the Second Amendment, making it read, "A well regulated Militia, being necessary to the security of a free State, the right of the people to keep and bear Arms *when serving in the Militia* shall not be infringed."

Some people believe that because there are no state militias, Stevens' amendment would effectively repeal the Second Amendment. Actually, it would probably have exactly the opposite effect and strengthen the rights of individuals to have guns. A well-established doctrine used by judges to interpret laws is that every word in legislation is presumed to mean something. Applying this doctrine, judges go to great lengths to uphold legislation that may seem to be outdated or nonsensical, rather than admit that legislators sometimes sloppily draft laws or deliberately pass laws that don't make sense just to gain some political advantage. If Stevens' amendment were adopted, a court that was asked to interpret the Stevens amendment would probably reason that if the people had meant to eliminate the right to have guns, they would have simply repealed the Second Amendment. The most obvious interpretation of the Stevens' amendment would be that the people adopted it in order to affirm the right of people to have guns and to form Militias. The amendment might be construed as requiring states to reestablish government-affiliated militias. It could also be construed as authorizing establishment of private armed militias. Stevens, who served on the court from 1975 until 2010, was among the dissenters in the *Heller* case.[163] He may have been looking for a simple way to undo that decision, but his proposal was not well thought out.

Jerry Large, staff columnist for the *Seattle Times,* wrote a 2014 column titled "Common sense calls for repeal of Second Amendment." He began, "I don't believe the Second Amendment was ever intended to support the kind of gun craziness we contend with today, but since it's always used to ward off any common-sense gun reforms, maybe we ought to just fix the Constitution and be done with it."[164]

Also in 2014, attorney and political consultant Rich Robinson wrote, 'Most importantly without repeal of the 2nd amendment mass gun violence will continue to plague America and the right of people to be secure in their homes, schools, places of worship and public gatherings shall perish from our nation."[165]

Columnist Steve Nelson argued in the *Valley News* in 2014 that repeal is needed because the Supreme Court has grossly misinterpreted the Second Amendment. "What is at stake is the very nature of our increasingly uncivil society. ...interpreting the Second Amendment to allow any idiot to carry a weapon to a school, church, home improvement store or restaurant is worse than infantile. It is crazy."[166]

Another columnist, Allan Goldstein, argued for repeal in *OpEdNews* in 2014. "[I]f a state wants, by popular vote of its citizens, to ban rifles, handguns, and/or automatic weaponry it should have that right as well. But it can't, because of the anachronistic, tyrannical Second Amendment. For freedom's sake, it has to go."[167]

A day after a Florida sheriff's deputy was shot and killed in an ambush, Columnist Gerald Ensley openly called for repeal in the

Tallahassee Democrat in 2014. "Gun freaks say if you take away their guns only outlaws will have guns. That's a chance worth taking. Because if we ban guns, eventually the tide will turn. It might take 10 years or 20 years. Hell, it might take 50 years. But if we make it illegal to own a handgun, eventually there will be no handguns...But those of us who think widespread handgun ownership is insane need to keep speaking up. We need to teach our children handguns are wrong. We need to support any measure that limits their availability—and work to repeal the Second Amendment. We need to keep marching forward until someday this nation becomes civilized enough to ban guns.[168]

Quaker Pastor Philip Gulley did not expressly call for repeal of the Second Amendment, but in 2014 he wrote that we didn't need it and would be better off without it. "...I've come to believe 'the right of the people to keep and bear Arms' no longer promotes our life, liberty and pursuit of happiness, but daily threatens them. How free are we when more people are shot and killed each year in America than populate the towns in which many of us live?...Our nation has outgrown its need for an armed citizenry. The disadvantages of widespread gun ownership far outweigh any perceived advantage."[169]

Tom Hastings, a member of the faculty of Portland State University, expressed his feelings clearly in the title of his 2014 article, "Shoot Down the Stupid Second Amendment." He wrote, "What country fetishizes, lionizes, valorizes, idolizes, and sacralizes guns as much as does our United States? OK, possibly Mozambique—the only country with an AK47 on its flag, but really, it's long past time to end this obsessive 'My Precious' attachment of Americans to instruments of death... Repeal the Stupid Second Amendment. Surround it, grab it, bring it in the back room, pull down the shades, and end it. OK, petition for it, get it on the ballot, and get it done by enough of the US populace, by enough people in enough states, to get it consigned to the dustbin of history."[170]

In 2015, columnist Bob Henry argued for repealing the Second Amendment in the California Desert Sun newspaper. "I would challenge any NRA member to give a rational explanation as to why a citizen needs an assault weapon or a 40-round magazine. The answers they do give are ludicrous—for target practice, as a collectible, or for hunting. The real reason is that the majority of these people are living in a fantasy in which they will need sufficient fire-power to protect them from their government. These people have sadly lost faith in their own democracy."[171]

Columnist Jamar Thrasher went even further, calling for banning all guns and amending the Constitution if necessary in order to implement a ban. "Gun ownership, as it stands is a constitutional right. But the United States Constitution is a working document and can be amended and revised as we see fit."[172]

The calls for repeal have seldom come from our politicians. The reason could be because they don't think the Constitution should be amended this way. It could be because they don't think their constituents want it amended. It could be because they don't think the majority of the country would support the amendment. It could be because they have some secret plan to solve the problem of gun violence that no one is telling us about, but I doubt it. Or—most likely—it could just be because they are afraid that the legendary NRA lobbying machine would pour so much money into ousting them from office that no one is willing to be a leader on the issue.[173]

It would be nice if the political elite would make some effort, but their silence shouldn't be taken as all that important. Every modern poll shows that the American people have lost confidence in their politicians. No one else expects politicians to display courage and vision. Why should we?

That the calls for repeal are coming from ordinary people is a good sign, if you believe, as I do and as our Founders did, that the ordinary people are the ones who should be running this country. We built this country. We own it. We run it. We the People, remember?

III. The Constitution and the people

HOW AMERICANS VIEW THEIR CONSTITUTION

Discussions of the Constitution and its amendments often assume that everyone understands what the Constitution is, just as everyone understands what a dictionary is. In fact, the Constitution is not so easily described. People have very different views of our Constitution. Their views differ not just because people have different outlooks and philosophies, although that does affect how we see the Constitution. Their views don't differ simply because some people are wrong and others are right, or because some people are more sophisticated than others or have a greater understanding of history or government. People's views about our Constitution do not just reflect their differences as individuals. Fundamentally, people's views of the Constitution reflect the different ways that they have been educated and indoctrinated to perceive the Constitution and the several different functions that the Constitution serves.

The Constitution as sacred text

Americans today are very reluctant to even think about amending the Constitution. They regard it as a nearly sacred document that was produced by a handful of remarkable men who were smarter than today's politicians and who knew two hundred years ago better than we know now what is best for us today. Americans hold both the document and the Founding Fathers in awe. They feel that it is akin to blasphemy to suggest that there might be a flaw in the Constitution, especially in the portion that is called the Bill of Rights.[174]

This attitude that the Constitution is quasi-religious is reinforced throughout our society. The document itself is displayed in the

National Archives in the rotunda of a building that was inspired by ancient temples. It is encased in a shrine of sorts—a marble structure that supports four gold-plated titanium and aluminum frames that are fitted with bullet-proof glass. The case is lowered each night into a steel and concrete vault. While on display, it is flanked by security guards. The Constitution is an icon, and millions of visitors hold it in awe, just as believers view the bone fragments of countless saints and martyrs that are enshrined in church reliquaries.

When sworn into office, every president, member of Congress, state representative, village trustee, and every other public official up and down the line takes an oath that includes a promise to uphold the Constitution. So does every soldier, sailor, airman, and marine. To graduate from grade school or in some states high school, students typically have to pass a test showing that they have some knowledge of the Constitution. To become a naturalized citizen, immigrants must show a rudimentary understanding of the Constitution. They don't have to know how to cross the street on a green light and stop on red, which is probably more important to their daily well-being, and they don't have to understand that murder is illegal, but they have to know that there are three branches of government, as the Constitution specifies.

The Constitution is regarded by many in a very similar way to the way they regard the Bible or other religious writings. People speak of the Constitution as if it was divinely inspired. Just as they would not endorse revising Holy Scriptures, they give almost no credence to the idea that there might be a need to change the wording of the Constitution.

The men who wrote the Constitution and the Bill of Rights didn't feel that way about it. During the drafting of the original Constitution, which took four months, there were vigorous disagreements about what it should say and how it should say it. The document that we now have was the result not only of lofty debate, but also of political maneuvering. Our Constitution wasn't written the way it was because that was the only way it could have been written. It is a compilation of compromises between idealists, statesmen, and powerful individuals who had their own personal interests and regional concerns to protect. We don't necessarily recognize their names today, but the people who took part in the Constitutional

Convention and the people behind the scenes had interests in agricultural, landholding, mercantile, financial, and other industries that in their day were equivalent to Monsanto, General Electric, Google, R.J. Reynolds, and other financial stakeholders. Many of their interests would today be the sort to be listed on stock exchanges or hidden behind family trusts.

One obvious example of how the drafters wrote our Constitution to protect entrenched interests is found in the very first Article, which states that representatives and taxes would be apportioned "by adding to the whole Number of free Persons, including those bound to Service for a Term of Years, and excluding Indians not taxed, three fifths of all other Persons." The drafters needed to find a compromise that would be acceptable to regions where there were many slaves and those where there were few or none. Slaves were a means of production, like machines are today. Counting the slaves, even as three-fifths of a person each, allowed the slave states to reflect larger population sizes, to achieve a greater number of representatives in Congress. The slaves were counted for the benefit of their owners, but they were not, of course, allowed to vote. Allowing slaves to be counted enabled the slave states to protect their agricultural interests and their economy. It also protected states that were dependent on the financing of the slave trade, rather than upon the direct labor of slaves.

The people who lived at the time the Constitution was adopted were not all actively involved in the process any more than people today are all involved in any particular political issue. In fact, the actual debates that led to the writing of the Constitution were carried out in secret, so that the public would not know what proposals were being considered before they were agreed upon. In the sweltering Philadelphia summer, they even kept the windows closed in the hall where they were meeting, to keep anyone from overhearing their discussions. The drafters, many of whom had a great deal of experience in government and politics, were afraid that too much disagreement would arise if the public became involved in the process, making it impossible to arrive at an acceptable final draft. The general public wasn't allowed to have any direct input whatsoever into the drafting of the Constitution. All they were able to do was either accept it or reject it through their representatives in conventions that were held in each state when the Constitution was presented for ratification.[175]

If a larger number of people had been able to become involved in the writing of the Constitution, it is not clear that they would have. Just as today, people then had a lot of things on their minds, like trying to raise crops, finance businesses, and cope with high mortality rates from untreatable and unpreventable diseases. Some were illiterate or barely literate.

But once the Constitution was published and sent by Congress to the states for ratification in conventions, a lot of people did get involved in the debate (excluding disenfranchised women, Native Americans, and slaves, of course).[176] There weren't a lot of people in the country back then, so those who were interested could be very intimately involved in the discussions. If you think the New Hampshire presidential primary today is retail-level politics, where interested voters can shake the hand of every contender, imagine how folks could have felt back then about the proposal for a Constitution. Every citizen could legitimately feel that it was their document and that they had the right to have it written exactly as they wished. They were eager to demonstrate their preferences to their ratifying conventions, which were convened in each state precisely so that people would feel involved.

Today, it would be hard to find many people who feel that they were entitled to a say in what the Constitution dictates. Even at the very pinnacle of our legal system—the US Supreme Court—where nine people have the power to apply the Constitution to situations that are brought before them, the justices speak of that document as if it had been carried down from a mountain carved on stone tablets. They never say, "Here is what I want the Constitution to say." Instead, they find rationales and excuses for "interpreting" the Constitution to mean what they want it to mean. The Supreme Court can and occasionally does abruptly change its mind about what the Constitution means, but it virtually never admits that it is revising what the words say. They do exactly the opposite, swearing up and down that all they are doing is reading the Constitution the way it is supposed to be read.

The many functions the Constitution serves

One of the impediments to amending the Constitution is that we are intimidated by it. Although we are taught in school that it is important and that it is the foundation of our democracy, we are also reminded throughout our lives that we don't understand it. Since only the Supreme Court can say definitively what the Constitution means, it follows that the rest of us can't, right? Not many people would try to fix their own malfunctioning television, because the workings of a TV are a mystery to us. So it is with the Constitution. We don't know what it is, how it works, or even what's in it. We keep our hands off, not daring to amend it, for fear that we might make things worse.

If you and I don't understand the Constitution, it is tempting to think that the nine members of the Supreme Court do, but the fact that they disagree among themselves so frequently casts some doubt. On almost every major issue that has come before them in recent years, they have split, usually along partisan lines. If the Constitution is so vulnerable to partisan interpretation, maybe no one can legitimately claim to understand it. Words should have meanings, shouldn't they? Since the Constitution is comprised of words, shouldn't someone be able to tell us what it means, and shouldn't intelligent people agree on that meaning?

Actually, the Constitution isn't just words. It is many things, and it functions in many ways. From time to time, we might focus on one or the other purposes that our Constitution serves, but we seldom take a holistic view.

One function of our Constitution is to serve as a record of our history. Almost everything that has happened since the founding of the US is reflected in some way in the Constitution. Just as the rings in a tree indicate which years during the tree's life had plentiful rainfall and which were dry, so the Constitution reflects the conditions of our country at various times. Slavery? Right there in black and white, although it is often only obliquely referred to. The word "slavery" didn't make it into the Constitution until the 13th Amendment was ratified in 1865, after the Civil War.[177] War? It's there. Changing views on taxation? Yup. Assassination? Absolutely. The Constitution provides for some of these things because the Founders anticipated them. Other eventualities were provided for through amendments to the Constitution after events occurred, as when we revised the provisions for succession of the Presidency, having realized that a President and Vice-President could become simultaneously or serially unable to serve, or that a President could become unable to serve due to a temporary disability.

You might have trouble pointing to words in the Constitution that talk about specific events or developments in our history. The "Great Depression" isn't there. Neither is "Cold War." You also won't find the words "telephone" or "computer" in the Constitution. But not everything in the Constitution is explicitly written in the document. Much of the Constitution is to be found in the laws that draw their authority from the Constitution and the court opinions that interpret the Constitution.

For example, the Constitution doesn't talk about diesel trucks. But the Commerce Clause of the Constitution provides the framework for a vast body of statutes and regulations that are just as important to the people who build and drive those trucks as the lug nuts that hold the wheels on. Here's why. The Constitution provides for the regulation of interstate commerce by the federal government. The Constitution could have said that no entity of government could regulate the roads. Or it could have given the power to the states. But the framers made a choice and gave the federal government primary control over commerce, although they also left room for the states to regulate in that area. When diesel trucks came into existence, the courts interpreted the Commerce Clause as giving Congress power to regulate their travel on interstate highways. Federal regulations range from the design of highway signs, to the number of consecutive hours a truck driver can be on the road, to the limits on carrying hazardous materials. And so, diesel trucks are captured in the history that is reflected in our body of law.

Not only does the Constitution reflect American history, it reflects the history of the world that led up to the formation of the United States. The US arose out of a rebellion against English rule, so a lot of what is in the Constitution is assumed to be a protection against similar governmental oppression in the future. The Fourth Amendment protects against unreasonable searches and seizures because the Founders either felt their English rulers were searching and seizing unreasonably, or they remembered when English rulers had acted that way in the past. The First Amendment protects free speech, also in reaction to perceived English oppression. But the bulk of the Constitution actually borrows from English law, giving the federal government and the states exactly the kinds of power that England had over its colonies, such as the power to impose taxes, form an army, and compel people to obey the laws by order of courts ruled over by judges and juries. The Founders drew upon what they knew, and that was predominantly the English legal system and body of law. Although the American Revolution certainly made some changes in the way government was organized, to a great extent the leaders of the revolution did not intend to alter the structure of society. They merely intended to substitute themselves for the power-elite that existed prior to the Revolution.[178]

Building on all of that history, the Constitution is a document that sets out the basic structure for our government and our country. The Constitution says there will be a Congress. If it didn't so specify, who would write the laws? Without a representative assembly for the entire country, we might only have whatever laws were written by the states. Or we might let the President make up the laws. Or we might have a direct democracy without representatives, where everyone voted on laws. Or, if the Constitution had not created the Congress, we might still have ended up with a Congress. It could have come into being on its own, by popular acceptance. But if it had, the courts might not have given as much deference to the laws Congress came up with as they do now. We'll never know.

Not every modern country has a Constitution. The United Kingdom, for example, still doesn't have one, and it manages to govern itself by referring to a long history of treaties, agreements, fundamental documents, and practices that serve many of the purposes our Constitution serves.

The US Constitution doesn't provide a very detailed description of our government. The original document, without amendments, is just over 4,500 words. It declares that there will be a presidency, but it says almost nothing about how the bureaucracy of the executive branch should be organized or how it should operate. The Congress set that up pretty much on its own. The Constitution also tells us very little about how the courts operate. The courts wrote their own rules. The Congress also operates according to their own arcane set of procedures that appear nowhere in the Constitution. All the

Constitution does is set out a very basic outline, which we as a country have elaborated on over the years.

The operating manual for a franchised sandwich shop is much more detailed than our Constitution. A franchise owner can pretty much run the shop's operations just by reading the manual and following the instructions. No one could ever recreate our current US government if all they had to go by was the Constitution.

There are a couple of very practical reasons why our Constitution is so devoid of details regarding how our government should operate. For one thing, there wasn't enough time to figure out all the details. We had to get the country going. In fact, we started running the country years before the Constitution was ratified. The Constitution was written in response to a perception that the country was not functioning well under the Articles of Confederation and might not survive. This wasn't just a matter of some people being discontented. Many of the people who had led the revolution and who went on to lead the country afterwards were convinced that the country was very close to collapse.

The other reason the Constitution lacks detail is that the Founders knew that others would understand what they had in mind. Leading up to the ratification of the Constitution, they debated fiercely, among themselves and in the press, about the many details of how the new government should be structured and how it should function. But since everyone was familiar with the fundamental concepts of the representative government that was being formed, it was possible to write a very succinct Constitution.

In addition, our Founders were wise enough to realize that they couldn't foresee the future, and that laying out endless details for the government of a growing and changing country wasn't feasible. If our Founders deserve credit for the wisdom they showed by drafting an enduring Constitution, they probably also deserve credit for saying to subsequent generations, "We don't know. Figure it out yourselves."

Our Constitution also contains some provisions that don't have anything to do with the structure of the government. These provisions cover topics that the Founders felt were important enough to include, or that the people felt were important enough to add. Most of the first ten amendments, which became known as the Bill of Rights, are generally thought to fall into this latter category. They weren't part of the original Constitution but were part of a deal that paved the way for the ratification of the Constitution by the original 13 states in 1788. The required number of states that were needed for ratification were only convinced to ratify based on an agreement that certain amendments would shortly thereafter be adopted. The Bill of Rights was passed by the first Congress that convened after the Constitution went into effect. They were ratified by the States by 1791, as promised.

There are some parts of the Constitution that both affect the structure of government and individual rights. They may do so directly, or indirectly by setting forth the powers that various branches of government have. For example, the Tenth Amendment allocates powers between the national government, the states, and the people, so it affects individual rights and government structure. Similarly, the 18th Amendment's prohibition of the sale of intoxicating liquors was an expansion of the power of government that also affected what could be seen as a very personal right of people to consume beverages of their choice. The Second Amendment (which was not actually the second to be proposed) was written primarily to describe the military powers of the states vis-à-vis the new national government, but it has come to be seen as a grant of individual rights, as will be discussed in more detail later on.

Our Constitution is also a codification of an ideal, not just a description of reality at the time that it was written. It gives us something to strive for. It is aspirational and inspirational. We can point to it and say to ourselves and the world, "This is what we believe. This is how a government should be run," even though we have never really followed through on all its promises.

The Preamble is the best example of this. It says, "We the People of the United States, in Order to form a more perfect Union, establish Justice, insure domestic Tranquility, provide for the common defence, promote the general Welfare, and secure the Blessings of Liberty to ourselves and our Posterity, do ordain and establish this Constitution for the United States of America." Isn't that lovely? It leaves out a few things, of course, like political favoritism, nepotism, cronyism, racism, and corruption that have always robbed some people of the Blessings of Liberty. But at least the Constitution says what we are supposed to be doing, and that is important. If it didn't, how would we know what to aspire to? How could anyone seek to unseat an ineffective or crooked incumbent if it wasn't written down somewhere what our politicians were supposed to be doing?

Our Constitution is and does all these different things. Any suggestion, therefore, that we change the Constitution is scrutinized by different people at different times with different philosophies, backgrounds, and outlooks according to different views on what a change will do. Think of the house where you live. You might want to paint a room a different color. To you, it might be just a matter of making the room look more contemporary. Someone else in the household might like a brighter color. Another person in the household, averse to change, might want to keep the room the same color. One of your family members might be concerned that the color you chose will make the room look dark and gloomy, so it would make the house harder to sell. Despairing of getting everyone to agree on a color, you may just decide to wash the walls and forget about painting altogether. Now imagine an entire country with different views on what the Constitution is supposed to do. Good luck on getting it changed.

THE SUPREME COURT'S ROLE IN CHANGING THE CONSTITUTION

It is hard to amend the Constitution, because millions of people have to agree to make the change. But over the years, a second method for changing the Constitution has been used that only requires five people to agree. Those people are justices of the United States Supreme Court. There are only nine justices at any one time, and if any five agree, they can rule on any provision of the Constitution and change its meaning.

Although the words of the Constitution only change when the Constitution is amended, the way the Constitution is interpreted can change with the composition of the Supreme Court, which changes as justices retire or die and are replaced. Every Supreme Court justice has an impact on the overall outlook of the Court. The majority view of the meaning of the Constitution can shift, not just because changing times require that Constitutional provisions be applied to changing conditions, but because the political makeup and philosophical orientation of the Court changes when new justices are named to the Court.

The Supreme Court and the Second Amendment

The history of the Court's rulings about the Second Amendment shows how the Court can change its mind about what the Constitution means. The Supreme Court seldom discussed the Second Amendment before the *Heller* case[179] in 2008, probably because most lower court judges knew how to read, and they understood and ruled that the amendment only guaranteed the right to guns for a "well regulated Militia." The only decision that directly answered the question of whether the right to bear arms was for militias affirmed the obvious and said that it was. This case was *United States v. Miller,* which was decided in 1939. It upheld the right of the Federal Government to regulate sawed-off shotguns and some other weapons, by upholding legislation passed in 1934 in response to the use of those weapons by Prohibition-era mobsters.[180]

But in the *Heller* case, the Supreme Court changed its mind and held that the Second Amendment gave people a personal right to have guns in their homes for their own protection, and that this right had nothing to do with whether that person belonged to any state militia.

Shortly after the *Heller* decision, the Court again upended prior Constitutional law and ruled in 2010 in *McDonald v. Chicago* that the Second Amendment was a limitation on the power of states to regulate guns.[181] Previously, it was understood and held that the Second Amendment only limited the federal government. Together, the *Heller* and *McDonald* decisions have imperiled gun control measures enacted over the last two centuries and have made the success of future efforts extremely unlikely.

Some people may hold out hope that in the future, the Court might change its mind again and reverse the decision that it handed down in the *Heller* case. This is not likely to happen for a very long time. Even when the composition of the Court changes, rarely does the Court overtly change one of its rulings as it did when it overruled the *Miller* case. One of the longstanding principles the Court follows is that it should try not to change what it says the Constitution means. It calls this principle *stare decisis*, which is Latin for "I already told you, and I'm not changing my mind, so don't bother me."

When the Court does change its mind, it usually tries to pretend that it isn't really changing its prior rulings, and it says instead that it is merely explaining its earlier decisions. That is what it did in the *Heller* decision. If, prior to the *Heller* case, there had been a whole series of cases holding that the Second Amendment was only for militias, instead of only one case, the Court would have had a harder time ruling as it did in *Heller*. It would have had to distinguish all those prior cases. With only one prior case to consider, the Court had a fairly easy time pretending that the 2008 *Heller* decision was consistent with the 1939 *Miller* decision, even though it wasn't.

How the Supreme Court avoids changing the Constitution

Although the Supreme Court can change the way the Constitution is understood, most of the time it avoids doing so. Historically, the Court has used a number of devices to keep from changing its pronouncements about what the Constitution means. In general, it avoids making these changes simply by avoiding taking cases that might result in change.

Actually, the Supreme Court hardly ever decides anything. In any given year, millions of cases are filed in the state and federal courts. In theory, cases can be appealed up through the various layers of courts. In the federal court system, cases start in the 94 District Courts, get appealed to the 13 Circuit Courts, and then can be appealed to the Supreme Court. Of all those cases, the Supreme Court considers fewer than 8,000 cases, and most of that number are thrown out without the Court deciding anything. The Court actually decides fewer than 150 cases a year, and it hands down a written decision explaining its reasoning in about 75 cases.

The Supreme Court has also developed a number of doctrines that it uses when it doesn't want to decide what the Constitution means. One of them is known as the "case and controversy" doctrine. Article III of the Constitution, which establishes the federal courts, says that the courts can decide certain kinds of cases and controversies. When the Supreme Court doesn't want to decide a case, it simply says that it is not one of those cases or controversies.

People who have cases rejected by the Supreme Court for this reason are sometimes surprised that whatever they have been arguing about is not a case or controversy. These cases sometimes involve a lot of money, or they involve disputes that affect people in important ways. Clients may have paid lawyers huge sums, having been told by those lawyers that they have good cases. But when the Supreme Court says your argument is not really an argument or at least not one that they have the authority to hear, there is absolutely nothing you can do about it.

Sometimes the Supreme Court rejects a case by saying that it isn't "ripe" for decision. This doesn't necessarily mean the Court will never take the case. But when the Supreme Court says, "not yet," it can really mean "not ever", or at least, "not your case."

There is yet another doctrine the Supreme Court uses to reject cases it doesn't want to decide. It can proclaim that the people who have brought the case to the Court are not the proper people to bring the case. The Court calls this the "standing" doctrine, meaning the parties don't have a right, or standing, to argue the case. In theory, this doctrine makes sure that people don't bring phony cases to the Court and then purposely lose them, like a prize fighter who has been bought off to take a dive and throw a fight. The Court says it is making sure that the people who bring cases will actually make a serious attempt to win them. But in practice, the standing doctrine is often used just to make sure that no one will be able to bring certain cases.

One of the requirements that the Supreme Court has imposed under the standing doctrine is that the individual who brings a lawsuit must be able to show he is complaining about something that will harm him in particular. If everyone in the US would be harmed in the same way, an individual complainant doesn't have standing to complain.

The Supreme Court has used the standing doctrine to avoid lots of controversies, including those involving the environment and taxes. It has held, for example, that no one has standing to complain about a law that will hurt endangered animals or even allow them to become extinct, because no one is harmed by this more than anyone else, even if they feel the harm more deeply or are more concerned about animals.[182] No one can complain that taxes are too high, because everyone could complain that taxes are too high.[183] The result of applying the standing doctrine can mean that an unconstitutional law cannot be challenged. In effect, the Court, by denying the opportunity to appeal, actually decides the issue and upholds the challenged law while saying it isn't deciding the case.

Even when it does take a case, the Supreme Court almost always avoids telling anyone what the Constitution means; this approach is sometimes referred to as "constitutional avoidance." It usually decides cases on other grounds, ignoring the Constitutional question entirely. It acts like a schoolyard monitor who is asked to decide which child should get the ball—the boy who claims to have been playing with it or the girl who he says grabbed it from him. The monitor may not want to spend a lot of time listening to these two kids or the others who may have witnessed the alleged offense, so she might just toss the ball into the air and tell the children to start over and play nicely together. This might be an acceptable solution during recess, but, as happens when the Supreme Court avoids answering questions about the Constitution, it doesn't tell anyone who was right or wrong, and it doesn't give any guidance for future playtimes.

Sometimes the Supreme Court avoids answering a question by using the "mootness" doctrine to let complainants know that the Court has lost interest in the case. The Court says that the case has become moot and that it no longer needs to adjudicate the controversy because something has happened that has already determined the outcome of the case. For example, several federal courts have decided that the Constitution does not give people a right to carry concealed weapons. When one federal court reached a different conclusion, there was the possibility that the case could be appealed to the Supreme Court.[184] But before the appeal was filed, that state's legislature enacted a law allowing concealed carry, so the anomalous court decision became impossible to appeal. The controversy was considered moot, even though the incorrect decision was still on the books and might be cited by later courts, and even though there was still a conflict between that one decision and all the other federal court decisions. Obviously, there was still an unresolved issue of constitutional law, but the Supreme Court's mootness doctrine allows the Court to pretend that there isn't. The Supreme Court also applied the mootness doctrine to avoid deciding whether the Equal Rights Amendment could be ratified after the congressionally imposed deadline for ratification had expired. It would seem to have been a fairly easy question to answer, but it was even easier for the Court not to bother.[185]

The Supreme Court also can apply what it calls the "political question" doctrine when it does not want to decide a case. This doctrine says that some questions are better decided by the Congress rather than by the courts. This doctrine was discussed by the Court in 1939 when it was asked to decide whether Kansas could ratify the Child Labor Amendment after that state had previously rejected the amendment.[186] The Court was trying to leave the amendment process in the hands of the Congress as much as possible.

With all these ways to avoid gun control cases, with a scarcity of Supreme Court decisions interpreting the Second Amendment, and with it being unlikely that the Court will overturn its recent pro-gun decisions very soon, people who are concerned about gun violence might think they should turn to other branches of the government for help in reducing gun violence. But the Court's recent decisions make it impossible for those other branches to act effectively in this area, because much of what could be done would likely be held unconstitutional. The option of amending the Constitution is now the only real option, just as it was the only option when the Supreme Court ruled in 1895 that the national income tax that Congress had enacted was unconstitutional.[187] You've probably noticed that today there is a national income tax. That's because in 1913, the 16th Amendment to the Constitution was adopted to allow the federal government to collect an income tax.[188]

Why the Supreme Court declines cases

Legal scholars tell us that the reason the Supreme Court doesn't decide cases is because it wants to let the other mechanisms of government function without undue interference. Although the Constitution doesn't actually say so, it was decided long, long ago that the Supreme Court has the power to tell other branches of the federal government and the states what to do, simply by declaring that whatever the branches and states have been doing is unconstitutional. The Supreme Court really is Supreme. It wields an awesome power.

Theorists tell us that the justices of the Supreme Court, because they have such respect for the concept of separation of powers and limitation of power of the government, go out of their way not to use all of the power they have. Instead, they only use as much of the power as they feel is absolutely needed. Perhaps. But the theorists also point out that while the Supreme Court can decide whatever it wants, it can't do anything other than issue opinions. The Court has no army to enforce its edicts and no money except what Congress gives it. If Congress got upset enough with the Court, it could revoke its funding. If the Court ticks off the President or Congress by declaring too many things to be unconstitutional, the President could evict them from their courthouse. The Constitution says the justices' pay can't be reduced, but it doesn't say that Congress has to pay the Court's electric bill, so Congress could turn out the lights, and all the Court could do about it would be to write an opinion saying, "Turn the lights back on!" So perhaps the Supreme Court is cautious in its use of power, not just out of respect, but out of fear that its authority could be diminished if the other branches of government stopped following its orders or even retaliated against it for being overly meddlesome. When President Franklin D. Roosevelt threatened to pack the Court by appointing additional members who were sympathetic with his policies, the Court suddenly started issuing opinions that were more favorable to those policies.

By leaving most questions about the Constitution undecided, the Court throws the ball back to the lawyers and their clients. This means that people who wanted answers either have to accept the answers that have been imposed on them by lower courts or find ways to settle their cases without ever getting their questions about the Constitution answered. This is consistent with the notion that our government should leave people with the maximum amount of freedom, including the freedom to interpret the Constitution for themselves until there is a necessity for a definitive ruling.

A problem arises, however, from the combination of giving the Supreme Court the final word on the Constitution and allowing the Supreme Court enormous latitude in choosing which cases to take and which issues to decide. It gives the Court the power to choose cases not just based upon whether there is a need to take the case, but also upon whether a particular case contains facts that will make it easy for the Court to change the law if it wants to. It makes it easy for the Supreme Court to act politically, rather than as a body that impartially seeks to determine the truth and mete out justice.

Approaches to constitutional interpretation

The Court has taken several approaches over the years to interpreting the Constitution. One approach, known as "strict constructionism" or "textualism," says that the meaning of the Constitution should be found simply by looking at the words of the Constitution without reference to historical context, and that once the Court has interpreted the Constitution, it should stick with that interpretation forever. This school of thought posits that the Constitution never changes. One big advantage of this viewpoint is that it would allow us to save a lot of money by only calling the Supreme Court into session on the rare occasions when someone finds a part of the Constitution that hasn't yet been explained. That wouldn't be very often. Over the past 225 years, almost every provision of the Constitution has been interpreted at least once.

The big shortcoming of this strict constructionist view is that it has never been possible to understand what the Constitution means without looking beyond the words on the parchment. It would be particularly difficult today, because some of the words don't have the same meaning they did when they were written, and it can be difficult to know how the words were understood in 1787, when it was written, or in 1789, when it went into effect. For example, scholars have argued that the word "infringed" in the Second Amendment may not have meant what we think it means today. They point out that "the right of the people to keep and bear Arms, shall not be infringed" may have meant that the Second Amendment would permit the regulation of guns but would prohibit total confiscation, and that if the amendment were intended to make sure that rights to gun ownership would not be limited, it would have said, "shall not be *impinged*."[189] The words "bear Arms" also do not have the same meaning today as when the Second Amendment was written. Back then, "bear Arms" had a definite military meaning that has not continued into modern times.[190]

Even if word usage and meaning did not change over time, which we all know they do, there are other problems with the "strict constructionist" theory. There are plenty of things that the

Constitution simply doesn't answer directly. The only way we have been able to perpetuate our government has been to allow courts to use the power of reasoning and inference to interpret the Constitution.

Some people think the solution to these problems is to interpret the Constitution according to what it was intended to mean when it was written, as in, "Don't tell us what it says, tell us what it was supposed to say." In order to uncover the intended meaning of the Constitution, they look to what the drafters said when they debated the various provisions of the Constitution. This approach is known as "original intent" interpretation. It also has problems. For one thing, the drafters weren't necessarily honest about what they intended. Like politicians in all eras, they were trying to get the provisions they wanted into the Constitution and keep other provisions out. What they said in public and what they had in their heads and hearts were not necessarily identical. It is impossible to know what the drafters intended because they didn't always want us to know.

Another problem is that the historical record of the debates over the Constitution, like all historical writings, are not complete, completely accurate, or free from reporting bias. It is impossible to know what the drafters intended because they aren't alive to ask.

Complicating the problem of figuring out the original meaning of the Constitution, either from a textual analysis or from contemporaneous writings, is that the drafters themselves never intended that the Constitution should be interpreted according to what they intended or what words meant when they spoke them. The drafters were quite familiar with the British common law tradition of interpreting laws according to what effect they would have at the time they were applied. The British system of deriving meaning of laws from the way that the laws were previously understood in other cases was well developed when the Constitution was written, and it was the foundation for the way the US courts would function from the very time the courts were created. US courts even mentioned British law when explaining what US laws meant. There weren't enough US court decisions to refer to, so they referred to the British antecedents to our laws. Some of the original state constitutions expressly incorporated English law, even though the states were founded in direct rejection of English rule.[191] The Founders were also familiar with other schools of interpretation, including Talmudic interpretation of biblical texts, which also applies meaning in the context of the times.[192] The Founders knew that whatever words they used to write the Constitution, future judges would have to make the Constitution relevant to future times.

All a person has to do is read a few Supreme Court decisions and they will see that in our times, the Court draws upon whatever theories of Constitutional interpretation will get them the results they want. Within a single opinion, you can frequently find justices claiming to be following strict constructionism, original intent, and other theories—often contradicting themselves.

Some people feel that if the interpretation of the Constitution can change, the Constitution ceases to be authoritative. But that has never been true. Throughout our history, no matter how it has been understood or misunderstood, our Constitution has always been regarded as the ultimate authority. If a mother tells her son that his bedtime is 9:00 and then one day changes it to 8:30, it doesn't mean the child is any less subject to his mother's rule. The mother is still in charge, and her dictates are still valid. If the boy is not persuaded by the reasons his mother gives for changing the rules, such as "you have to get up earlier to catch the school bus," the boy can start to view his mother as arbitrary, but he will quickly learn that arbitrary rules are just as enforceable upon children as rules that children agree with. When the boy grows up, he will probably understand why his mother sometimes changed the rules. If he has children himself, he'll probably do the same thing.

Similarly, the interpretation of the rules the Constitution imposes on us can change to fit circumstances, or for no apparent reason. We may like a new interpretation less than we liked the old, but we are all still subject to the new interpretation, and it is still just as legitimate under our system of government.

The will of the people and the law of the land

Although in any particular case the Supreme Court has the final word on what the Constitution means, ultimately, taking a broader perspective, the Supreme Court's opinion about the Second Amendment or any other part of the Constitution is no more important than what the people think the Constitution means or want it to mean. Ours is a system of government that depends upon the will of the people. That is what was supposed to distinguish it from the British monarchy and feudal societies that preceded it. By the time of the American Revolution, the subjects of the British Empire had made some progress in demanding that the government respond to what the people wanted. The American revolutionaries intended to extend this theory, and they enshrined it in a Constitution that lacked any governmental authority that was not chosen by and responsible to the people.

The desire for popular sovereignty would not have been served by creating an unchangeable Constitution that would be interpreted by a Supreme Court without regard to changes in the populace over time. Nor would it have been served by creating a government that centralized all decision-making in a Supreme Court. What the Founders had in mind was a country in which people made their own decisions as much as possible, generally at the most local level possible—both individually, in agreement with one another, and collectively. It mattered to the Founders what the people thought the Constitution meant. That's why they insisted that the Constitution would not go into effect unless and until it was adopted by a supermajority of states representing the people all across the country. That's also why they provided that it could be amended—so that the people would always be able to control their government. No part of the new government was supposed to be imposed on the people. It was all supposed to grow from the assent of the people.

But even beyond the idea that the people should interpret their own Constitution, the Founders anticipated that the people should make decisions without any regard to the Constitution, or even without regard to the laws and the government. Nothing in the Constitution says that all decisions would be made by the government. It would have been totally impractical. But it was not beyond contemplation. Some of the American colonies did in fact place nearly all decision-making power in the hands of the local governor or the religious elders or the local community. By the time the Constitution was written, Americans had experimented with centralized decision-making and had rejected it. The Tenth Amendment plainly says that "The powers not delegated to the

United States by the Constitution, nor prohibited by it to the States, are reserved to the States respectively, or to the people." Our Constitution assumes that all power that has not been enumerated as being given to the federal or state governments remains with the people. This is entirely consistent with the First Amendment, which preserves the right of free speech and the press.

Although Supreme Court decisions get on the front pages of newspapers, they are a minuscule portion of the decisions that are made in this country. Business people decide millions of disputes without ever bringing suit in court. They are able to do this because they are free to interpret the Constitution and laws themselves. In fact, the reason laws and judicial opinions are published is so that people will be able to read them and conform their conduct to them. The old expression, "Ignorance of the law is no excuse," points out that Americans are expected to familiarize themselves with the laws and to understand them. When laws are too complex for ordinary folks to understand, they hire lawyers to advise them, but the decision-making power still resides with individuals. It is lawyers' responsibility to explain the laws to their clients so that they can understand them and apply them to their own circumstances. Only in extraordinary, rare instances do people have to go to courts to find out what the law is. When it comes to the law, we live in a "do-it-yourself" country. We are only supposed to use the courts as a matter of last resort, if we fail to handle things ourselves.

This is not, however, the same as saying that we live in a lawless country. Far from it. Our notion of individual liberty includes the equally important obligation of communal responsibility. But we are not supposed to merely obey. We are not supposed to leave it to law school professors or other experts to tell us what our Constitution means and what should be in it, although we can certainly gain insight from them. We are expected to understand and to participate in the creation of our laws and the functioning of our government. That's why we have a right to vote and to amend the Constitution. The Constitution was never intended to be the property of the original drafters. It belongs in every era to the people whose lives it touches.

THE SUPREME COURT'S RADICAL SHIFT

Discussions about the Second Amendment naturally tend to focus on the question of the extent of people's right to have guns. That's what the amendment says it is about. But taking this view excludes far too much. Because the Constitution serves multiple functions, any Supreme Court decision that changes the Constitution has far ranging impacts and reflects broad and deep changes in societal and political attitudes.

Although the Supreme Court is generally spoken of as if it were the non-political branch of government, any observer of the modern Court knows that it is at least as political as the other branches. It shouldn't be surprising that the effort that led to the Court changing the meaning of the Second Amendment in the *Heller* decision wasn't just a matter of lawyers writing briefs in a case and making arguments to the Court. The effort can better be understood if it is viewed as a political campaign. A lot of work was done behind the scenes far in advance of the Court's vote. Just as political candidates work to build images of themselves that will be appealing to the public, the pro-gun forces paved the way for the *Heller* decision by manipulating the historical record so that the Second Amendment would be misunderstood in a way that the Court and the public would accept.

How was the Supreme Court persuaded to change the Second Amendment?

When the Supreme Court ruled in the *Heller* case that the Second Amendment gave individuals the right to have guns, it changed a "collective" right into an "individual" right. This was a revolutionary change, and as with almost all significant Supreme Court decisions, this decision did not arise in a vacuum. It was the culmination of a long struggle between the pro-gun and anti-gun folks. Over a period of years, each side strategically worked to lay the groundwork for a decision on this issue, anticipating that one day a case might make it to the Supreme Court that would allow the Court to either follow the age-old understanding of the Second Amendment or to change the way the amendment was to be interpreted.

Because the meaning of the Second Amendment, which favored the anti-gun side, was well established, the pro-gun folks had more work to do than the anti-gun folks. They had to make sure that if the Supreme Court wanted to side with them, it would have a body of "scholarship" that it could point to as justification for their position. They set about writing law review articles and publishing opinions that expressed their views. They had so-called conservative think tanks and opinion leaders lend their names to this revisionism. The legitimacy of these distortions of history was criticized by the academic and legal establishment, but that didn't really matter. The pro-gun folks accomplished what they wanted just by publishing their theories, regardless of whether they were accurate. Historian Gary Wills has eloquently criticized their so-called scholarship: "Time after time, in dreary expectable ways, the quotes bandied about by Standard Model [pro-gun] scholars turn out to be truncated, removed from context, twisted, or applied to a debate different from that over the Second Amendment. Those who would argue with them soon tire of the chase from one misquotation to another, and dismiss the whole exercise—causing the angry reaction from Standard Modelers that they are not taken seriously. The problem is that taking them seriously is precisely what undermines their claims."[193]

Once the theoretical "scholarship" was in place, the pro-gun folks set about to find a case that the Supreme Court could use to change the meaning of the Constitution. They were careful not to bring a case that contained facts that might tempt the Supreme Court to decide against them. The anti-gun folks were engaged in the same task from the opposite position. They wanted to make sure that if a case made it to the Supreme Court, it would be a case that would make it easy for the Court to affirm its longstanding position—that the Second Amendment was only intended to apply to guns held for militias. Groups that advocate for all sorts of causes are constantly on guard in this way, watching the lower courts for cases that they might be able to use on appeal or that might hurt them on appeal.

The pro-gun folks finally found their case[194] and pursued it through the courts. Initially they had some hesitation, fearful that they might get a decision they wouldn't like. Although the Court had turned decidedly conservative by the time the case came up, there is always some uncertainty when dealing with the Supreme Court. The pro-gun folks were confident that the justices in this Court, who had a strong record of deciding cases on partisan political lines, would favor their side. But they couldn't be sure.

People sometimes assume that when the Supreme Court decides a case, it is merely deciding what the law means. But Court decisions are always made by applying the law to a particular set of facts, and the facts of a case can move the Court to decide in one direction or another. The case that the Court used to reinterpret the Second Amendment had facts that favored the pro-gun side. It involved Mr. Heller, a special police officer in Washington, D.C., who had applied for a permit to have a handgun at home but had been turned down because a Washington, D.C., law did not allow people to have handguns at home. As a police officer, Mr. Heller held the position of being presumptively credible and responsible. He did not appear to be just some gun nut. It seemed reasonable for him to have a gun at home, because D.C. law allowed him to carry a gun while he was working. If he wasn't a threat while at work, why should he be considered dangerous when he was at leisure?

It also probably helped that when the case made it to the Court, Washington, D.C., was well known as a city that suffered from considerable gun violence. The justices would all have known this, since D.C. is where the Court is located. So it would have seemed reasonable that a responsible, law-abiding, law-enforcing officer would want to have a gun for protection, not just for the reasons that anyone might want a gun, but because he might need to defend himself from some criminal who was seeking revenge.

The Court, in a 157-page decision (including two dissenting opinions that take up 90 pages) decided five to four that Mr. Heller had a constitutional right to have a handgun in his house so that he could protect himself. The bulk of the decision dealt with the question of what the Second Amendment meant when it was originally put into the Constitution.

The dark origins of the Second Amendment

In order to reach its conclusion in the *Heller* case, the Supreme Court had to deal with the language in the Second Amendment that said that the right to bear arms referred to militias. As a historical matter, there are a handful of explanations for why the language about militias was included in the Second Amendment. One of the most important reasons the amendment was adopted was that in regions where people owned slaves, the slaves occasionally would try to escape from their masters. They would flee either to territories, states, or countries that did not enforce slave owners' rights to own other humans, or to wilder areas of the young country where they could live as free people with relatively little danger of being captured. Prior to the American Revolution, the French, who were skirmishing with the British along the Canadian border with the American colonies, gave escaped slaves their freedom, in return for the intelligence or military service the escapees provided. Similarly, the Spanish, who were fighting the British in Florida, rewarded escaped slaves with their freedom, and they armed and encouraged them to attack their former owners. During the American Revolution, the British encouraged slaves to escape and fight on the British side, promising them freedom in return for their military service.[195]

Because slaves had value, the people who owned them were apt to try to recapture them. They also wanted to discourage the very notion that slaves could gain their freedom by escaping or by rebellion. If slaves grew hopeful, there might be more and more attempted escapes and revolts, of which there had been quite a few. Some of the revolts had included bloody massacres of slave owners and had been widely reported and discussed among whites. Slave owners and a significant portion of white society were terrified. So people who supported the system of slavery were inclined to form posses—or militias—to help their neighbors track down and re-enslave the escapees and otherwise use deadly force to prop up the institution of slavery.[196]

States that depended upon slavery for their economic viability were so supportive of these militias that they wanted the new Constitution to explicitly allow the militias to continue to exist. They felt that the very existence of slavery would be threatened if the slave owners could not forcibly maintain it as part of their way of life.[197] England had begun outlawing the slave trade, and abolitionism was gaining ground both in England and in its American colonies.[198]

Slave states insisted on a Constitutional provision that would allow them to retain their militias so that they could protect slavery on their own. Some pro-slavery states may not have trusted the anti-slavery states to help them in this regard, and they may have been concerned that a federal government, influenced by anti-slavery states, would not do the job. They agreed to allow the federal government to call the militias into action in the event that slave uprisings expanded beyond local boundaries. The fact that the Constitution provides for federal control over the militias may indicate that the slave states were powerful enough that they were able to prevail upon the Founders to write the protections for slavery into the Constitution. It may also indicate that the Founders thought that slavery was so important to the entire country that the entire new federal government needed to be able to protect it, or that they were as afraid of slave uprisings as anyone else.[199]

Although the Constitutional provisions for militias allowed slave owners to own guns so they could hunt down their slaves, there was no concern that the Second Amendment would also allow slaves to own guns. The Constitution did not give any rights at all to slaves; they were considered property, not people.[200]

Modern supporters of gun rights seldom talk about this important motivation behind the Second Amendment. Actually, they never talk about it, and there is little mention of it in history books. It doesn't sound particularly noble in today's post-slavery America, but it was undoubtedly one of the reasons why some states felt that the Second Amendment had to be adopted. It likely wasn't, however, the only reason the Second Amendment became part of our Constitution.

The Second Amendment was also needed to assure people that they could have guns so that they could murder Native Americans. Killing Indians was important to people in many parts of what would come to be known as the United States, not just in areas where owning slaves was socially acceptable.[201] It was so fundamental to the very presence of European settlers that it was taken as a given. When the Constitution was ratified, the number of people who were considered American citizens was fairly small, and though a few had explored other parts of the continent, most of them lived on a narrow portion of the land along the East Coast. They had been welcomed onto some parts of the land by the native inhabitants. But most regions were settled and then defended or taken by force.[202] Guns were very useful to settlers and their new country because guns could be used to take whatever land was needed or desired, both with and without the blessing of the state governments.

Pro-gun explanations for the Second Amendment

Gun rights supporters don't talk about killing Indians any more than they talk about perpetuating slavery. Instead, they like to point to other reasons underlying the adoption of the Second Amendment. In general, they point out the concern some people had that the newly formed federal government might not function the way they envisioned it.

It is difficult to say to what extent the Second Amendment was meant to address this concern. As we will see below, some people thought the government might encroach on their lives too much. Others thought it might not be powerful enough to serve the needs of the growing nation. There was a broad diversity of opinion about what powers the new government should have and what restrictions should be placed on those powers. People in rural areas, which were mostly agricultural, differed on this topic from people in urban areas who were more likely to be engaged in trade. Wealthy people, who were well represented among the drafters of the Constitution, had different views from most of the rest of the country, which had much less land and other wealth. People in the South, who wanted to be able to ship their agricultural commodities interstate and internationally without burdensome tariffs, had very different views from people in New York, which derived a great deal of revenue by levying tariffs on goods moving through its waterways and harbors.

These days we tend to praise the Founders for creating a Constitution that allowed our country to grow to great wealth and power. But what many of the Founders wanted was to create a federal government that wouldn't do much of anything at all, except in limited matters where the state governments had been having difficulty, such as controlling the currency, managing debt, and establishing relationships with foreign governments. They wanted the states to continue to operate mostly autonomously, as they had up until that time.

Many of our early political elite were reticent to create a new federal government that might interfere with their attempts to profit from speculation in land that had belonged to Native Americans. They had put a great deal of effort into developing influence and connections in a political world that was organized around independently governed colonies. They were particularly wary of creating a federal government that might interfere with those efforts.[203] Others among the Founders envisioned a much more significant role for the federal government and hoped it would develop into something resembling European governments of the time.

It has become popular in recent times for pro-gun folks to argue that the Second Amendment guarantees the right to have guns so that people can overthrow the government. There undoubtedly were some early settlers who were afraid that the new federal government would gain more power over the individual states than they thought was desirable. Even though the Constitution was intended to form a "more perfect Union" than had been assembled under the prior Articles of Confederation, there was still some concern that that Union could become overbearing and deny the rights of individuals, as they felt they had experienced under British rule.

In modern times, the concern about an overbearing government is expressed as if the Founders were concerned that the Congress would overstep its legitimate role. When the Constitution was written, the more pressing concern was that an overly strong national military could stage a coup or simply gain too much power. Americans had seen this sort of thing happen in other countries, just as we continue to see any number of instances today where a country's military supplants its civil government. In response to this concern, the Constitution was written to include limitations on the funding of a standing army. The Constitution provided from the outset that Congress could only fund the army for two years at a time.[204]

Some people who did not have full confidence in the notion of a federal government may even have wanted to be prepared to destroy that government by force and revert to rule by the independent states if they felt the new Union was not respecting the idea of popular sovereignty. But those people would have been few, and that notion would have had little appeal to the men who drafted the Constitution. Those men were well aware of the history of the Old World. They knew firsthand that peasant revolutions could threaten a regime and that armed peasants were the most dangerous kind. Heck, they had just overthrown the British themselves, and their success was due in large part to the availability of guns. They knew about the armed revolt that had taken place in Boston in 1689 when the people heard the news of England's "Glorious Revolution" of 1688 and decided to rise up in arms against the English governor and his troops.[205] They were also quite aware of Shays' Rebellion, one of a multitude of violent rebellions against tax and debt collection that had been taking place within the states immediately preceding the Constitutional Convention.[206] They knew, also, about the boundary disputes that had festered for years between neighboring colonies, such as the competition between Pennsylvania and Virginia over control of land around Pittsburgh.[207] If the Founders really wanted the new United States to succeed and prosper, they would hardly have been enthusiastic about guaranteeing that people would be equipped to make it fail. As pointed out by historian Gary Wills: "Only madmen, one would think, can suppose that militias have a constitutional right to levy war against the United States, which is treason by constitutional definition (Article III, Section 3, Clause 1)."[208]

The drafters of the Second Amendment may have been pressured to insert the Second Amendment to appease people who, for a variety of reasons that didn't have anything to do with guns, were reluctant to have their own states be part of the new nation. The drafters were unquestionably not, however, going to back off from the idea of a nation governed by laws, so it's preposterous to think that they would propose an amendment that would empower anti-American vigilantes to destroy the nation they had just risked everything to bring into being. Nor, as we learned during the Civil War, did the Constitution contemplate that individual states, once they had joined the Union, could leave it.

The other concern that some of the Founders actually had about the way the new federal government might function was just the opposite from the fear some dissidents had that the central government would become too powerful. They feared that the new federal government might simply not function at all. If that happened, the states wanted to be able to run things themselves without a federal government, until they either formed a better federal government or they figured out some other scheme. For this, they might need militias, and hence the Second Amendment.

At the time the Constitution was being written, some people were afraid that England or France or other European powers would attack the new country, and they wanted to be prepared to defend what they had just won. This would not have been a foolish concern. European governments had been squabbling over territory for a long time, and they might well have decided to try to wrest control of the new country or some of its territory in the future. The War of 1812 between the US and England can be seen as just such a conflict.

The federal government was formed in part so that the country would be able to mount a unified defense against hostile foreign powers. It would have been odd, in a time when the technology of warfare was rapidly advancing, if the new country were to trust its defense to any degree in a bunch of independently operating state militias made up of farmers with muskets. It didn't. In Article II, the first power the Constitution gave to the President was the power to command the military, and, importantly, the state militias: "The President shall be Commander in Chief of the Army and Navy of the United States, and of the Militia of the several States, when called into the actual Service of the United States..." Among the powers it immediately gave to the Congress in Article I were the powers to declare war and to tax the people to support the national military: "The Congress shall have Power To lay and collect Taxes, Duties, Imposts and Excises, to pay the Debts and provide for the common Defence..." Indeed, the first Congress funded a standing national army just four days after it adopted the Second Amendment and sent it for ratification.[209] The Founders may have been idealistic, but they weren't fools. They knew they couldn't rely on individuals with squirrel guns to defend the US territory and its new government. But some people wanted to have their state militias just in case.

Some people argue that the Second Amendment was adopted so that the national government could call upon the states' militias if they were needed for the national defense. While that may have been the case early in our history, before our national military was well-established, it would seem an odd way of doing things from today's perspective. Since the Constitution gave Congress the right to raise money for an army and navy and gave the President the power to use the military, it would seem more efficient to simply have a strong military rather than rely upon a bunch of uncoordinated state militias. But at the time, this was a new and not particularly prosperous or even self-sustaining country. The expense of maintaining a sufficient national military could be significant, and it wasn't clear what level of taxation the citizens of the new country would tolerate. The Boston Tea Party, which was a protest against taxes, was still a fresh memory. A reasonable solution could have been to allow the states to retain the militias they had formed for recapturing slaves and killing Indians, but to make it clear that the national government could call upon those quasi-military resources if needed for the national defense.

Although we don't know precisely why the Second Amendment was included in the Bill of Rights, we can be certain that the Founders were not interested in creating a country where every person who had a gun would be a law unto themselves, which seems to be what today's advocates of concealed carry and stand your ground laws want. Ever since the earliest European settlers came to this country, the rule of law had been entrenched as solidly as the rule of God, often inextricably. Under British rule, the colonists had been governed. They were not by any means just a bunch of individuals doing anything they saw fit. There were governors, courts, jails, and punishments to deal with violators. Similarly, once the US was a country, it was not a "free country," it was a governed country.

Although the American Revolution was in part a rebellion against repressive measures, it was never a rejection of the notion that people could be governed by a central authority and that they should rely upon each other and their government for their protection. If it had been, there would never have been a Constitution. America was an attempt to create a country that, to a greater degree than the European countries where the settlers came from, was governed by the will of the masses of people instead of by hereditary monarchies.[210] Anarchy was never an option. America did not adopt the Second Amendment so that people could shoot tax collectors.

Textual origins of the Second Amendment

Admittedly, it is difficult to know which of the several reasons for the Second Amendment being adopted was the most important at the time. The record of the debate in the House of Representatives does not answer the question, and no record was made of the Senate's deliberations about the amendment.[211] In fact, there is very little record of the debates over any of the amendments that became the Bill of Rights. Those amendments started out as a proposal that James Madison compiled and presented to the first Congress. He drew upon more than 200 proposals for amendment that had been suggested by the states' ratifying conventions. There was a lot of duplication among those proposals, but they included about 100 distinct ideas. Many of the ideas were already contained in various states' constitutions.[212]

Although several of the state constitutions mentioned militias, only five mentioned bearing arms, and only one spoke of an individual right. The Virginia state Bill of Rights of 1776, Article 13, did not give individuals a right to guns. It only spoke of guns in the context of a state militia: "That a well regulated militia, composed of the body of the people, trained to arms, is the proper, natural, and safe defence of a free state..." This provision was the basis for item 17 of the list of proposed amendments that the Virginia ratifying convention sent to Congress. It referred in two clauses of one sentence to the right to bear arms and to a militia, but the clauses were in the reverse order from the way they would eventually appear in the Second Amendment. The text of the Virginia proposal read, "That the people have a right to keep and bear arms; that a well regulated Militia composed of the body of the people trained to arms is the proper, natural, and safe defence of a free State."

The Declaration of Rights and Fundamental Rules of Delaware also speaks only of a militia and does not mention arms: "That a well regulated militia is the proper, natural, and safe defence of a free government." The Declaration of Rights and Constitution of Maryland of 1776 also mentions a militia but not guns: "That a well regulated militia is the proper and natural defence of a free government."

The New York Constitution of 1777 speaks only of a militia but says it should be armed: "And whereas it is of the utmost importance to the safety of every state, that it should always be in a condition of defence; and it is the duty of every man, who enjoys the protection of society, to be prepared and willing to defend it; this convention, therefore, in the name and by the authority of the good people of this state, doth ordain, determine and declare, that the militia of this state, at all times hereafter, as well in peace as in war, shall be armed and disciplined, and in readiness for service." The New York ratifying convention recommended including in the Bill of Rights a provision for bearing arms for the common defence: "That the People have a right to keep and bear Arms; that a well regulated Militia, including the body of the People *capable of bearing Arms*, is the proper, natural and safe defence of a free State."

The only mention of guns in the Massachusetts Declaration of Rights, which was adopted along with the state Constitution in 1780, was in the context of defense of the state: "The people have a right to keep and bear arms for the common defence." North Carolina's Constitution of 1776 similarly mentions guns only for the purposes of collective defense: "That the people have a right to bear arms for the defence of the state ...." The North Carolina ratifying convention recommended including in the Bill of Rights a provision that was nearly identical to that which was recommended by Virginia: "That the people have a right to keep and bear arms; that a well regulated militia composed of the body of the people, trained to arms, is the proper, natural and safe defence of a free state."

The Pennsylvania Constitution contains perhaps the broadest right to guns: "That the people have a right to bear arms for the defence of themselves and the state ...."[213] The Pennsylvania ratifying convention did not recommend that a right to bear arms be included in the Bill of Rights, but a minority report did make such a recommendation. Notably, their recommendation was not for an absolute right to have guns. It recognized that that right could be limited, in the interest of public safety: "That the people have a right to bear arms for the defence of themselves and their own State, or the United States, or for the purpose of killing game; and no law shall be passed for disarming the people or any of them, unless for crimes committed, or real danger of public injury from individuals ...."

New Hampshire's Constitution of 1776 was a bare-bones document which did not mention arms or a militia, but its ratifying convention recommended that the following provision be included in the nation's Bill of Rights: "Congress shall never disarm any Citizen unless such as are or have been in Actual Rebellion."[214]

Madison did not confine himself to just the proposals the states had made. He added some amendments of his own that no state had suggested, and he left out some of the proposals that were most important to many states.[215]

The wording that Madison used for a right to bear arms is not the wording that was ultimately adopted. Madison recommended the following language: "The right of the people to keep and bear arms shall not be infringed; a well armed and well regulated militia being the best security of a free country..." The remainder of the amendment dealt with the question of whether a conscientious objector could refuse to take up arms. That part of the amendment did not make it into the Constitution.

Madison's wording was modified by the Select Committee of Congress that considered his proposals. The Committee inverted the clauses, so that the amendment would read: "A well regulated militia, composed of the body of the people, being the best security of a free State, the right of the people to keep and bear arms shall not be infringed..." The House of Representatives passed the Select Committee's version, with the only change being to capitalize the word "People" and add a comma after the word "arms." The amendment passed by the House read: "A well regulated militia, composed of the body of the People, being the best security of a free State, the right of the people to keep and bear arms, shall not be infringed..." The Senate changed the wording of the Amendment so that it read as follows: "A well regulated militia, being necessary to the security of a free State, the right of the people to keep and bear arms, shall not be infringed." A conference committee capitalized the words "Militia" and "Arms." The conference committee's changes were accepted by the House and Senate, and the Bill of Rights was sent off to the states for ratification.

Over the entire course of the debate over ratification of the Constitution there is little indication that the right to bear arms had a high priority to very many people or states. Other issues were considered much more important. Those issues included whether the federal government could raise direct taxes without first seeking revenue from the states; whether Congress could prescribe the times, places, and manner of holding elections for Congress; whether jury trials would be guaranteed; whether it would be explicit that powers that were not delegated to the Federal Government were reserved to the states or the people; and what the size of House districts would be.

Although there was no particular concern about the right to bear arms during the debates over ratification, there was debate about the power that Article I, Section 8 of the Constitution gave Congress to "call forth" and organize, arm, and discipline the state militias for national service. Some opponents of the Constitution seized on this provision as an indication that the new federal government would become too powerful. They argued that if the federal government could command the state militias, even temporarily, the federal control over the militias could become too great. They also argued the contrary position, that if the federal government was given power over the militias, it could undermine and perhaps eliminate them. The Founders explained that because the federal government would have state militias at its disposal, it would have less need to establish a permanent standing army—a possibility that supporters and opponents of the Constitution were both worried about.

By the time the first Congress met after ratification, there was less concern about militias and the right to bear arms than there had been during the debates over ratification. Indeed, interest in the entire topic of amendments had waned. People had quickly grown comfortable with the new Constitution, and they patriotically supported it. Nothing had happened that made the absence of amendments a problem, and Congress had more pressing business to attend to than passing amendments.[216] But during the debates that had occurred in the state ratification conventions, James Madison and other supporters of the Constitution had mollified the opponents of the Constitution by promising that amendments would be proposed at the first Congress. They made that promise in order to get the Constitution ratified and to avoid the need for a second convention to consider amendments, and they followed through on their promise.

Although Madison had promised to come up with amendments, he did not say what those amendments would be. The documentary record from the time of the Second Amendment does not answer the question of why the Second Amendment was among those that Madison proposed, but it does suggest that if the Second Amendment had been left out of the first group of amendments, there might not have been any strong objection.

It could be that the Second Amendment was included in order to reassure people who were still concerned that the state militias were at risk—that risk deriving from the power that Congress had over militias, as outlined in Article I of the Constitution. This theory is supported by the record of the brief debate in Congress about the Second Amendment.[217] That debate focused entirely on militias, which, contrary to what some modern commentators suggest, was obviously what the first Congress thought the amendment was about. Although the Second Amendment didn't contradict Article I, it may have been comforting to those who still worried about their militias to have an amendment that said that militias were a "right." Similar language to the Second Amendment had appeared in some state documents, where militias were among the enumerated rights of states. The Second Amendment might have been included among the first amendments to the Constitution simply because it looked reassuringly familiar, without any real thought that it would ever be significant. In fact, until the *Heller* decision, it never was.

The Supreme Court reanimated a dead Second Amendment

Although the Court pretended that it was simply explaining what the Second Amendment meant in the *Heller* case in 2008, clearly it was changing the amendment. Entire books could be written trying to explain why the Court took such a radical step at that particular moment in time.

In one sense, the Court should be seen not just as changing the amendment, but as rescuing it from oblivion. As discussed above, the militias that the Second Amendment refers to are a thing of the past. They just don't exist anymore. This means that if the Second Amendment only refers to militias, it is meaningless today. As one federal appellate court judge said, "There are few more antiquated constitutional provisions than the Second Amendment."[218]

There have been other parts of the Constitution that have lost meaning over time. For example, when the 25th Amendment was adopted in 1967, it rendered obsolete prior provisions on succession in Article II. In the *Heller* decision, the Court could have upheld the challenged restrictions on gun ownership and, as a result, simply let the Second Amendment fade away. That the Court did not do so suggests that the Court may have been deliberately siding with the pro-gun lobby, for whatever reason, rather than simply interpreting the Constitution. It could also be that the Court has become so attached to the Constitution that it just couldn't bear to face the truth. The Court might have simply been incapable of letting even a small part of the Constitution go, even though it was already obsolete.

It may be helpful to draw an analogy between the way that the Supreme Court viewed the Constitution when it handed down the *Heller* decision and the way that some people view sacred scriptures, as discussed above. Numerous passages in the Jewish and Christian Bibles, for example, refer to practices that have no counterpart in the modern world. Neither Jews nor Christians sacrifice animals at a temple, and it is unlikely that such a practice will ever be revived. What do today's Jews and Christians do, short of ignoring those passages? They don't erase the passages, and for the most part, they don't admit that the passages are obsolete. Instead, they find ways to derive meaning from them or at least to explain them, through creative (and sometimes tortured) reasoning. The Supreme Court did the same thing. It reinterpreted the text of the Second Amendment to give it a meaning it didn't originally have.

THE IRRELEVANCE OF THE SECOND AMENDMENT TODAY

Aside from the historical significance of the Second Amendment, what purpose does it serve today? In other words, if we were writing the Constitution today, what reasons would we give for including a right to have guns? This is the question that will and should be at the center of the debate on whether we should repeal the Second Amendment or retain it.

The Constitution has already served the interests of Americans who lived in the 18th, 19th, and 20th centuries. It can't do anything more to influence events that occurred in the past. It can and will significantly impact future events, however, so it should include provisions that will help today's and tomorrow's Americans to live in the kind of country that they want, in the context of a world that would barely be recognizable to the people who wrote the Second Amendment.

Guns as a right of individuals

Before we consider what purposes the Second Amendment serves today and why we might want to keep it, we should note that the pro-gun side does not concede that this is a legitimate question. They assert that owning guns is a right that does not have to be justified. They believe that just as artists can rely upon the right to free expression as a component of the First Amendment's right to free speech, gun ownership is a matter of personal expression and belief that is guaranteed by the Second Amendment, regardless of whether anyone who doesn't own guns sees value in that right.[219] No one has to explain why they want to go to church, and gun owners don't feel the need to explain why they want to have guns.

Gun owners view gun ownership as a matter of personal freedom. What they fail to realize is that every freedom that is enjoyed by one person has the potential to limit the freedom of another. Our Constitution, though, does reflect an understanding of this tension, and it deals with it by allowing the government to maintain a balance between competing claims of freedoms. The classic example, used by Supreme Court Justice Oliver Wendell Holmes Jr. is that free speech does not include the right to falsely yell "fire" in a crowded theater. Such an action would impinge upon the rights of others to peaceably and safely enjoy the show without the danger of being trampled in a stampede.[220]

There are plenty of other examples we encounter in daily life. A person might think she has the right to drive her car however she wants, but she doesn't, because other people's safety is at risk if she drives dangerously. A person might think he has the right to raise his children however he wants, but it has long been established that parents cannot ignore laws that require children to receive an education. The rights of the children to be able to function in society outweigh their parents' rights.

So it is with guns. Whatever interest gun owners have in their guns must be viewed in relationship to the fundamental rights of people around them to live unmolested and unthreatened, which is the essential aim of the entire Constitution. This concept is clearly and boldly stated in the Declaration of Independence as the unalienable right to "life, liberty, and the pursuit of happiness." How can we experience liberty and pursue happiness if guns are causing us to live in fear?[221]

By framing gun ownership as a matter of freedom, gun owners have gained the upper hand in the public debate. Americans love the idea of freedom. When George Bush spoke to the nation just after the September 11th attacks, he laid the groundwork for war by telling us that terrorists had attacked us because, "They hate our freedoms: our freedom of religion, our freedom of speech, our freedom to vote and assemble and disagree with each other."[222] I recall hearing an elderly veteran make a statement that reflected our country's strong belief in freedom (coupled with what he felt was our country's commitment to violence): "If you don't believe in freedom, we'll blow off your head."

The gun owners' may have succeeded in framing the debate so far, but the tables can be turned, as they have been in the past. Prior to Prohibition, everyone assumed that individuals had a right to drink alcoholic beverages. With the passage of the 18th Amendment, they learned that the government could limit their rights.

The public passed Prohibition based in part upon the notion that drinking alcohol to intoxication was interfering with all sorts of rights that other people had. Alcohol was blamed for impoverishing families, for degrading the nation's workforce, for violence on women and children, for public brawling, and on and on. Some proponents of Prohibition saw drinking as a threat to the very existence of America. When enough people felt that alcohol was getting in the way of what they wanted in their lives and in society, they got rid of alcohol.[223]

Although Prohibition was repealed, it was never held to be unconstitutional. We could enact it again tomorrow. So it is with guns. We can either allow them or outlaw them.

Guns for personal defense

When gun owners do answer the question of what purpose the Second Amendment serves today, one of the answers they give most frequently is that they want to have guns so that they can defend themselves from criminals.

Clearly, we have better ways to defend ourselves from criminals than letting everyone shoot them. Notably, we have police departments that increasingly consist of officers who are trained to do their jobs. Police today are almost always selected by an extensive process that includes interviews, tests, and psychological examinations. They are required to have a certain level of education, oftentimes a college degree. They must go through months of training and are often hired on probationary status so that their fitness can be evaluated. They are overseen and regularly evaluated, and they must undergo periodic retraining and testing. They are subject to discipline and dismissal if they don't perform to departmental standards. Although we know that not all cops are perfect, at least there is a system for keeping them on the right track.

Compare this to the private gun owner, who can in many parts of this country legally own a gun without satisfying any of the above criteria. To these people, what the Second Amendment means is they have a right to own a gun, no matter how inept, stupid, erratic, and dangerous they are. They think the Second Amendment isn't there to guarantee that the modern professional police officer will be able to defend the people; it is there to assure that totally unqualified people will be able to own guns and be a menace to everyone within shooting distance of them.

Lest this sound biased to you, let me point out that this is exactly what huge numbers of gun owners believe and what their organizations lobby for on their behalf. They openly protest in speech, in print, and on the airwaves that no government bureaucrat should be able to decide whether people can have guns, what kinds of guns they can have, whether their guns should have safety features, how many guns they can have, how they should store them, or where they can carry them. They complain that gun licensing fees violate their constitutional rights to bear arms. They are very quick to point to their Second Amendment rights as the source of their entitlement. Many of them, based either on past encounters with the police or on political rhetoric they share with each other, believe that the police are their enemies precisely because the police want to be the ones society relies on to do the job of policing. They want to be the "good guys" who stop the bad guys, and they don't want the police getting in their way.

How do the police feel about this? Responsible police tend to have a very different view of guns. It is drilled into them that guns are dangerous. They are told to not even take their guns out of their holsters unless they feel a very serious threat is imminent. Many police departments require officers to file a report each time they shoot their guns.[224] They understand that their guns and their jobs can be taken away quickly if they misuse their weapons, and that a single weapons infraction can end an entire career. They do not view guns as something they are entitled to have, let alone to use. They see guns as something they must earn the right to carry. They also tend to be very concerned about proliferation of guns in the civilian population, because they know that there is a difference between the way they view and handle guns and the way non-professionals do.

The evidence shows that having a gun so that you can defend yourself from bad guys is mostly a fantasy in the minds of gun lovers. Even though a few million people in the US have guns, they almost never use their guns in self-defense, according to the FBI, which keeps track of shooting incidents. Far more often than they are used defensively, guns are used offensively to threaten and shoot people. This offensive use of guns isn't what gun owners say they have their guns for. It isn't what the Supreme Court said the Second Amendment protects. But it is the grim reality that is finally leading people to call for a change to our Constitution.

Defending our country from tyranny

The other main reason gun owners give for wanting to have guns is so that they can use their guns to prevent tyranny from overtaking America. Their arguments usually don't focus on using their guns to repel a foreign invasion. Instead, they talk about shooting our own government officials, in the event that our state or federal governments become tyrannical. You won't find very many police officers, FBI agents, or other law enforcement professionals who share this view, because they understand at a very personal level that they are the ones who would be shot.

In the abstract, many of us could concede that it's theoretically possible that our government could someday turn tyrannical. We have seen plenty of dictators and totalitarian states. But there is nothing in US history that gives any credence to the fear that our own government would or could get to the point that every citizen would need to be armed so that they can shoot their way to liberty.

We have had a few eras when our government suppressed

people's rights. The McCarthy era blacklisting and the World War II internment of Asian Americans quickly come to mind. But we shouldn't overlook that in each instance, the wrong was righted by the political process itself and not by armed insurrection. No one shot their way off the blacklists. They sued in the courts and pressed their cases to the public and to the government itself. Sometimes people suffered. Too often the government did not respond as it should have. But ultimately, things resolved themselves without shootouts in the streets against representatives of the government.

In reality, the few times that people have tried to resist our government with guns have all been catastrophes for the armed resisters. Roaring Twenties bootleggers, 1980s drug lords, survivalist militias, and a few militant religious sects have all had their shootouts with the government. They all lost, and the American people cheered when they did. The public does not want a Second Amendment that would guarantee anyone's right to violently resist the government, and the courts will not uphold such a right if it is ever seriously asserted.

When people take up arms against their own government, they give the government legally accepted cause to suppress them as rebels, insurrectionists, and traitors.[225] Governments—ours included—do not hesitate to put down such uprisings, using whatever force they deem necessary. The very existence of a government depends upon its ability to prevent its people from directing violence towards the government. Absent this ability, states degenerate into what we have come to know as failed states, where force is used to terrorize the populace. The gun lovers overlook the fact that just as they view government tyranny as a threat to them, governments view uncontrolled violence as a threat to the government. As long as the general populace views the government as legitimate, the gun lovers will be viewed by the populace as a threat.

Will gun owners save America?

What if the government did turn tyrannical, beyond the control of its civil law and institutions, and the people were unable through non-violent means to restore democracy? Think for a moment about what an armed resistance would look like. Picture in your mind the people you may have met at gun shows or shouting at village board meetings about their rights. Are these the people you would want running the show? Do they seem like the sorts who would act in a deliberative fashion, listening to the concerns you have and protecting your rights? Have they ever shown that they have any appreciation of minority rights? Do you think they would fashion a shadow government that would in any way resemble the America that they would claim to be restoring?

Hardly. They are renegades—and proud of it. Today, they revel in imagining that one day they will be called on to save society from the legal and governmental establishment. They are arming themselves now because they think the country is going to hell, and they want to be ready to shoot anyone they perceive to be trampling their rights.

What rights do they claim are being infringed? I can't recall ever hearing one of these folks talk about anyone else's rights besides their own. I'm certain I never heard them argue that they need guns to make sure minority voting rights aren't interfered with. I never heard them say they need guns to defend the right of same-sex couples to marry. They never seem to profess any interest in the rights of immigrants. It's just as well. I'd hate to imagine the scene if a self-appointed posse showed up at a polling place or a wedding chapel or a community college, guns drawn.

As for their own rights, other than the right to not wear a motorcycle helmet, you don't hear much from them about any rights except gun rights, which makes their arguments kind of circular. Their logic is that they need guns to protect them from people who would take away their guns. Obviously, if they didn't have guns in the first place, they wouldn't be at any risk. They'd have nothing to lose and nothing they needed to defend.

Let's take a closer look at how we responded when Senator Joseph McCarthy led a nationwide terror campaign against ordinary Americans in the 1950s. He spurred our national government to deny fundamental rights to a significant segment of our population and to intimidate an even larger group. He helped create a hysterical fear of communism after World War II, pointing to the murderous abuses of Russian dictator Joseph Stalin to frighten Americans into acceding to abuses of authority.

McCarthy, with the assistance of the US Congress and state and local governmental units all across the country, pushed people out of jobs and sometimes into prisons, ignoring the due process of the law that Americans would normally have insisted upon. McCarthy was able to do this because, not too many years before, the public had learned of the Nazi death camps. They had seen the Russians overrunning large swaths of post-war Europe, ousting governments and installing their own regimes. People didn't want to see Nazism or communism coming to the United States. So when McCarthy and his followers equated progressivism with communism and socialism and said that harsh measures were needed in order to preserve democracy, people accepted those measures. Just as they had during the war, when they had accepted governmental restrictions on their own liberties as necessary for national security, people let themselves be led away from protecting one another's freedoms. They accepted that they would have to give up their own freedoms to keep communism at bay. The US government treated its own people tyrannically and got away with it for a while by making people afraid that foreign tyranny was a greater threat.

When all this was happening, the pro-gun guys didn't come to our rescue. Why not? For one thing, they weren't the same pro-gun guys who are around today. In the 1950s, there were more war veterans than at any prior time in our history. We had drafted and accepted millions of enlisted men into our armed services to fight in World War II. More than 400,000 Americans died in that war, so when the war was over, millions came home—some with their guns, but nearly all of them with some training and familiarity with firearms.

All of these soldiers, sailors, airmen, and marines had been part of an unprecedented military campaign using the most highly developed guns in history. They had all been indoctrinated in the military outlook that the US was virtuous and justified in using deadly force to defend itself, its allies, and its concept of individual freedom. Except for a very small number of conscientious objectors who served in the war effort, the veterans had participated in or supported operations that killed millions of enemy combatants and civilians. You might think that these guys would have jumped at the chance to take up arms to defend their own countrymen against the kind of tyranny they had just fought against overseas.

But they didn't. A lot of them probably just weren't paying

attention and didn't see McCarthy's antics as a real threat to liberty, or at least to their liberty. How many of them really cared if a few Jewish screenwriters in Hollywood or liberal newspaper writers in New York lost their jobs? And besides, why should they believe the accounts that said that the very government they had just risked their lives for was wrong when it told them that a worldwide Communist conspiracy was plotting to take over the world? They had just fought against one madman who really was trying to take over the world—and who came too damn close to doing it.

Some of the veterans undoubtedly were concerned about what the Red Scare was doing to America. But, like concerned citizens in every era, they found a way to convince themselves that they didn't need to put themselves at personal risk. They had just gotten home from some pretty frightening situations. They weren't jumping at the chance to take up arms to defend anyone or anything, even their own country.

That is the big flaw with the NRA's argument that everyone should have guns so they can defend the country and everyone in it from government tyranny. Most people simply won't do it. They'll let the next guy take care of himself. They'll convince themselves that someone else will do what needs to be done. They'll avoid concluding that anyone is really being abused, or they'll convince themselves that the tyranny isn't that severe and that the victims brought their trouble on themselves. They'll decide they aren't quite prepared enough yet and need a few more meetings to discuss it.

Your average gun lover did not kiss his wife and kids goodbye and go to the aid of the people who were persecuted by McCarthy, the Japanese-Americans who were sent to American concentration camps during World War II, the civil rights workers who were fired upon in the South, the anti-war protesters who were spied on by police and FBI Red Squads, the students who were beaten by cops at the Democratic National Convention in Chicago, the students who were fired upon by the National Guard at Kent State in Ohio, the kids who were rousted by New York police during the Occupy movement, the minorities who were racially profiled in Los Angeles, or the majority of Americans, including themselves, whose emails and phone calls were intercepted for no reason.

There are more privately owned guns in this country right now than ever before, and there is absolutely no reason to think, based on anything that has ever happened in American history, that any gun owner will ever use his guns to protect anyone else from government tyranny. All we can expect is that occasionally a desperate gun owner will take a shot at the police in a futile attempt to avoid being arrested. That's not patriotism. It's not heroic. It's just tragic, sad, and a danger to the public.

There are other reasons why all the veterans never strapped on their guns to form a citizen's freedom brigade. As I have been told by more than one veteran, once you have seen what guns can do to people, most people aren't eager to start a gunfight. A minority of the veterans who came back from Europe after World War II ever saw combat, but those who did had memories that would have a lasting influence on how they viewed guns. A lot of the other veterans heard stories and saw pictures that affected them the same way.

War vets also learn how ineffective violence can be. They see the battles start and stop and start again, often without any enduring gain. They see new wars start up, as if countries can never learn the lesson that every combat veteran learns, that war is hell. Eventually they see the wars they fought in settled by diplomacy, and they wonder whether the fighting and dying was necessary.

What does stop tyranny?

What has always stopped abuse of government in the US is that the abuse has been exposed, the abuser has lost the support of the people, and the abuser has been peaceably removed from power by the very forces of government that the Constitution created. Oftentimes we have followed up by enacting reforms to prevent the abuse from recurring.

Joe McCarthy's tyranny wasn't stopped by armed individuals. It was stopped by journalists and government officials who did the methodical work of interviewing people, observing events, reviewing documents, holding hearings, and interpreting the facts to the American people. It took time, but eventually McCarthy was censured by the Senate and he ceased to be a problem. Those in government who had stood by his side faded away. The people whom he had intimidated into testifying against their co-workers stopped feeding him information. News outlets stopped printing what he gave them as if it were true, and they stopped praising him as a savior. Instead, they printed the truth, and the truth won out. Not a single shot was fired in defense of freedom in America, but freedom was restored.

Richard J. Daley, who presided over the Chicago police during the 1968 Democratic National Convention as they beat peaceful protesters, was not shot. He died years later, still in power, from a heart attack. Although he wasn't removed from office through any governmental process, his abuse of power was limited to some extent because it was exposed in the press. While his police were brutalizing protesters, the protesters chanted peacefully, and the whole world was watching. The courts also played a part in restoring honest government to Chicago by enjoining some of the abuses of the Daley political machine and making it more difficult for him to act as a dictator.

Daley's power wasn't ever totally eliminated. His son inherited much of it, and he himself served as mayor for even longer than his father did. The son's administration was also tainted by abuses, including its tolerance for police who beat false confessions out of suspects. But eventually, some (although not all) of his abuses were addressed in non-violent ways.

Richard Nixon, whose reelection committee employed burglars to break into the offices of his political opponents and who then tried to cover up the crimes, resigned from office in disgrace. The mere threat that he would be impeached was enough to force him out of power, once it became apparent that the public had lost confidence in their president.

Over the years, various governors, mayors, congressmen, and city council members have been sent to jail for their corrupt acts, which sometimes rose to the level that they could be considered tyranny. Too often it has taken too long to cleanse the government of those who abused their power. But the abuse has never gone on forever, and it has never gotten as bad as in some other countries. Most important of all, in our country the transition of power and restoration of legitimacy has never required violence. Provisions in the Constitution, not including the Second Amendment, deserve the credit.

The Founders set up a system of shared power, often referred to as "checks and balances." Power is shared at the federal level among the President, Congress, and the courts. At various times in our history, each has stood in the way of the abuse of power by one of the other branches. For a long time, the courts were viewed as the main protector against tyranny because the other branches of the government were the ones acting directly upon the populace. The courts decreed that legislatures couldn't enact laws that interfered with voting rights.[226] The courts declared that the police couldn't prevent people from assembling to protest.[227] The courts stopped local officials from condemning private property without compensating the owners.[228]

For a period of time, the courts were so prolific in protecting individuals' rights that some came to view the courts as themselves becoming "tyrannical." They complained that the courts were usurping roles that the Constitution assigned to the legislative and executive branches of government. This backlash against the courts, particularly the Supreme Court and its perceived liberal leanings, led to more conservative justices being appointed to the Court. The Supreme Court as it is now composed is viewed by the pro-gun folks as less tyrannical, because it has protected gun owners from legislation that would limit their ability to have guns. Whether it will protect them from other actions by the government is questionable.

The Constitution also limits the powers of both the federal and state governments vis à vis each other, establishing a balance between centralized and diffused power. Furthermore, each state has some sort of constitution or charter that limits the ability of individuals or the state itself to become tyrannical. Different parts of our government have instituted protections against abuse of power in addition to those that are mandated by the federal Constitution.

Some states use term limits to keep administrations or representatives from becoming too entrenched and beyond control. Some give their people the power to initiate legislation directly by petitions and ballot initiatives. The power to advise and consent to appointments and the power to fund or de-fund programs is used throughout government to keep a level of control.

Throughout its history, our country has not needed to resort to violence to restrain government oppression. Every succession of power has been orderly and peaceful. It is a record that we have every reason to believe can continue.

America's wars against tyranny

There have only been two instances in American history when large segments of the population took up arms to resist what they called governmental tyranny. The first was the War of Independence, which the American colonists fought for many reasons, among them to free themselves from having to pay taxes to the British. The American Revolution is generally seen in the US as a successful violent revolution that resulted in a stable and enduring government. This success no doubt strongly influences Americans to view violence favorably. It gives many Americans the conviction that if something is worthwhile, we should be willing to fight for it. It leaves the impression that violence is the only possible avenue to success, and there is no reason to look for peaceful alternatives. In America, if something works, we keep doing it over and over. We don't argue with success.

We do, however, overemphasize the role that violence played in the American Revolution, ignoring all the other factors. We also ignore the possibility that America might have been able to win its independence without a fight. The American Revolution was an armed struggle. But the fighting was done in the midst of ongoing multinational political dialogue and negotiations, and in the context of a philosophical debate on the nature and legitimacy of various forms of government. There might have been another way. Nonetheless, battles make vivid stories and they are easy to report on, so they tend to get prominent places in history books and they have tended to dominate our understanding of our national origins.

The only other time Americans fought against so-called tyranny was the Civil War, which is sometimes still referred to in the South as the War of Northern Aggression, or the Recent Unpleasantness. That time, violence failed to achieve the desired result, at least from the perspective of the Southerners, who fired the first shots, claiming that the tyrant was the North. If the Confederacy was correct that its own government, the United States, was tyrannical, then tyranny won. Most people today would agree it's a good thing the North was victorious. If the Confederacy had been able to defeat Northern "tyranny," the United States would not have survived.

A very important lesson can be derived from our Civil War—that although violence can defeat opponents, it does not convince the opponents that they were wrong. By resorting to violence, people admit that their arguments do not have the power to persuade, so people have to be forced to accept them.

People who resort to violence should not be surprised when their violence does not win over their opponents. If you can recall losing a schoolyard fistfight, as many of us can, you probably remember going home and brooding about getting even. You probably didn't decide that the other kid was right just because he won. If, on the other hand, you won the fight, you may remember walking to school the next day, worried that your opponent would be lying in wait for you, perhaps with a few friends ready to provide backup.

Victories that are won by violence also tend to be temporary. They leave the victors in the position of having to constantly maintain strength to be ready to fend off future challengers. Those challengers may be previously defeated foes or newcomers who want to take from the victors whatever they took from someone else. In the context of countries, every military victory invites a challenger to step forward. Whatever is won must be protected, because it was won through strength, not merit, and there is always the possibility that someone else will come along who will be stronger.

We should also have learned from our wars that violence tends to plant the seeds of resentment in vanquished opponents. Like the children who get into schoolyard fights, families, tribes, and countries all react the same way to violence. They despise the act and the actor who used it, and except under extraordinary circumstances and leadership, they feel the urge to retaliate and seek revenge. Southern whites feared that just such a backlash would occur after the Civil War and expected that newly freed slaves would seek revenge for the deprivations they had suffered. To their astonished relief, no such large-scale vengeance ever took place. Whites in South Africa also feared retaliation after the end of apartheid. Nelson Mandela's commitment to reconciliation is generally credited with avoiding a dreaded bloodbath of retribution. All sides in the seemingly endless violence in the Middle East understand this dynamic, and they all seem incapable of overcoming it.

The vanquished Confederates in the U.S. never mounted a large-scale effort to retaliate against the Union army after the war was over. However, the resentments that were generated by the violence of that war and the humiliation felt by the South did not disappear. Some of it found expression in violence against blacks, and some of it became the basis for the anti-Yankee feelings that are still expressed today. At some deep level, basic issues remain unresolved more than 150 years after our Civil War ended. Although people in the South were not convinced that it was wrong to hold slaves, they were forced to relinquish their control over their slaves and to restructure their society. The seeds of resentment that had been sown in the violence of the war germinated in the South's involuntary capitulation to its Northern conquerors.

That resentment is still being played out today by many on the pro-gun side, even by people who have no historical connection with the Old South. As people all over our country fall into despair due to the situations they find themselves in, they are identifying with the vestiges of southern resentment, and they are spreading it well beyond the boundaries of the old Confederacy.[229] When we hear discontented people using phrases like "states' rights," their position can be traced back to the rhetoric that led the South into war and later birthed the Ku Klux Klan. When people adorn their properties with Confederate flags and join organizations that glorify the Old South, they reveal their resentment at being told what they can and cannot do. When people rail against other people collecting "entitlements," there are obvious echoes of Southern resistance to Reconstruction. An intransigent core of revanchists has not given up the dream of resuming the fighting and reestablishing their white male world view. That's why they still have guns.

America has labeled the Revolutionary War as a fight against British tyranny, and the Confederacy saw the Civil War as a fight against Northern tyranny. In both cases, the label was applied in order to make the wars seem meritorious. But if the idea of tyranny is to have meaning, it must be viewed from all perspectives, and it must be viewed fairly.

Even today, most Americans would have difficulty viewing the American Revolution from the perspective the British government had at the time. I doubt that many Americans have ever tried. The

British government didn't see itself as tyrannical; it viewed us as disloyal, selfish, irresponsible, deadbeat tax-dodgers. British loyalists in America tended to agree with the British government, but their view of the situation is not a major part of the narrative that is taught in American schools. It has been ignored through the ages, and it was suppressed at the time by the propagandists for our revolution, who worked to discredit or silence their opposition, refute their arguments, and discourage the spread of their opinions.

We have also not paid much attention to other opinions that were held at the time. Not all Brits agreed with their government's actions in America. Some, although it is difficult to say how many, were sympathetic to us. The taxes the British government imposed on its American colonies were supposedly to pay the costs of administering those colonies, not to pay for Britain's many wars. But the line between those expenses was not altogether clear, as Britain had been fighting its European rivals not just on their home turf but also in America. The British people were being taxed to pay for the wars, and they did not always feel that the Parliament was adequately representing their interests. They were receptive to our complaints about taxation without representation and about having to house British troops in private homes. To the extent that our claims of tyranny were based on tax policy, plenty of people in Britain were feeling similarly tyrannized. Just prior to Thomas Paine's publication in America of *Common Sense*, a pamphlet often credited with articulating the argument for revolution to ordinary Americans, pamphleteers in Britain were articulating very similar grievances.[230]

In fact, complaints about quartering soldiers and taxation without representation had become a staple of British political thinking. Eighty-eight years earlier, such practices had been among the issues that had led the British to overthrow their own King James II in the "Glorious Revolution" of 1688. As news of that revolution spread to America in 1689, it prompted scattered mini-rebellions in New York, Maryland, and throughout the New England colonies. Those rebellions, like the British revolution, complained of government abuses and taxation without adequate representation.[231]

As for the Civil War, although the South viewed the North as tyrannical, others perceived the South to be the tyrants. You won't see that viewpoint expressed in history books, where the dominant story is about a struggle between two powers—the North and the South—and where the South is never seen as tyrannizing the North. But from the viewpoint of the southern slaves, it is obvious that the South was visiting tyranny upon them, and it was a tyranny that was far more offensive than simply burdensome taxes on tea. Every possible type of mental, emotional, cultural, and physical violence was inflicted on the slaves. It was done not by rogue lunatics acting beyond the reach of a civilized government. The violence was inflicted at will by individuals who had the permission, cooperation, and assistance of the government, and by the government itself. Although not everyone in the South owned slaves or approved of owning slaves, the entire Southern society was organized around the keeping of slaves. The violence was inescapable, pervasive, and incontestable.

Some argue that the violence that imbued the system of slavery was not viewed in this way among white Southerners at the time, and that in the context of their society, the violence was normal, permissible, and unobjectionable. Even if that view was held by white Southerners, it would be completely beyond the point, for two reasons.

Firstly, violence must be evaluated from the perspective of the recipient. Whether a victim seeks revenge will depend upon whether he feels he was victimized, not on whether the perpetrator feels he was justified. That probably explains why the British did not pursue vengeance to a very great extent after they were forced to give up their American colonies. The British interest in America was at its core a mercantile endeavor. The British were sophisticated in geopolitical trade and politics. Although they may have taken offense at the American Revolution, they were practical. They understood the realities of the situation, and they quickly accommodated the new American states so that British financial pursuits could resume. At the conclusion of our Revolutionary War, the British had lost some land and potential revenue. Its military had lost some of its prestige. But neither the British government nor its people had suffered any humiliating degradation that they felt had to be avenged. They were in a very different frame of mind from that of the African Americans, who by the close of the Civil War had been abused by the slavery system for more than 200 years.

Secondly, violence must be evaluated from the perspective of humanity today, because this is where we are in time. We do not accept the same level of violence today that was deemed acceptable when either the American Revolution or the Civil War were fought, and at those times, society did not accept the level of violence that was deemed acceptable when Genghis Khan slaughtered his way to power or when the ancient Hebrew kings laid waste to tribes that opposed them.

Just as violence has always been present to a degree in all societies, so has the level of violence that societies accept been variable. In general, the trend over a very long period of time has been towards less and less acceptance and use of violence, and consequently less resentment and retaliation, although there have been moments in history when sentiments swung the other way.[232] To our great fortune, the entire history of the United States has taken place during a few centuries when society was moving away from accepting violence as a matter of principle, even though in practice violence has always had a major role in our country.

Will we need guns to fight the next Hitler?

When the pro-gun guys have used up all of their arguments to justify the use of violence by individuals and they have still failed to convince people that guns are the answer to potential abuses by governments, they always play what they think is their trump card. "What about Hitler?" they say, pointing out that it took guns to remove him from power.

There are many flaws in that argument. Let's look at just a couple of big ones. To start, it should be remembered that at every step, Hitler used violence to get his power. In the early days, his thugs intimidated political opponents. Later, his secret police used violence to silence opposition. His propagandists staged parades that showed off the German military's ability to use overwhelming violence against its enemies, in order to earn Hitler the admiration of the German people. His military used violence to invade other countries. His SS organization used violence to rid the world of people they considered undesirable. It was the acceptance of violence that enabled Hitler to become a problem. Had the world rejected his violence, we would never have learned his name.

Far from being an argument in favor of guns and violence, Hitler is actually the perfect argument against them. People living in Germany today understand this. They have been teaching their children about peace ever since the collapse of the Reich. They have had to live with the shame of being associated with monumental violence. They faced up to their past, and they have changed.

It is also a mistake to assume that the only way Hitler could have been kept out of power or removed from a position of power once he had attained it was through violence. Hitler's regime depended upon assistance from foreign financiers in Switzerland and elsewhere. If the flow of funds had been cut off, he would have quickly withered. Hitler also required markets, fuel, material, and political recognition from outside Germany that could similarly have been denied him. There were many approaches the people, businesses, and governments of the world could have taken that would have undermined Hitler and robbed him of the power he had amassed.[233]

The world not only was slow to condemn Hitler's racial policies, it didn't raise much of an objection to his violent methods, because most governments at the time used violence to get what they wanted, and most people were OK with that. For the most part, Hitler was not breaking the rules of civilized society; he was following the rules that the rest of society was following while they called themselves civilized.

In the fifth century, Saint Augustine articulated a Christian theological justification for state violence that has become known as the "Just War" theory. It bestowed religious blessing on brutality in an age when the Catholic Church found such justification very useful. Augustine wrote, "We go to war, that we may have peace." The Just War theory has survived to present times.[234]

Mao Zedong, the Chinese Communist revolutionary, summed up the philosophy that China and much of the world followed—in Hitler's time and up to the present day—when he said, "Political power grows out of the barrel of a gun....We are advocates of the abolition of war...but war can only be abolished through war. In order to get rid of the gun, it is necessary to take up the gun."[235] That philosophy was used by Britain, France, and the Allies to justify World War I as the "war to end war."

In the United States and in much of the rest of the world, there has been a longstanding belief that violence is an appropriate way for countries to pursue their goals. It is thought to be effective and to be justifiable from a moral and religious point of view. Like other countries, we are quick to ask God to help us achieve military victories, and to proclaim that God was on our side when we won. It is important for Americans to feel that war and violence are OK. Our country was born of violence, and it has been at war for a large part of its history. We are always preparing to start another war. We proudly speak of ourselves as a military superpower, and when the Soviet Union collapsed, we exultantly boasted that we were the only remaining superpower. Our entire national identity is tied up in the idea that war is good, and that we are good when we go to war.

Gandhi preached a different approach as he built his campaign of non-violent resistance, which ultimately ousted the mighty British Empire from India. It took many years, and along the way, the British caused suffering and death as they used violence against Gandhi's non-violence. But eventually Gandhi's Satyagraha movement proved successful. The British tyrants withdrew because they were shamed and because they could not govern a country that refused to be governed. Gandhi followed this path not just because it was dictated by his Hindu faith, but because as a student of history and a capable politician, he knew that it would succeed and he believed that it was the only strategy that would work. He had seen violent resistance against the British crushed. He proved that non-violent resistance was superior.[236]

The superiority of non-violence over violence was demonstrated long before Gandhi's time, though. Famously, in the time of Jesus, the Jews employed non-violent tactics to protest against the mighty and unquestionably tyrannical Roman Empire. When Pontius Pilate, the Roman official with jurisdiction over Jerusalem, erected images of Roman power that offended the Jews, the Jews called a general strike. Their work stoppage threatened to reduce the yield of the crops from which Rome derived much of its tribute. After five days, Pilate attempted to break the strike by threatening to kill the protesters. The Jewish people did not respond by trying to defend themselves. They did not attack the Roman soldiers. Instead, they explained that they would allow themselves to be murdered before they would give up their protest. Upon seeing such a powerful show of solidarity, Pilate relented.[237]

The same lesson has been learned repeatedly in recent times.[238] The Berlin Wall did not come down because West Germany's military attacked. It came down when peaceful protesters refused to walk away. Poland did not win its freedom from the Soviet Union by force of arms. It won because the Solidarity Movement showed the world its resolve, without any show of force. Blacks in South Africa did not overcome apartheid by rioting, shooting, or bombing. They won because they and their international supporters convinced the minority white ruling class that the time had come for a peaceful transition. All enduring modern liberations have come through non-violent action.[239] All modern armed attempts at internal rebellion have been bloody disasters.

Certainly not all non-violent protests against repression have succeeded. As spectacular as the Tiananmen Square protests were, China remains a state that severely limits the freedom of its people. The protest was put down. But it's not clear that a violent protest in China would have had any greater success. Violent revolutions have a mixed record throughout history.

Another distortion of history that some pro-gun groups have been circulating is the notion that Hitler was able to slaughter Jews because he had enacted laws that allowed him to take away their guns, leaving them defenseless once the extermination plan was put into effect. This is not only offensively historically inaccurate, according to a number of scholars and the Anti-Defamation League, it is also ridiculous.

When a small number of Jews, armed with what guns they could find, resisted the liquidation of the Warsaw Ghetto, Hitler's forces didn't square off against them in rows like the British did during the American Revolutionary War. They used artillery to reduce the ghetto to rubble.

At what point could the Jews of Germany have used handguns to save themselves? When their books were being burned in the streets and the rest of the German population looked on approvingly? When laws were being enacted that forced them out of their jobs at universities and as government civil servants? When they were being denied exit visas so that they could leave the country? When they were being forced to wear armbands? When their hair was being cut in public to humiliate them? When they were told to vacate their homes so that Christians could move in? When their children were being expelled from schools? When their shops were looted and their synagogues burned? When they were being loaded onto trains heading (little did they know) to concentration camps? At any of these times, could the Jews have simply picked up their guns and shot the police? No, they would have been arrested or simply killed.

It seems glaringly insensitive for the pro-gunners to suggest that the Holocaust was the fault of the victims because they failed to arm themselves against a government that had the will and the ability to quash any such resistance. Insensitive, but not surprising. Today's pro-gun movement is not known for its sensitivity. Regrettably, in their desperation to find justification for their violent proclivities, today's pro-gun folks miss the real lesson that we can learn from Hitler: guns and violence enabled Hitler to become who he was. If there is ever another monster like Hitler, he will grow out of a society that values guns and violence, not one that rejects them. Now would be a good time to make sure that America is not the kind of place that could spawn the next Hitler. Repealing the Second Amendment, so that we can start to rid our country of guns, would be a good start.

IV. Overcoming fear and moving forward

GUNS AND FEAR

Gun ownership has been declining for years, despite everything the NRA has been doing. Even our veterans who have returned from wars have, for the most part, lost their interest in guns, despite having been indoctrinated that their use of guns was necessary for the suppression of tyrannical governments. They took up bowling, golf, tennis, and jogging instead of shooting sports.

In very recent times, though, the rate of decline in gun ownership may have slowed, due to guns becoming a symbol of the alienation that the angry white guys are feeling.[240] The gun industry has capitalized on the alienation and has aggressively promoted gun violence as a response to it. The vitality of the gun industry today depends upon people feeling afraid and angry.

The gun industry thrives on fear

Just as advertising in the 1960s convinced women to start smoking cigarettes by labeling them as a sign of independence and sophistication, advertising has convinced some people that guns are the symbol of manliness. This link in advertising between violence and manliness has gone way beyond the subtle posing in a photo of a man, his gun, and his woman. The Bushmaster Firearms company, which manufactures the assault weapon of choice for mass rage killers, ran an ad for more than two years that promised to issue "man cards" to men who didn't let women control them. The ads promised that a man could renew his manliness by purchasing a Bushmaster rifle.[241] What could be more potent than a guy who resents women and is ready to kill other people? It doesn't get any more primitive than that.

The gun industry has taken advantage of several opportunities that have come its way. The economic decline in the US that began in the 1970s left a lot of people feeling helpless, as did the Iranian hostage crisis that began in 1979. By then, people in the US had been schooled to reject any kind of communalism as communism, and unions were on the decline. Working people did not view each other as fellow members of a support group as they had in earlier economically difficult times. Solidarity was replaced by lonely solitariness.

The gun industry also capitalized on fear of crime. The inner-city battles among crack cocaine sellers in the 1980s fed the perceived need for handguns for personal protection. The spread of methamphetamine labs to more dispersed locales in the 1990s strengthened this marketing opportunity.

Isolated people felt besieged and unable to defend themselves in a time when commentators on both the left and the right were expressing alarm at what they saw as a deterioration of America and of civilization in general.[242] Guns were offered as a way for individuals to feel powerful and safe.

Firepower, as portrayed in movies like *Rambo* in 1982, gave some men a vicarious flush of testosterone. People started buying army-style rifles and talking tough. The gun industry was delighted to find that there was a market for expensive semi-automatic rifles, at a time when their military markets seemed uncertain due to reductions in Cold War tensions. Gun manufacturers began a nationwide effort to encourage people to keep guns in their homes and carry them in public. They lobbied for legislation, and by 2013 had succeeded in legalizing the open or concealed carrying of guns in all 50 states.[243]

Just how big a change this was for the US is not always appreciated. It is easy to overlook the fact that for almost the entire history of the US, there have been local restrictions on carrying guns.[244] Among the most famous bans were those in Tombstone, Arizona, and similar frontier towns, which had outright prohibitions on carrying guns into town. These towns had gotten fed up with gun violence in the form of cowpokes looking for a good time on the weekends, getting drunk, and getting into gunfights. Consider for a moment that a town named Tombstone banned guns, and the situation becomes clear.

Most people in the US simply didn't carry guns, especially in more densely populated cities. Even so, the police in these cities struggled to maintain order among rapidly growing populations of immigrants from many countries, who spoke many languages and often brought their dislike of each other's cultures along with them to their new country. Not infrequently, immigrants were resentful of each new group that came ashore, seeing the new arrivals as competition for jobs. They tended to fight. The situation got so dangerous that cities and even states banned all sorts of weapons that people could conceal on themselves, including saps, billy clubs, knives, brass knuckles—and guns.

No one doubted that governmental authorities had the power to enact and enforce such regulations or doubted the wisdom of doing so. No one other than thugs subscribed to the idea that everyone would be safer if there were more weapons in everyone's hands. We were trying to be a civilized country, so we naturally rejected the idea of brute force having a place in day-to-day affairs. The courts certainly didn't interfere with the enforcement of regulations that were enacted by towns and states attempting to reduce violence.

These regulations continued to expand during the lawlessness of the Prohibition era. The public was horrified by machine guns, so Congress all but outlawed them, along with sawed-off shotguns, another favorite of rum-running gangsters. These were the first federal gun regulations, and they had widespread support.

But, remarkably, in our lifetimes, things have changed. Public opinion swung, and we are now at the point where on any street in any town, people may be carrying guns in their pockets, and there is nothing anyone, including the police, can do to stop them.

What the gun industry wants us to believe is that they want people to live peacefully. What it has never admitted is that the more violence there is in America, the more money they make selling guns to people who are afraid of the violence. In frontier times, Tombstone could outlaw guns because the gun lobby was not as developed as it is today. Today, the gun lobby is going from one state capital to another, giving campaign contributions to politicians who are passing laws that prohibit municipalities from regulating guns and that result in more people shooting each other.[245] The gun lobby is making it impossible for towns to make their streets safe from gun violence, because the gun sellers depend upon violence to spur demand for their products. Would anyone buy a gun to protect themselves if they already felt safe? Of course not. Only frightened people buy guns for defense.

How can we overcome fear?

The dependency that the gun sellers have on people feeling frightened points toward one part of the solution to gun violence. If we would all just stop feeling so afraid of one another, we would stop buying and carrying guns. Why weight yourself down with a couple of pounds of metal if you don't need it? Why waste the money?

Some people undoubtedly think it is the height of naiveté to think that if we just decide not to be afraid, we won't have anything to be afraid of. Maybe these people never sang the Star Spangled Banner, which, like all national anthems, is meant to strengthen people's courage and faith in their government, especially during frightening times. "The flag was still there..." Maybe they never prayed and felt safer just because they affirmed to themselves a belief that they might be protected. Maybe they never cuddled a frightened child or soothed a pet that was terrified of lightning and thunder. Maybe they don't understand what President Franklin D. Roosevelt meant when he said, "the only thing we have to fear is fear itself."

The fact that our view of guns has shifted in this country stands as evidence that we can in fact reject fear and the guns that falsely promise to shield us from whatever makes us afraid. We have rejected the fear before. We can do it again. There is nothing about Americans today that makes us less capable than any other generation of dealing with the uncertainties that life throws at us. Indeed, we have learned so much and have such marvelous resources available to us now, we should be more able than ever before to control ourselves and the way we respond to our social environment.

Perhaps wild animals do fight or flee when they feel threatened, but we don't have to. Our brains are more developed than theirs. We should have some options they don't.

What *should* we be afraid of?

We have eliminated from our lives many things that used to make us feel afraid. When I was a child, parents were afraid that their kids would contract polio. Few of today's young parents probably have any notion of what a huge threat polio used to be. When my parents were kids, their parents worried that kids would contract whooping cough, scarlet fever, measles, mumps, and other diseases that are almost unheard of today because of vaccination programs. A generation before, their parents worried that their kids would get beaten up by Cossacks or drafted into the Russian army. They were so afraid that they fled their homelands and families and immigrated to this country, as did millions of others who were afraid of such things as starvation due to potato famines. Throughout our history, during recessions and the Great Depression, many parents worried about how they would feed, clothe, and house their families.

Today, parents fear that chemicals in the foods their kids eat will poison them. They worry that their kids won't be able to afford college and that they'll never find jobs. They have plenty to worry about without having to worry about burglars invading their homes, but that is what the gun industry urges them to fear—so that they will buy guns to overcome the fear.

No one in the US worries about the Cossacks much anymore. But people find things to worry about. I suppose we always will. Rational fear can be productive and lead parents to protect their young. It can prompt people to demand that their governments implement programs to protect them. Irrational fear, however, can lead people into very foolish directions.

Distortion and manipulation

The gun industry doesn't generate fear in people about things that we might reasonably be afraid of. Instead, they tell us to carry guns to protect ourselves from gangbangers, doped up meth-heads, and others who would do random violence to us. Are there really that many of those folks around? Actually, there is a lot less of that sort of street crime now than there was just one generation ago.[246] Stiffer jail sentencing, coordinated law enforcement, drug treatment programs, and other factors have resulted in the number of these types of shootings being drastically reduced over the past few decades. Murders in Chicago, for example, are down almost fifty percent from what they were at their peak. The rest of the country has also experienced a significant reduction in crime in recent years.[247] So although there is still criminal violence in our country and always will be, people probably have much less reason to be afraid of this sort of thing than they used to, and much less reason to carry guns.

But fear mongering is an art, and the level of fear that can be induced in people does not need to be very closely correlated with the actual threats that exist. For years, we lived in fear that the Soviet Union would attack the US, possibly with nuclear weapons. It never did. Was there ever really much cause for us to be afraid? Our defense was based on what was called the doctrine of Mutually Assured Destruction. The doctrine began with a traditional idea that if we built enough nuclear weapons, the Soviets would fear that if they ever launched one against us, we would be able to launch one back against them. That is just traditional deterrence. But in the nuclear age, both sides built enough weapons and delivery systems that each side was supposed to be afraid that if they ever launched against the other, both sides and possibly the rest of the world would be totally destroyed. No one would win.

The acronym for the doctrine was MAD, and it was madness. No one could rationally justify following such a policy. But both sides based their national defense on it. Why? Because we were led to be so afraid that we could be convinced to act irrationally. Neither side was ever at the level of risk that each side perceived itself to be. There was never that much of a threat.[248] But the war profiteers were able to instill fear beyond what the situation called for.

Not only can people be convinced to be unnecessarily fearful, they can also be persuaded to fear people whom they need not fear. In the lead-up to World War II, the weaknesses in the German economy made people afraid for their futures. The Nazis found it useful to direct that fear towards ordinary Jews, many of whom were living very modest lives and almost none of whom were in any position whatsoever to influence the economy.

People who are in fear can also be encouraged to take action—including irrational action—to reduce their fears. The slaughter of Jews during the Holocaust did nothing to improve the German economy and alleviate the German people's fears for the future, but the German people allowed their government to follow this extermination policy. Fearful people are easily led astray.

Hermann Goering, a leader in Hitler's Nazi party, gave a very succinct explanation: "Why, of course, the people don't want war. Why would some poor slob on a farm want to risk his life in a war when the best that he can get out of it is to come back to his farm in one piece. Naturally, the common people don't want war; neither in Russia nor in England nor in America, nor for that matter in Germany. That is understood. But, after all, it is the leaders of the country who determine the policy and it is always a simple matter to drag the people along, whether it is a democracy or a fascist dictatorship or a Parliament or a Communist dictatorship...[T]he people can always be brought to the bidding of the leaders. That is easy. All you have to do is tell them they are being attacked and denounce the pacifists for lack of patriotism and exposing the country to danger. It works the same way in any country."[249]

Does the gun industry really not understand that we are more secure in our homes and on the streets now than we were a decade ago? Haven't they noticed that there are a lot more security cameras around? Don't they realize that more than a hundred million people carry around cell phones that they can use not only to report crimes, but also to take photos and even videos of offenders? Don't they realize that stolen vehicles can be tracked by satellites because they have built-in electronics, that credit cards can be instantly located when they are used, that license plates can be scanned at whatever speed people are driving, and that the police can identify fingerprints and faces much more quickly than in the past, with the aid of computers? In many respects, we are probably safer than we have ever been.

Why is the gun industry so successful in making us feel afraid?

The gun industry has been using an old debater's trick. They have been setting up a false object—a straw man—and gun opponents have been wasting their time knocking it down. They tell us to be afraid of gangbangers, armed burglars, and other physical threats when what people are really frightened of is economic insecurity. We end up talking about protecting ourselves from the violence, and we argue about whether we can do it with guns. We don't talk so much about the economic threats, which we obviously can't shoot at. Our attention is diverted, and our efforts to solve our problems are fruitless. Even if we managed to lock up all the "bad guys with guns," we would still be afraid, because the bad guys aren't carrying guns, they are carrying our mortgages, student loans, and credit card debt.

Although gun owners will say they have guns to protect themselves from violence, there is nothing about the way they act that is consistent with their living in fear of violence. People who are afraid that someone might act violently towards them stay in their own homes. When they are with other people, they speak cautiously. They avoid confrontations. Gun owners, in contrast, strut around the streets attending rallies, instigating confrontations, and trying to intimidate people.[250] It's pretty obvious that today's gun owners are not afraid of what they say they are afraid of.

Whether people respond to the world by living in fear depends in part on whether they feel alone. These days, even when living in the midst of an ever-growing population, many people feel isolated.[251] We don't have the support we would like to have, which may have always been the case, but we feel vulnerable because we are convinced that we don't even have the support that we had a short while ago. It feels to a lot of people like the world—or at least their world—is going to hell, for lots of reasons including those discussed earlier in these pages. They don't want to go to hell with it, and they don't have a lot of people propping them up and telling them that everything is going to be OK.

A couple of generations ago, when this was more a country of immigrants than it is now, people tended to live surrounded not only by their immediate families but by extended families. Grandpa and Grandma might live in the same house as their children, or in the apartment upstairs in a two-flat building, or at least in the same neighborhood. These days, not so much. Some towns even use zoning laws to keep people from building mother-in-law apartments on their properties, isolating aging parents who could otherwise help care for grandchildren as well as benefit from the oversight and care of their own children. We fragment families in an attempt to preserve all-important property values.

There are lots of other ways that people today are separated from potential supporters. Children are bused to schools outside their neighborhoods, away from people who know them and might watch over them. School boundaries are redrawn, separating kids from other kids they grew up with. Young adults go away to college to live among strangers, with little or no adult supervision. People are so busy juggling careers and family responsibilities that they find it difficult to get to know their neighbors.

When their schooling is over, young adults, often burdened with large debts they incurred to pay for their educations, feel pressured to travel to distant cities to find work. Companies encourage employees to transfer to locations where the company needs them, which may have no relationship to where their families or friends are. Or companies close facilities, leaving employees either without work or, if they are lucky, with an option to transfer to another facility far away.

Frequently, companies don't even give people the security of making them employees. They let them work as contractors for whatever period of time they are needed, then terminate them. Not only do workers not have the support they might once have had as members of unions, they aren't even considered part of the company they are working for. Workers today understand from the outset that they have no realistic expectation of a career with a company. Everything is temporary. No promises are made, so no promises can be broken.

These arrangements can lead people to feel they have no one they can depend upon, other than perhaps a spouse, who might just divorce them. Adding to this feeling of insecurity is the elimination of benefits that, though not providing human support, gave workers important financial support. Hardly anyone gets real pensions anymore. Lots of people don't get decent health insurance. Sick days and paid days off are disappearing. Social Security is threatened, as is Medicare.

If today's workers feel they are on their own, they have good reason. A strong person can survive under these circumstances. People form friendships and build networks. But not everyone is so strong, and even strong people can have moments of weakness, especially when life gives them a bad hand to play. Knowing how little support they can call upon can lead people to become anxious. If pushed, they can become angry and afraid. That's where the gun industry finds its opening.

Seeking comfort from guns instead of from people

Contrary to the Beatles' song lyric, happiness is not a warm gun. But some people who feel isolated can buy a gun more easily than they can form new relationships. They can look at a gun and hold it and tell themselves that it is there to protect them even if no one else is by their side. They can believe that because it is a physical mechanism that follows the laws of physics, it will function reliably when needed, unlike people who may not be there when you want them. I have heard lots of gun guys say they'd rather have their guns to protect them than have to rely on the police. They put more trust in steel and lead than they do in flesh and blood.

What they miss, of course, is everything that makes humans the social animals that we are. People aren't reliable in the same way that a precisely machined piece of metal is. But some of us try to help others in their time of need. We don't always act the way others want, but on the whole we find ways to work together. We aren't always sympathetic or empathetic, but sometimes we are, if you give us a chance.

The gun industry doesn't make money by encouraging people to call their mothers if they feel blue, or to invite a friend over for dinner if they feel lonely. It doesn't boost the industry's profits to urge people to become involved with their local churches or to volunteer for charities. The gun industry thrives when it can get people to buy guns instead of build trust.

The gun industry's rhetoric graphically illustrates how it wants people to view each other. We are told to mistrust strangers because they could attack us. We are told to mistrust family members and friends because they are unpredictable. We are told to mistrust repairmen who we pay to come into our homes, people who stop to help us when our cars break down on the highway, and police who are supposed to protect us. We are told to be suspicious of everyone, all the time, under all circumstances, because they might just be lunatics. And we sure as hell can't trust government or God, because they sometimes let us down.

So when the gun industry tells people that the world is all one person against another—us against them—some people will see things that way, especially if they don't have a sense of unity or of community support. If they see themselves as being at odds with the world, and guns are offered as something to even out the odds, they may buy the guns. Especially if they feel that they don't have anywhere else to turn.

But some of us are not afraid

No, and it makes the gun lovers crazy that we are not. Our fearlessness refutes their fear mongering. If the world were as dangerous as they paint it, we'd be afraid, wouldn't we?

In general, there are some regional and historical differences that tend to explain why guns are more prevalent in some parts of the country than others. But I am not aware of any studies that explain why any particular person becomes a gun lover vs. a lover of people. People with similar backgrounds, incomes, social statuses, educations, religious orientations, and other characteristics can fall into one camp or another. We all have a great deal in common. We are all living in an isolating world. We all face economic insecurity. How is it that some of us just don't feel the need to buy guns and make ourselves dangerous?

It could simply be a matter of happenstance. Some people affiliate with the Democratic Party and others with the Republicans. Some people are selfish, and others are more generous. Some people are introverts and others extroverts. Although there are clear differences between people on each side of this issue, it is not obvious what leads people to sign on to one view or the other.

You might think that people who claim to have guns as a defense against a frightening world would simply switch sides when they see that some of us are not frightened. That doesn't happen a lot, any more than Republicans become Democrats. Once these kinds of identities are formed, they are largely entrenched.

The hope for the world lies in the fact that many people, probably most, do not choose sides on the gun issue. They don't really pay much attention. Until they do, they can be influenced. Over time, there is hope that people who may feel the need to align with one side or the other will choose the side that seems happiest and most secure. If the people on that side of the issue also happen to have the truth on their side, along with a convincing moral and social argument, all the better. This is how progress is made, and it is one reason why gun ownership has been declining over time. People who are uncommitted choose to go with the happy, sensible people, not the angry, unhappy, illogical ones. We win!

ALLIES AND OPPONENTS OF REPEAL

A successful effort to repeal the Second Amendment will require more than just a conviction that guns are bad and the people who have them are wrong. We also need to take a close look at how the pro-gun forces are organized, how they are led, and why they have succeeded. We also need to know who is with us and who may be persuaded to join in a coalition that will support the repeal effort. We need to be honest about our strengths and weaknesses, and to fairly assess our current status.

What can we learn from the NRA?

The NRA does so much that is offensive that I am reluctant to hold them up as a model in any way. But it is important to understand how they do what they do, not only so that those of us who want to live in a safer country can counter their maneuvers, but so that we can replicate what is useful.

What the NRA does right is no different from what any other interest group does. It articulates a viewpoint that represents its members' views, or at least it represents enough of what its members think that they remain part of the organization. At the very basic level, although NRA members have varying views about what they consider to be acceptable restrictions on the use and ownership of guns, they all agree that they don't want to completely lose their ability to use and own guns.

When non-NRA members hear the NRA screaming—literally—that they won't let anyone take away their guns, it is perplexing. Although getting rid of guns seems more and more like a good idea, the proponents of gun control have not even come close to taking this position. The NRA may seem crazy to keep making this fictional claim year after year. Crazy like a fox.

The reason the NRA goes to great lengths to frighten its members that "gun grabbers" are trying to take away their guns is because this is one thing that their members can all agree shouldn't happen. Even though the NRA gets a great deal of its money from the gun industry, it must have individual members in order to effectively convince legislators to support its agenda. The NRA's most consistent and successful way to get members to join and renew their memberships is to frighten them into thinking someone wants to separate them from their guns. It doesn't matter to them whether their hysterical claims are true or not. They appeal to the paranoid. They appeal to hunters. They appeal to target shooters. They appeal to everyone they want to appeal to.[252]

The NRA is not the only group that uses scare tactics. Other groups are constantly trying to frighten people that someone is trying to destroy the environment, or take away their right to control their reproductive organs, or do a whole lot of other atrocious things. If they can convince people that what they cherish is in danger, people will be ready to help protect it. All that the NRA and these other groups have to do is to appear to be the group that is best able to protect their interests.

With its history as a staunch and reliable advocate for gun owners, the NRA is well positioned to scoop up the membership dollars and donations of the people it has frightened. It takes effort, of course, to collect the money, so the NRA runs sophisticated mail, email, phone, and online operations to reach potential supporters. For years it has collected the names and contact information of gun owners from the government agencies that issue gun and hunting permits and from instructors who the NRA certifies to teach gun classes. Even though the NRA strongly opposes any governmental efforts to keep track of who owns guns, it nevertheless benefits by using information from those records for its own purposes.[253]

Again, the NRA is not unique in trying to assemble lists of people to solicit for support. Just about every online petition anyone signs does the same thing. So does every warranty registration card that comes packaged with every toaster. So does every stadium scoreboard that gives away T-shirts to whoever tweets them to try to win a contest. Organizations gather contact information along with as much information as they can get about people's preferences. They use that information, and they also sell it. Many businesses exist just for this purpose, although they put up a front so that people will not realize what is going on. Facebook and Google make a fortune selling lists to companies that want to contact potential customers.

Once it has a member, the NRA tries to get that member to be active. They ask members to phone their representatives in Congress, sign up other members, put bumper stickers on their trucks, and use association-sponsored credit cards—anything to reinforce the identification the member has with the group. Again, lots of groups do this. It is very useful to the organizations, because the more times people take affirmative steps, the more they feel they are part of the group. That's part of the reason why clergy want people to come to church regularly. That's why some advocacy groups send out emails to their members almost every day asking them click on something. It doesn't really matter what they click on, so long as they click. A person who feels strongly attached to a group is more likely to stick with the group and support it in the future.

The NRA doesn't just sign up members; it puts its membership to good use. It brags about how many members it has. It holds rallies to show off to the press how many people it can assemble in matching T-shirts. It encourages members to write letters to the editors of their hometown newspapers. This is Organizing 101, and it works. Organization members may ignore fundraising letters or emailed solicitations, or they may even turn down phone calls asking them to take specific actions. But if you ask them often enough, some of the people will respond. It's a numbers game, just like cold calling for product sales. The NRA has enough resources to keep asking and asking, and as a result, they keep receiving. The meek may eventually inherit the earth, but in the meantime, the persistent get what they want.

But beyond all this rudimentary work that many advocacy groups do, the NRA specializes in doing the dirty work that its members want done but are too timid or embarrassed to do themselves. This work is the type that extremists are much more likely to undertake than more moderate individuals and groups.

A lot of racists might have wanted to stand in the door of the schoolhouse and prevent black students from entering, but Governor George Wallace was gutsy enough to do it. His supporters were so grateful that they gave him a long political career. A lot of environmentalists might like the idea of riding a rubber boat and getting between a whaling ship and its intended prey, but few would actually risk their lives the way that Greenpeace volunteers have done.

A lot of people who were against the Vietnam War were happy that Father Daniel Berrigan destroyed draft board records, but few took part in his protests. A lot of recent anti-war activists applaud Kathy Kelly for symbolically planting corn on a missile silo in Missouri, but not many joined in her protest or went to jail with her.

In a society that applauds courageous public outcry, the person or organization that actually cries out will get applause. So the NRA succeeds by making outlandish statements that its members wish they had the courage to make. When, in the wake of mass-shootings, the head of the NRA says that we need more guns, not fewer, his critics may think he is out-of-touch and insensitive. NRA members think he is great.

Meanwhile, what has the anti-gun violence movement been doing? Our rallying cry has been, "Common sense gun laws!" Nice sentiment, good idea—but hardly the sort of phrase that goes down in history the way "Give me liberty or give me death" does.

Should the folks who want less gun violence become as obnoxious as the NRA? I hope not. But the organizations and leaders of the pro-peace movement could imitate the NRA by proudly and repeatedly saying what our most peace-loving people might be hesitant to say themselves. It might seem odd that people would be reluctant to say things like, "Stop killing the children." But most people simply don't feel comfortable taking any public stance. There is a role for people who will represent their views in a way they can be proud of. That role has been largely vacant.

Another lesson that can be learned from the NRA is to keep the big picture in mind. They have a very clear idea of what they want, which is for people to be able to own and use guns with a minimum amount of governmental interference. By defining their objective this way, they can simultaneously address any number of smaller issues as they come up and also respond to challenges.

For example, in recent years the NRA has been working to get "stand your ground" laws passed in as many states as possible. These laws basically say that if a person feels threatened, that person doesn't have to run away or use less than lethal force to defend himself. He can just shoot his way out of his anxiety. These laws run counter to long-established legal precedent that requires people not to use force or to use only the minimal amount of force necessary to resolve a situation. [254]

Stand your ground laws also are contrary to what most people would consider to be common sense, because most people realize that they are far more likely to escape harm if they deescalate a violent situation than if they increase the level of violence. That is why banks tell their tellers not to resist robbers and to just hand over the money. The bank may have already included a dye-pack that will explode harmlessly later and mark the money and the offender, making capture more likely, or it may have planted a transponder in the bag with the loot, allowing police to locate the offender, or another employee may have triggered a silent alarm. Or the robber may just get away with the money, which most people would consider a better outcome than having a bank teller get shot.

Stand your ground laws are a fairly modern phenomenon, the first such law having been passed in 2005. They were adopted based upon assurances that they would reduce crime, especially serious crime that involved or threatened the use of violence, such as residential burglaries and homicides. Not only were these assurances contrary to common sense, they have turned out to be contrary to reality. By 2012, the 23 states that enacted such laws were adding between 500 and 700 additional homicides a year to the national total. The killings were not, as the pro-gun folks predicted, killings in self-defense. They were just self-declared "good guys" killing other people, who may or may not have been "bad guys."[255] These laws have had tragic consequences, as exemplified by an incident in Detroit. A 19-year-old black woman who was in an automobile accident knocked on the door of a nearby home in a largely white neighborhood, hoping to get help. The homeowner who answered the door shot her in the head with a shotgun, killing her. The Detroit police were reluctant to charge the homeowner with a crime, because the law said he had the right to stand his ground.[256]

Telling people that they can stand their ground doesn't just run contrary to logic and experience, it also defeats the potential for violence reduction that a number of technological advances have made possible in recent years. Probably the best known of these devices is the Taser, a personal defense weapon that shoots a barbed dart into a person's skin that can then transmit an electric shock to temporarily disable the "offender." This is hardly a non-violent alternative, and it has proved fatal in a number of cases. But it is far less lethal than a standard issue handgun.

Many police forces are now equipping their officers with Tasers, so that they will have non-lethal alternatives available to use when appropriate. The military and some police forces also have other non-lethal devices at their disposal, including sound cannons that use sound waves to disable individuals or even crowds. They also have microwave transmitters that burn but do not kill. More non-lethal innovations will no doubt be available in the future. But by insisting on the expansion of people's right to use deadly force, the NRA sidesteps the entire question of whether there is first an obligation to act more humanely and whether technology can help us to fulfill that obligation.

While the NRA has been promoting stand your ground laws, it has simultaneously been promoting concealed carry laws, immunity for gun dealers and manufacturers, and other changes to the body of law.[257] They don't feel the need to pursue only one type of legislation at a time, because these pieces of legislation can be seen as complementing each other, and they all fit within the general scheme of more guns everywhere.

The folks on the gun control side have tended to take a much more fragmented approach. They think that they are being practical by using their limited resources in a focused way. Often they find themselves concentrating on defeating one of several NRA initiatives in a particular state. The result is that they are often on the defensive. If they win on that single issue and the NRA does not get a law passed that it wanted, all it means is that the NRA can come back the next year and try again, and the gun controllers will have to play defense all over again. Meanwhile, the NRA can pursue the same initiative in other states.

But if the NRA has several initiatives and the gun controllers only put up a struggle on one of them, the result is that the gun controllers automatically lose on the others. It's like trying to rid a cockroach-infested apartment of the pests one at a time. You might stomp on one, but the others get away. Once a legislative battle is won and a law is passed, it is very hard to get it repealed in later years. The NRA boasts, for example, that no state has ever repealed a law permitting people to carry concealed guns once the law was passed.

The other problem that arises from the fragmented approach is that various gun control advocates don't agree on what their highest priority should be. They don't work together as an effective coalition, and each group pursues its favorite issue without offering to help the other groups. Legislators, like jackals, are quick to sense when the herd is not united. This gives the NRA an opening. As a unified group, the NRA is able to take advantage of the lack of unity among its opponents. Every time disunity hampers the gun controllers' efforts, they get discouraged by their losses, and they blame the other gun control groups for not working with them or for dissipating the available public support. Instead of fighting the NRA, the gun controllers fight each other.

Gun control groups are not the only ones that have been missing the opportunity to form coalitions and pursue multiple goals. All sorts of groups all over the political spectrum follow this route. Some of their lack of unity is due to their having legitimate differences of opinion on what course of action to follow. But some of the disunity is caused by less noble considerations. Groups often scramble rather than coalesce with one another because each group wants to be able to boast that their group was the one that actually scored a victory, so that it can then attract donations that might otherwise go to other groups. Ego can also lead people to work on their own rather than working as a team. In our celebrity-oriented culture, everyone wants to be a superstar. The NRA is actually unusual in the success it has had in recent years of getting various potentially diverse groups such as hunters, rifle shooters, shotgunners, pistol shooters, and vigilantes to work together toward a well-defined, common goal.

By defining their objective, the NRA also manages to exclude other objectives from debate. They don't talk about public safety; they talk about gun safety, which frames the issue as only being a concern of people who have guns. If people who aren't gun owners get shot, that's OK with them. In fact, they think that there are a lot of people running loose in society who should be shot, and that it is just as well if private gun owners do the shooting instead of the police.

One way to counter the NRA's tactics would be for the gun controllers to mimic them. If we stopped arguing among ourselves about whether it was more urgent to ban assault rifles or require background checks on gun purchasers or limit the places where people could carry concealed weapons, we would have a better chance of accomplishing all these things. Solidarity would yield more progress on all these issues. Having an agreed-upon agenda would allow us to work together.

In truth, the people who are on our side really are concerned about lots of these things, because we see them all as part of the issue of public safety in peaceful communities. With a bit more discipline, we should be able to work together more effectively.

Our organizational limitations

There aren't any fundamental or insurmountable problems with what we have been doing or the way we have been doing it. We just aren't organized well enough yet. As for why, the answer to that question changes all the time. To an extent, organization depends upon conditions in society that are beyond the control of organizers. During the presidency of Barack Obama, which has been supported by many on the left side of the political spectrum, people have found it difficult to simultaneously support his presidency and insist that he act more boldly on gun issues and other issues. He has tried to urge his base to get organized and pressure him and Congress to act.[258] But progressives have had trouble pressuring him without feeling they were undermining him.[259]

During the presidency of George W. Bush, the nation was led to panic in response to the attacks on September 11. Then we were led into war. Then we suffered an economic collapse. The nation wasn't able to catch its breath long enough to organize on the issue of domestic peace, and the usual proponents of war did an effective job of preempting us by branding any criticism of the administration as treasonous and cowardly.

During the presidency of Bill Clinton, we were in the unusual position of having the administration champion gun control with significant support from the opposition Republicans in Congress. Clinton championed the Brady Bill, which required background checks before gun purchases[260] and a ban on assault weapons.[261] He also delivered on a promise to have the federal government pour money into local police departments to crack down on crime and violence.[262] None of these measures solved the entire problem, but in politics, if you do anything, it is generally seen as doing enough. Once the federal government took these steps, it was hard to ask for more, and it was easy to feel satisfied with what we had accomplished.

And so it is during any period of time. Circumstances dictate actions. Of course, we can't blame everything on circumstances. There is always more that can be done, and there are always plenty of explanations for why things played out as they did. After any electoral campaign, the pundits go on and on about the reasons why one candidate or party won and the others lost. The only sufficient answer was given years ago by Chicago's Mayor Richard J. Daley, who was also the head of the local Democratic machine. Whenever he was asked why any particular candidate lost, he would always respond that the winner got more votes.

One systemic problem that the anti-gun movement has had is that in its efforts to imitate the NRA's organizational strength, it has built organizational bureaucracies that have tended to over-emphasize the building of the organizations themselves. This is a problem that all sorts of bureaucracies have to cope with, whether they are non-profit or for-profit. The people at the top build their staffs so that they can accomplish their goals, but it takes increasingly more money and energy to keep the organizations functioning. In the non-profit world, the organizations become increasingly dependent on grants and large donors, which are notoriously fickle. The money can dry up, or the funding sources can exercise too much influence on how the organizations operate, leaving the grass-roots membership dissatisfied and forcing staff to spend time on efforts that they don't feel are productive. When needed funds don't materialize, staff cuts rob our organizations of accumulated knowledge and demoralize the people who are left behind.

And then there is the tendency of the people at the top to spend too much of their time doing glamorous things like attending congressional events and not enough time doing the mundane work of keeping in touch with the membership and building the base. As the pressure builds, it is easy to be seduced away from the grunt work.

Organizers also learn, just like corporate managers, that it is a good idea to always be on the lookout for the next job. So the initiatives that staff members take may be tempered by a concern that they don't want to get reputations as radicals or people who are difficult to deal with. Better to go along to get along and become one of the in-crowd.

We have also made a few mistakes in the projects we undertook and the messages we championed. Although it makes sense to look at gun violence as just a subset of violence, at times we have let our focus be diverted onto issues that were not productive. For example, parents have the right to decide whether their kids should be allowed to play with water pistols, but as a movement, spending energy on this issue doesn't get us very far.

What we are doing right

Everything we do is right. We just haven't been doing enough. And we could do what we do better. It would be a mistake to dwell on our mistakes.

The most important thing that we are doing right is that we are acting out of conviction. No one is working against gun violence to get rich. Rather, we are spurred to action by our outrage that others are suffering unnecessarily. That righteous motivation is powerful. In the history of the world, no political force has ever matched the intensity of people who are indignant at a perceived injustice.

The pro-gun folks may seem to have this same zeal, but there is a crucial difference. We know we are right, and they know they are wrong. The sources of our belief in peace and non-violence are deep; they run through every religion and every enduring social movement.

The expression of violence, on the other hand, has been universally condemned, even though it is often tolerated. The pro-gun folks know that what they are advocating is destructive of every institution from the family to the nation. They know that what they are supporting grievously harms individuals. They have all sorts of justifications for it, but they know that it is indefensible. They may claim that guns and war make peace, but in making those claims, they affirm that our goal—peace—is the ultimate goal, and that their methods are what we all want to extinguish. In a world that believes that two wrongs don't make a right, their logic is flawed.

The pro-gun folks like to say that violence is just "human nature."

They say the same thing about small-scale violence in our neighborhoods and about war. To them, people are just naturally violent towards one another, just as animals in nature are violent. There was a time in history when that view was popular, but it has been losing ground as we learn more about both animals and people.

Undeniably, predators use violence to capture prey for food. But they use only as much violence as they need, while expending as little energy as possible. Some animals also use violence to establish and protect territories. But in the vast majority of instances, no actual violence is used. Only threats of violence or ritualized behavior are used, and in almost all cases, the dispute is resolved without bloodshed.[263] There is really no analogue in nature either to the random violence, pointless malicious violence, or organized mass violence that people display.

More importantly, although people are animals, we need not be overly modest about the fact that we have certain capabilities that no other animals have. Whatever tendencies towards violence we may share with our fellow creatures, we also have the ability to act non-violently by choice. Just as humans are the only animal that has developed guns, we are capable of being the only animal to reject guns.

The pro-gun folks look at the world as it is and see it as confirming their viewpoint that people are, always have been, and always will be violent towards one another. They fail to distinguish between the violence of a predator, which is necessary to sustain life, and the violence of a vigilante, which destroys life and the society that makes life possible. The anti-gun folks have a different view. They look at the violence we are experiencing today and see the world as it could be and someday will be. They see violence as an aberration from the peacefulness that characterizes life as we want to live it.

Another thing we are doing right is keeping our emotional balance. It is great to be outraged at the violence. It is proper to be indignant at the way the pro-gun folks act, but it would be a shame if we started to act the same way they do.

At one point in our efforts to keep Illinois from adopting a concealed carry law, I was surprised at how many pro-gun folks started posting comments on our Facebook page. I wouldn't mind if they had posted reasonable comments and joined in the debate, but almost all of their comments were insulting and even threatening. Lots of them said I should be shot. I was surprised to notice that the comments were coming from all over the country, until a friend who had been working in the peace movement for a long time tipped me off to a tactic they use. When the pro-gun guys want to disrupt an anti-gun online presence, they reach out to their compatriots all around the country and mount campaigns to flood the sites that they don't like with so many comments that they halt the anti-gun discussion. It is akin to hackers' "denial of service" attacks that are used to shut down websites; these attacks are generally considered to be electronic sabotage. I'd never want people on our side to do that.

Pro-gun guys also show up at our anti-gun meetings and rallies and shout down our speakers.[264] Their behavior is rude, and it stifles legitimate debate. I don't want us doing that, either.

After one public forum, a woman who had spoken out against guns told me that when she went to her car, she was followed by a pro-gun guy who made a show of writing down her license plate number. She was afraid that he was going to find out where she lived or follow her home, or who knows what else, and she was concerned for the safety of her family. It seemed unlikely at the time that this guy would do her any harm, but I couldn't think of any legitimate reason why he would want her license plate number. He was just trying to scare her. We won't be doing that kind of thing—no way. Nor will we be intimidating people by standing outside their meeting places with guns drawn, the way some pro-gun folks have been doing in order to harass people who belong to gun control groups.[265] That's not effective advocacy. It's just terrorism.

There is a balance to be found between expressing oneself strongly and letting one's frustration degenerate into conduct that frustrates other people's expression. I see nothing wrong with holding signs so that people can see them, but that is not the same as holding them in front of people's faces so they can't see anything else. I recall being chased down the street by a woman who was shoving a sign in my face. I have had a congressional candidate's campaign aide wave his hands in front of my camera so I couldn't take a photo at a public forum. I hope we don't stoop to doing these sorts of things.

The depravity of the pro-gun folks is not just a matter of a few kooks acting badly. It is engaged in and encouraged by the very top leadership of the pro-gun movement. When Academy Award winning actor Philip Seymour Hoffman was found dead from a drug overdose, most people were sympathetic. Mr. Hoffman had gone through drug rehab and remained clean for 20 years before relapsing. He was survived by three young children. But Richard Pearson wrote in his official capacity as the Executive Director of the Illinois State Rifle Association, an NRA affiliate, that he was not mourning, because Hoffman was in favor of gun control. "The death of actor Phillip Seymour Hoffman, who died Sunday with a syringe full heroine [sic] stuck in his arm, is being lamented by many, but not by me. Hoffman narrated an antigun cartoon which demonizes gun ownership along with actress Julianne Moore and of course, it was financed by MAIG [Mayors Against Illegal Guns]. The media is falling all over themselves saying what a wonderful guy he was, what a wonderful actor he was, and on and on. I disagree. People like Hoffman are part of the drug culture that is destroying our young people and tearing the fabric of this county apart. As far as I am concerned, he played his last and greatest role—that of a bad example. Hopefully he willed his 'stash' to some of his drug addicted antigun buddies in the entertainment 'industry'."[266] Mr. Pearson sent this warped and hateful message to all of the members of his group so that they would know that anyone who supports gun control deserves to die.

Fortunately, the folks on our side have been consistently civil for long enough now that we have a reputation that serves us well. Police know that they don't have any reason to be concerned when we assemble. This is quite a change from when the earliest protests against the invasion of Iraq were held and police showed up in large numbers with shields, horses, and dogs ready to arrest massive numbers of us if we rioted. Eventually they learned that the folks on the peace side are the peaceful ones. We're not the ones talking about violent overthrow of the government; that's the pro-gun guys.

We have also, for the most part, avoided the trap of extremism. The pro-gun folks fall into this trap all the time. One shining example was the state of Iowa, which was so eager to give everyone the right to carry weapons that they passed a law allowing blind people to carry guns in public. The pro-gun folks looked a bit foolish when it was pointed out that Iowa law did not allow blind people to drive cars. The public was incredulous, and the newspapers had a field day. But, consistency being more important to the pro-gun folks than common sense, they held to their position, dismissing concerns about public safety.[267]

We on the anti-violence side have earned a reputation that the pro-gun folks can't always match—for acting in good faith and keeping our word. Their modus operandi has often been to say and promise whatever they think is needed in order to obtain the legislation they want, and then change their rhetoric and to renege on those promises whenever it is convenient.

At the end of a recent legislative session in one state, their chief lobbyist boasted of the legislation they had been able to get passed and announced to his membership what legislation on the same topic they were going to pursue in the next session. "We got our foot in the door. Now we are going to break it down," he announced to a roar of approval. He neglected to mention that he was only able to get the legislation he wanted passed based on an agreement with the legislators on the opposing side that he would not seek modification in the upcoming session. When he returns to seek the new legislation, his duplicity may hamper his efforts with legislators who will feel they were lied to. I don't want our side to get in that position. If we are confident that our positions are valid, we have no need to engage in tactics that are not legitimate.

Who is on which side?

Some women, some men, some blacks, some whites, some poor folks, some rich folks, some people of every religion and every category are in favor of gun control, but no group as a whole has been working to rid our world of violence. The only commonality that the opponents of gun violence hold is that they are all people of good will. This is significant, because many of the people on the pro-gun side are not.

A large number of pro-gun folks are just in it for the money. About 13 billion dollars worth of guns are sold in the US each year to individuals, in addition to the huge number that are sold to police and other law enforcement agencies.[268] A much, much bigger pile of money goes to buy weapons of various sorts for our military. And a huge but unknowable amount of money flows for the purchase of guns for the CIA and other "national security" agencies, in addition to an enormous amount of money that comes into the US from people in foreign countries who buy our guns.[269] Then there are the guns that our government purchases just so it can give them away to other countries as foreign aid.

Guns are big, big business. How big? Most of the money the US government spends on programs other than Social Security and other public benefits is spent on our military, and a huge chunk of that goes to buy and maintain weapons. The next time you hear someone from the NRA claim that they are standing up for the rights that individuals have under our Constitution, keep in mind that most of the NRA's money comes from companies that want to sell as many guns as they can to whoever they can sell them, public safety be damned. And damned it is.

Although this book focuses mainly on the effects of guns within the US, the trade in US guns is international, and the effects of our guns are being felt all across the world. The rest of the world is concerned that we are exporting our level of violence to them, and they are taking steps. One response to international gun violence has been the Arms Trade Treaty that the United Nations General Assembly adopted on April 2, 2013. It became effective on December 24, 2014 when the 50th country ratified it. To date, it has been ratified by 65 countries. It's been signed by the United States, but the US Senate has not ratified the treaty.

The treaty has a very limited scope and concerns only guns that are destined for use by warlords, pirates, terrorists, and their friends—those who violate human rights and commit genocide in conflict regions and failed states.[270] Nonetheless, the NRA strongly opposes the treaty, and its opposition is giving the entire US a bad name in the international community. Oscar Arias Sanchez, former President of Costa Rica and Nobel Peace Prize winner, directly addressed the NRA's efforts to block the treaty: "To the N.R.A., I say: Inflict your agenda on your own nation if you must, but spare the rest of us. Spare us the notion that the interests of a single interest group, in a single nation, should trump the rights of all other nations to protect their citizens. Spare us your misguided references to a

Constitution whose brilliant authors would be aghast to see you equate the right to put a rifle in your gun case with the right to put an AK-47 in the hands of a child soldier."[271]

To the gun manufacturers, guns are just business. These companies are just in it for the money. But to a lot of pro-gun folks, guns are very personal. Among the ranks of pro-guns folks are not only angry guys who resent minorities while denying they are racists, but also folks who are out-and-out white supremacists, women-haters, and religious bigots.[272] It is easy for them to buy commercially produced targets that cater to their particular malice, like targets with pictures of imaginary ex-girlfriends, pregnant women, and gun-control lobbyists. Those with other fixations can buy targets with images of children, teenagers, corporate executives, cubicle workers, or the elderly on them. They can also get targets with pictures of real people, like Barack Obama and Trayvon Martin.

Sadly, there are also a good number of former law enforcement people on the pro-gun side who seem motivated not so much by a continuing concern for public safety as by a lingering resentment of the ones who got away. One former police officer laughed as he told me that he considered violent neighborhoods of Chicago to be open-air shooting galleries, the implication being that anything that moved was subject to being shot, like a deer in the woods during hunting season. There have been enough reports recently of police-involved shootings that there is reason to suspect that many current and former police are quick to pull the trigger if they think someone in their sights is not an ally in whatever they think we are at war against.[273]

On our side are not just people who have personally suffered a loss to guns. There are also many people who are with us out of sympathy for those who are suffering, and those who can imagine what it would be like to lose a loved one to gun violence but who don't want to find out firsthand. They don't want any additional victims to have to suffer, and they want people to be able to live without fearing violence.

I spent the better part of the year that preceded the writing of this book organizing opposition to the expansion of concealed carry laws. Initially, I was shocked at the number of people I heard from who had experienced a shooting within their family or close circle of friends. But upon further examination, I realized that these people were only a tiny portion of the thousands of people who signed on to help in these efforts. As I spoke to people, I came to understand that the largest number of our supporters by far simply wanted the violence to end because they understood how destructive it was. They weren't necessarily afraid for themselves or for anyone in particular. They were just fed up.

The anti-gun people all across America have that in common with people who are against war, torture, racism, and many other political causes. They aren't primarily active because they think that they will suffer under the policies of our country. Few whites who are against racism, for example, think that they will ever be discriminated against the way blacks have been, but they still are in favor of fair treatment for everyone. Few people who opposed our country torturing Arabs fear that they will themselves be tortured, but they care about the people who have suffered. Almost none of the people who opposed the invasion of Iraq expected that the US would in turn be invaded, and unlike the Vietnam War protesters, they knew they would not be drafted to fight in the war. All of these individuals are, instead, active because they feel an obligation to do what is right, regardless of whether they expect to personally benefit from a change in the policy or be harmed by the present policies of their government. They are altruistic in the truest sense of the word. In days gone by, they were derisively called "do-gooders" by right-wing propagandists, but that is exactly what motivates them—they want to do good.

Certainly there are some altruists on the pro-gun side, but the leaders and the most vocal supporters on the pro-gun movement tend to make distinctly self-centered arguments. They speak of defending themselves and of their rights much more quickly than they speak of other people's rights. Their favorite catch phrases, such as "I'll give you my gun when you pry it from my cold, dead, hands," betray their inward focus. They aren't concerned about a gun victim's dead hands. Certainly not about the 30,000 pairs of hands of people that die each year in the US from gun violence, or the 60,000 pairs of hands belonging to people who are wounded by guns each year.

The difference between the outlooks of the people on the different sides of this issue is reflected in the way that they associate with others. The NRA is often given credit for running a well-organized, citizen-centered lobbying group. But the organizational strength of the pro-gun lobby is largely due to the fact that there is a pro-gun culture in parts of this country upon which the NRA can draw. Members of the gun culture, being in the minority in America, do what other minorities do. They seek validation and political power by associating with others who share their values. They mimic the calls that other minorities make for civil rights and insist that their efforts to secure their "gun rights" are equivalent to the struggles for voting rights and other civil rights that black Americans engaged in. They tauntingly ask anti-gun activists what other constitutional rights they want to take away from people. They cast themselves in the role of a put-upon, discriminated-against minority, because they perceive that the political process favors minority interests.

There is no comparable anti-gun culture, just people who want to reduce gun violence. Their view of themselves is not nearly as centered around one concern. Their interests are much more varied and diffuse. They don't go to anti-gun shows or anti-gun ranges or anti-gun shops. They aren't as likely as gun owners to put bumper stickers on their cars expressing their views on guns. They see themselves as people, not just as non-gun-owners.

Are there any reasonable gun guys?

It's hard to say how many gun guys would support the repeal of the Second Amendment, because there hasn't been much discussion on this topic yet. But a lot of gun guys do support various proposals to reduce gun violence. These gun guys aren't the ones who are angry at the world. They aren't racist. They aren't paranoid. They are pretty ordinary folks. And they are tired of everyone thinking that they are like the goofballs who get in the news carrying assault weapons to the grocery store.

Until just a few decades ago, people with guns didn't think of themselves as being any different from anyone else, anymore than people with brown shoes thought of themselves as being very different from people with black shoes. People had guns mostly for hunting or target shooting, and that's what the National Rifle Association promoted. When it was formed in the 1870s, the NRA, according to its own history, was concerned with rifle marksmanship.

It helped organize amateur shooting clubs and sponsored competitions. Back in 1934, the NRA supported federal regulations of firearms to stem Prohibition-era gangster violence. In 1938, it supported federal licensing of firearms manufacturers and dealers. In 1968, it supported the Gun Control Act, which imposed further restrictions on interstate sale of guns.

Then things got crazy. There was what has been described as a coup at the NRA. Right-wing ideologues took over the leadership and changed the organization from a membership-led group to one that was increasingly a lobbying group for gun manufacturers and sellers. The new leadership shifted the emphasis of the group from sportsmanship to protecting the "rights" of gun owners against efforts by liberals to reduce gun violence.

As the focus of the NRA changed, so did the composition of its membership. The group began attracting people who were more interested in hunting other people than they were in hunting deer, or who imagined that other people were hunting them. As the organization changed, some gun owners dropped their NRA memberships, most famously President Richard Nixon and President George Herbert Walker Bush, who publicly resigned in protest when NRA President Wayne LaPierre referred to federal law enforcement agents as "jack-booted government thugs."

But, inertia being what it is, many gun owners stayed with the NRA, even though a lot of them disagreed with the organization's shift to the right. There was and still is no competing national organization of gun owners with anywhere near the membership of the NRA, though the more reasonable gun owners have made frequent attempts to organize new groups. Just like many people stay with either the Democratic or Republican parties even though they disagree with some of their policies and practices, many gun owners have stuck with the NRA.

It is not unusual, though, to hear gun owners voice their disagreement with the NRA. One told me he thought that a lot of his fellow gun owners were "nuts" for promoting the carrying of concealed weapons in public. Others, like former Seattle police chief Norm Stamper, have taken public stands against the NRA and the policies it supports. "We are in denial about our duty to stop gun violence. We're awed by what we perceive to be the power of the

National Rifle Association, and the political clout of those members of Congress whose loyalty has been purchased by the NRA. So we wait. We wait for the next slaughter, knowing it will surely come. Nothing has changed, nothing will change. Not unless we resolve to become, in the president's aspirational words, better than this." Stamper has proposed that we repeal the Second Amendment.[274]

Paul Sterne, a gun owner who boasts of being a member of the NRA for 50 years, sponsored a petition in 2012 on the White House website calling for repeal of the Second Amendment. He says, "With respect to firearms, the rule of law is the problem. It is perpetuating gun violence across America and creating a climate of fear. When the law is the problem; the law has to be changed."[275]

Many gun owners support a range of gun safety and control proposals such as requiring safe storage of guns so that children cannot get hold of them, requiring background checks for every gun purchase, limiting the number of people who can carry concealed handguns and the places they can carry them, outlawing civilian use of certain military-style, semi-automatic assault rifles, etc. It is difficult to know how many of these reasonable gun owners there are. The extremists on the pro-gun side have not only managed to suppress research about guns, they have also convinced a lot of gun owners that they should remain silent and avoid being identified, because if the government can find out who they are, it will be able to confiscate their guns. But as the discussion of repealing the Second Amendment grows, we can expect to find many supporters who own guns. Once gun regulations depend not upon a constitutional dictate but upon the reasonableness of the regulations, reasonable gun owners will be eager to support regulations that are aimed at the problems guns cause. They will be willing to make compromises rather than worry about guns being banned completely.

WHAT'S THE PLAN?

The particulars of the strategy that will be followed for getting the Second Amendment repealed will continue to take shape—evolving as the effort moves forward. The campaign to repeal cannot be entirely planned out in advance. It will have to be dynamic and responsive to the events that unfold over time. But the history of how other amendments were adopted sheds light on how the effort to repeal the Second Amendment will emerge. The conditions that will be needed for the effort to succeed are already observable in our society.

Lessons from previous amendment efforts

Throughout our history, amendments have come about in pretty much the same way that most change comes about. People work for it. Some amendments, such as those that changed the succession to the presidency, have arisen from among the ranks of Congress itself. But amendments that affect the social order have generally arisen from small groups and coalitions of activists, such as slavery abolitionists, advocates for the prohibition of alcohol, and suffragettes seeking the vote for women. Fervent speakers organized committees at churches and in social clubs, wrote letters to the editors of newspapers, held public rallies, visited their representatives, leafleted, and wrote books. They used the media of the day to gain broader public attention to their causes. They got arrested and were sometimes abused for speaking their minds. They adapted their tactics as they learned from experience. They welcomed converts into their ranks. They interpreted religious teachings as supporting their views. They injected their issues into public campaigns and debates. They drew parallels to preceding historic struggles. They believed in the righteousness of their goals.

But despite their commitment and their passion, they made mistakes. They fought among themselves. They misjudged their audiences and were embarrassed. Some of them grew discouraged and abandoned the effort. They ran out of funds. They put forward arguments that could be countered. They overstated their claims and misjudged the extent to which the public agreed with them. They allowed themselves to be tricked, co-opted, and fooled. They allowed their egos to interfere with their work. They made every mistake in the book and invented new ones as they went along.

They could have failed. Sometimes they did. Besides the 27 amendments that have become part of the Constitution, there are many more that were dreamed up but never got off the ground. There were even a few proposed amendments that could have been part of what we now call the Bill of Rights, but which never made it into the final draft.

But most important of all, they didn't give up. The movement for the prohibition of alcohol, for example, was active in the US for more than sixty years before it finally achieved the goal of a nation-wide ban. The early temperance movement, which preceded the prohibition movement, focused its efforts on action by state legislatures. By 1851, its proponents were able to get variants of prohibition enacted into law in 13 states. By 1860, every one of those prohibitions had been repealed. The focus was then broadened to include the national level. A resolution calling for a prohibition amendment to the Constitution was introduced into every Congress beginning in 1876. By 1916, 23 States had some form of prohibition. Finally in 1917, the prohibition amendment passed both houses of the US Congress. The ratification lasted into 1919, and the amendment went into effect in 1920.[276]

As much as I would like to suggest that repeal of the Second Amendment is inevitable, that is a claim that will have to be considered by historians after it has happened. All that we can say now, in light of history, is that repeal is possible. Maybe even likely. That is saying a lot.

What happens if we don't do anything?

If we do nothing, the violence will continue, probably at roughly the same rate that it has been. The country seems to be willing to live with the level of violence we have, so we could probably go on like we have been, indefinitely.

Over time, there may be some slight increase in fatalities in mass-shootings at schools, movie theaters, and other public places. It seems that the young men who engage in that sort of thing like to try to run up impressive total numbers of victims, as if they were trying to beat the best score on some vile video game. They have noticed that the news barely reports anymore when only a handful of people are shot. The numbers of dead have to reach over a dozen before the national news runs the story.

America's seeming complacency may make it sound like there is no urgency and no reason to expect that a movement will build around the idea of repealing the Second Amendment. But there is one other factor to consider, which is that once the movement to repeal begins, all events that relate to it become subject to being interpreted in relationship to it. This factor is what led, for example, to the amendment that gave 18-year-olds the right to vote.

Once it was proposed that those disenfranchised citizens be allowed to vote, they had a "hook" to get into the newspapers. Every time another body was brought home from the war in Vietnam, the pro-vote activists could protest that young people were being sent to die without having a say.

The same thing will happen once the movement to repeal the Second Amendment gets going. There are plenty of activists who know how to stage events and interest the media. They have essentially been in training over the past several decades, working on issues like war, immigration, and racism. They are a force with great potential, ready to dig in and work on a cause that they consider worthwhile.

The dynamic that can propel this issue is the sense that people do not want to feel that their country has lost its legitimacy. This is what led to the cessation of our involvement in Vietnam. It led to the Republican Party disassociating itself from Richard Nixon, which resulted in his resignation. It has been leading to the recognition of the rights of the LGBT community, the condemnation of torture by our military, and the legalization of marijuana for medical purposes.

It seems that Americans are quick to criticize their government, but in fact we are strongly nationalistic. We identify with our country, and we want to feel that what our country is doing is defensible and just. People in every country feel this way, but it is especially true in countries that want to view themselves as democracies. If our government is not acting as it should, it's our fault, isn't it? As people come to view gun violence as an offense against not just the immediate victims but against the entire society, they will join the effort to eliminate the violence. Not to take action would require us to see ourselves as callous and insensitive. We'd rather view ourselves as concerned and responsive.

How long will it take?

Some amendments have been passed through Congress quickly and been ratified almost immediately. Some have taken longer. Of the 27 amendments that have been added to the Constitution so far, the longest time between proposal and ratification is 203 years. The 27th Amendment was submitted to the states for ratification in 1789 and was finally ratified in 1992. The story of how it came to be ratified is rather remarkable.

The 27th Amendment provides that the pay of senators and representatives cannot be increased or decreased until after the next election. It was probably intended to discourage congressmen from increasing their own pay, because they would have to stand for reelection before they could receive the increase, and they would therefore have to answer to the people for any increase before they received it.

The amendment was actually the second amendment ever submitted to the states for ratification. It was among the twelve that were submitted for ratification in 1789, ten of which eventually becoming the Bill of Rights. At that time, there were only the 13 original states, so only ten states would have needed to ratify the amendment for it to become part of the Constitution. But only six states ratified it initially. As the number of states in the union increased over the years, more states would have had to ratify. For a long time, none did. The amendment had lost its momentum. Then, in 1982 an undergraduate student at the University of Texas wrote a paper about the amendment, suggesting that the amendment might still be ratified. He received a "C" grade for the paper, reportedly because his professor thought the idea was unrealistic.

Apparently the student was not happy with the criticism he received, so he began a letter-writing campaign urging that states ratify the amendment. His idea caught on. In the next ten years, enough states had ratified the amendment for it to become part of the Constitution.[277]

When people ask me how long I think it will be before we are able to repeal the Second Amendment, I acknowledge that the 27th Amendment took a long time to be ratified. Hopefully, people will feel that the slaughter that is taking place in our country on a daily basis presents a more urgent need for change than the concern that members of Congress will grab a few too many dollars for themselves. Hopefully, it won't take 203 years to repeal the Second Amendment. Perhaps it will take a much shorter time. The 26th Amendment, which lowered the voting age to 18, was ratified by the states within four months after they received the amendment from Congress.

Why repeal is likely to happen

Gun lovers are quick to point out that Americans own a huge number of guns. There may be more guns than there are adults in this country. They follow this observation with an argument that because there are so many guns, it would be futile to try to get rid of them all. How could anyone retrieve 200 million or more guns that are already in circulation all across the land? How could anyone expect the police to confiscate all those guns, and what makes anyone think that gun owners would voluntarily give up their guns?

Good questions. Fortunately, there are good answers. Although there are a lot of guns in the US, gun ownership really isn't nearly as widespread in this country as the gun owners think. Only a small minority of Americans owns any guns at all, and the numbers of guns that Americans own includes guns that are inoperable and are kept only as mementos of past wars or as part of antique collections.

The ownership of guns is also not as geographically dispersed as some gun owners would like to think.[278] Gun owners are concentrated in southern and western states, and generally in rural parts of states. In many of the highly populated urban parts of our country, where most of the population growth has been taking place for several generations, very few people own guns.

Some of the reasons for these geographic differences are obvious. For example, people in cities don't hunt for their food, and they depend upon their police, not their marksmanship, for protection. But other reasons may not be as readily apparent. There is some scholarship that indicates that the geographic differences in attitudes about guns are due to the countries of origin of the people who settled in those areas, and the religious beliefs and cultural attitudes that they brought with them. People who settled the southern US, for instance, are thought to have brought with them a culture of "honor" that led them to engage in duels and that is still more sympathetic to personal violence than the cultures that settled other parts of the nation.[279] States where that culture of honor is strong have passed laws that are consistent with the culture and that allow people to use guns to defend themselves and their property without having to retreat or first try less violent measures. In those parts of the country, the value of honor was higher than the value of life when dueling was in vogue, and for some it remains more important than public safety today.

In addition to the geographic trend away from gun ownership, other demographic trends are heading in a good direction. Young people show much less interest in guns than older people do, and their interest in guns has been declining.[280] As older gun owners die off, they are not being replaced by new generations of gun owners. Also, immigrants from other countries, almost none of which allow private ownership of guns the way the US does, have no experience with guns and show almost no interest in them. Immigrants are a major source of population growth in the U.S. The larger their percentage of the population becomes, the smaller the percentage of gun owners there will be in the U.S.

Gun ownership has been steadily declining in this country for all of our modern history, and it continues to do so.[281] This trend points favorably towards the possibility of repeal of the Second Amendment. Most people don't want guns, and they don't see any reason the Constitution should guarantee anyone's right to own them. In states that allow people to carry concealed weapons, only a tiny percentage of people even bother to get the permits, let alone to carry the guns.

But the most significant reason it will be possible to repeal the Second Amendment and eventually to rid our country of guns is that more than half of the people in this country are women. They will continue to lead the public movement to control guns until victory is achieved, just as they have implemented gun controls within their families. No one knows how many men have been persuaded or coerced to get rid of their guns by women, but there are so many stories of this happening that it can't be doubted. Typical is the story of a new mother who comes home from the hospital with a baby and insists that her husband get his guns out of the house—for the child's safety. While she's at it, she also makes him stop smoking in the house. You'll see these guys sitting and smoking outside—on their porches in the middle of winter, and even at gun shows—trying not to look as emasculated as they feel.

The angry white guys who own guns are not very happy that

women are on the ascendancy politically. They aren't in favor of immigration. They don't like to see their violence-oriented culture disappearing. But they can't stanch the demographic trends that are all leading towards a future with fewer guns in fewer hands.

Where can we find inspiration?

In any movement, it is helpful to look back in history to see what progress has been made, by whom, and how it was made. Unfortunately, our recent history gives us very little to draw inspiration from. Not only have we not been making gains, we have been losing ground.

But we need not only look at recent history. Looking just a little further back in time, there are plenty of success stories, where our country's policies were more attuned to its people's desires to live without the constant threat of gun violence. States and the federal government accepted the responsibility to enact laws to protect people, and they acted in accordance with this responsibility. The recent retreat by our government from its responsibility does not erase the fact that progress was once made, and that history of action teaches us by example that there can once again be progress. There is no reason to believe that what was once possible is no longer possible. Just as the recent reversal of our gun policies teaches us that reversal is possible, it teaches us that we can turn those policies around once again.

There are few obvious leaders and groups in the gun control movement that we can point to. We do not have a central figure like Martin Luther King Jr., as the civil rights movement had. We do not have a Caesar Chavez, as the farm workers had. We do not have a Frances Willard or a Women's Christian Temperance Union, as the prohibition movement had. We do not have a Susan B. Anthony or an Elizabeth Cady Stanton, as the women's suffrage movement had.

This may leave us without an acknowledged iconic personality, but that is not important, because in one sense, each of the people mentioned above led our society to the point where we were able to make progress in reducing guns and violence. Dr. King clearly was working to reduce violence in the black community and in all of America. He spoke and wrote of the harm that violence did to black family life, and he repeatedly reminded us that harm that was experienced by any portion of our society was ultimately felt by all of society. His entire movement was for non-violent resistance to racism and to the violence that was both an instrument of American racism and that perpetuated that racism. He also spoke out bravely against America's projection of violence abroad, particularly in Vietnam, helping us to understand that the war was corrupting the core of humanity of which we are all part.

The movement for equal voting rights for women, led by Anthony and Stanton, also was a movement for a reduction in violence. The economic dependency of women, who were not only denied voting rights but were also excluded from much of the labor force, was enmeshed with their susceptibility to violence. Women did not seek the vote merely as an academic matter. They sought it so that they could exert pressure upon governments to address issues that concerned them. Violence was one of those issues.

Similarly, Willard and the prohibition movement had as one of their goals the reduction in drunkenness that led intoxicated men to inflict violence upon each other and their families. Alcohol was viewed as an evil because it had led directly to an abundance of violence, and also because imbibers were too often left in financial difficulties that led to violence within the home.

Those who had experienced and witnessed violence had a strong desire to eliminate the conditions that contributed to the violence, and that desire fed all of these social movements. We can therefore look to each of these movements as the forebears of our struggle, and we can draw inspiration from their victories. None of them would mind. Each of them saw themselves as leaders of movements not just for the objectives we associate with them, but of a broader movement for the advancement of humankind. That's what we are all about, too.

We can also examine the methods that were used in each of these movements and apply to our struggle the lessons they teach. Though each movement must employ strategies and tactics that are appropriate to its own time and challenges, there is much that we can borrow from the past. Each of these successful historic movements required leadership, organization, inspiration, communications, and persistence, and each of them looked to the movements that preceded them to learn all of these things. Sometimes the connections were very close, with people who were instrumental in one struggle moving on to work on the next.

Although they are mostly not internationally known, there are plenty of heroes of the anti-gun violence movement on a more local level. Father Michael Pfleger, a Roman Catholic priest, has been inspiring the movement for decades. In 1981, Father Mike, as he likes to be called, was assigned to St. Sabina Church in a depressed area on the south side of Chicago that is known as Auburn Gresham. He was given the assignment to prepare the church for being closed because of the low number of parishioners who were attending Mass and participating in congregational life. Instead, he turned it into one of the most vital, socially involved churches anywhere.

During his time leading the Faith Community of St. Sabina, Father Mike has led protests against a nearby gun shop that was reputed to be selling guns to criminals. He has helped people who have lost family members to guns to form support groups to help themselves and each other and to become politically active in the struggle to reduce gun violence. Tragically, one of the children who was in his foster care was shot and killed in gang crossfire in 1998.

To hear Father Mike preach to a packed church any Sunday morning about what God and his religion have to say about peace and violence and what we are supposed to do about them is a thrill. To walk with him through neighborhoods that are frequently the scene of shootings is a privilege. To listen as he speaks truth to power is inspiring. He may be a saint, but he is anything but sanctimonious. He has a wonderful sense of humor and is always welcoming. He never gives up, and despite all the pressures on him and all the demands on his time, he is always there when he is needed.

Other clergy all over the country also inspire their congregants and others to stand strong against violence in countless ways that are just as important and inspiring. Wherever you find a vigorous protest against guns, you are likely to find one or more faith leaders taking a leadership role, setting a tone of steadfast, fearless vigilance.

Among the protesters, you are also likely to find people who have lost family members to gun violence. They often bring framed photos of the loved ones they have lost. Despite the pain it must cause them, they are determined to tell about the ways the shootings took place, so that people will understand. Years after the shootings, they still show up to tell their personal stories and evoke the pathos that just might help someone understand violence in a new way and be inspired to help end it.

Among the people who are organizing and protesting and trying to stop the violence, equally inspiring are the dedicated volunteers who show up not because it is the calling that they were ordained to, and not because the violence has touched them personally, but just because they care and they know they are needed. The press counts them and shows them marching by, as if they were just extras in a movie, unworthy of notice. But they matter. The victims always greet them with hugs, expressing thanks to them for just showing up and reminding them that they are not alone. They are the "little people," as politicians sometimes refer to them—the ordinary folks who never get in the limelight and seldom are handed the bullhorn. The anonymous people who hand out fliers and hold signs and join in chants, rain or shine. The people who forward emails announcing demonstrations and invite their friends to join them on a march. They keep the movement moving. They are the connection between those in the midst of the violence and the rest of society.

But the Constitution is so hard to amend

Hard, but not impossible. Our Founders set up a government that drew upon the participation and consent of the governed. That's why they provided for elections, representation, the right to petition for redress of grievances, and the rights to free speech and to peaceably assemble. The Founders wanted to make sure that the people would have the ability to influence their government.

But the Founders went even further and provided in the Constitution itself a means by which the people could alter the very structure of the government. This was perhaps the boldest innovation in the entire Constitution. It allows the people to go beyond merely petitioning for fundamental change. It allows us to institute change directly. It even allows us to remake the governmental structure that we inherited if it has proved not to be suitable to our needs.

The Constitution provides methods by which it can be amended, but it is protected from being changed on whimsy or by transient public alarm over unusual circumstances.[282] Following the September 11th attacks in 2001, President Bush took advantage of the public's shock and was able to implement policies that otherwise would have been difficult to put in place. He was even able to convince Congress to pass certain laws that would impinge on Americans' civil liberties and alter our policies abroad. But he didn't even try amending the Constitution, because it would have taken too long and been too difficult. Thank goodness that more than 200 years earlier, the Founders had foreseen what kind of mischief someone like George Bush might have done if the Constitution had been easier to amend.

Although we often refer to the events of 1776 as a revolution, they really were more of a rebellion. The people who formed our new government didn't stray very far from what they had known before. They were actually a rather conservative bunch. The Constitution they wrote embodied their views, and they intended that those views would remain the basis for the new country for many years to come. They set up a structure that would accommodate needed revisions, but they didn't look forward to a whole lot of radical change. So they provided a mechanism for amendments, but they made it cumbersome and difficult to use.

Our country today is to a great extent even more conservative than it was when it was founded, in the sense that conservatism means keeping things the same. We have gotten to the point where the government hardly changes anything, and although people complain about the irritating legislators who engage in partisan "gridlock," we keep electing the exact same people over and over again. We don't seem to want a lot of change. So the prospect of passing any new amendment seems limited. This essential stability is what the Founders wanted. They only wanted amendments that were absolutely necessary and nearly universally agreed upon. If they lived today and saw the havoc guns are wreaking, they would have wanted us to repeal the Second Amendment, because they would recognize that clinging too hard to the status quo is threatening the integrity of our society.

How repeal will affect gun ownership

No doubt, the gun lobby will take this call for repeal of the Second Amendment as a call for the prohibition and confiscation of all guns. We could take that step by including in the repeal amendment some kind of language that bans guns. But by itself, a simple repeal of the Second Amendment would have no impact on gun ownership. The day after repeal, unless new laws were passed, gun owners would be totally unaffected. All that the repeal would accomplish would be to allow the states and the federal government to pass gun laws that people want.

Some states would probably do little or nothing. Many state constitutions contain guarantees of the right to bear arms that are very similar to the Second Amendment in the US Constitution. If those states didn't repeal their constitutional provisions, the repeal of the federal Second Amendment might not mean much within those states. But other states might move very quickly to pass laws that they have wanted for years but were unable to pass. In our country, each state legislature acts independently of the others. The notion is that the states will experiment with the laws that seem to be useful, compare each other's ideas and experiences, and allow good ideas to propagate across the country. We are supposed to be akin to an experimental laboratory, discovering solutions to problems and rejecting proposals that prove unworkable or unwise.

If a repeal is passed, the federal government will likely act slowly, as it tends to do, enacting legislation only when needed to solve problems that remain unsolved by inconsistent state laws or that call for a nationwide policy. No one can say what laws will be passed by either the federal or state governments. All that repealing the Second Amendment will do is to allow them to try to make a positive change. Right now, they can hardly try.

It will be open to debate which measures the states and federal government should take immediately and which should be deferred. As tempting as it is to dream that we might outlaw all guns, that is probably the least likely course that events will take, not because it is the wrong thing to do, but because we still live with the memory of Prohibition, mandated by the 18th Amendment.

Prohibition did do some good. As a result of the temperance movement and the campaign to pass the 18th Amendment, the public gained a new understanding of the problems caused by alcohol. This knowledge led us to drastically reduce our national consumption of alcohol, which was a good thing.

But there were also notorious bad effects that were associated with Prohibition. The most well known is that it created an environment that led to the growth of a nationwide organized crime syndicate that continues to plague our country nearly a century later.

We should not get carried away with concern that just because Prohibition failed and was repealed, eliminating the right to own guns would fail and that the Second Amendment would be restored. Prohibition was undertaken in the wake of World War I. The entire world was traumatized. Alcohol was consumed by a much larger percentage of Americans than the percentage that now have guns, and it had a much more diverse place in the culture. The federal law enforcement system was in its infancy and unable to effectively respond to the black market that developed for alcohol.

Federal and state law enforcement is much more capable today. Perhaps most important of all, any new gun laws would only get passed after debates that would benefit from consideration of our experience with Prohibition. Legislators are not omniscient, but they are capable of learning from the past. Because Prohibition was not entirely successful does not mean that there is no hope that we will ever be able to pass effective and enforceable gun laws. The fact that the NRA fights against gun laws so relentlessly should make it obvious that they think we could pass effective laws. If they thought the public wouldn't support gun laws, the NRA probably wouldn't bother fighting against them.

The time is now

When I first started talking with people about repealing the Second Amendment, I found almost no one who thought it was worth the effort to try. This surprised me, because the first people I asked were activists who I knew didn't like guns. I had worked with several of them on various gun safety initiatives. I had expected them to be more enthusiastic.

As I talked with these people, I knew that their reticence wasn't because they thought we needed to protect people's rights to have guns. Most of these people would be happy to eliminate guns altogether. They just didn't believe that we would be able to amend the Constitution. It seemed like an impossible idea.

As I tested the idea on more people, I realized that the activists weren't just discouraged because gun control efforts have failed so often. Their pessimism went much deeper. Having endured years of a poorly performing economy that followed the 2008 stock market crash, the rise of obstructionism in Washington politics, our never-ending and pointless military adventurism in the Middle East, the decline of the middle class, and the continuing struggle and failure to get the political machinery of this country to respond to these and other problems in a productive way, they had largely given up hope of bringing about any needed change.

The activists were fatigued. Rather than thinking about how repeal could improve people's lives, they were content to argue that we didn't need to repeal the amendment; we just needed to get the Supreme Court to change its mind about what the amendment meant. That gave them an excuse for not doing anything, because they knew that there was nothing they could do to accomplish that goal other than sit back and hope that some new justices would someday be appointed to the court who would view the Second Amendment differently than their predecessors had. The activists had not stopped dreaming, but they were quick to find reasons why repeal would not be possible. Having largely been raised on the standard community organizer's playbook, which says people should demonstrate their power by winning small victories, the activists rejected repeal out-of-hand because it could not be achieved within a short period of time—the period defined by a funding grant or a political campaign.

As I continued to talk about repeal, however, I found that the general public was much more enthusiastic about the idea than the activists were. Most people were quick to tell me that they would be happy to get rid of guns, but they didn't know how it could be done or that it could be done. When I pointed out that we could eliminate the underpinning of the gun lobby's power by amending the Constitution, and when I showed them that the Constitution could in fact be amended as it has been in the past, they did not hesitate to pledge their support for the effort. People are overwhelmingly ready for this change, even though many activists and politicians are skeptical. The people know what they want, and they want gun violence to end.

Although some people's energy for a cause dissipates when they face setbacks, other people respond with renewed zeal for an even bolder vision, especially when they see that other people have not given up. We need not be despondent that some activists are flagging. They will revive as they witness the commitment that the public has for repeal, and they will carry the mission forward.

"Make no little plans. They have no magic to stir men's blood and probably will not themselves be realized." These words by Daniel Burnham, the architect who drew up the master plan for Chicago, were reflected in a later generation by the mission of the Starship Enterprise, to "Boldly go where no man has gone before." They speak of what we love to think is the courageous, visionary American spirit.

These words may seem to bear little resemblance to what is found in public life today, which would more accurately be phrased as, "Maybe we could try to accomplish some tiny thing and make it look like more than it is." Our political realm has become the playground of the timid, where no one will take any risks because they are convinced ahead of time that they will fail. Small wonder that we are making so little progress.

But every activist has probably heard and been stirred by the quote from sociologist Margaret Mead, "Never doubt that a small group of thoughtful, committed citizens can change the world; indeed, it's the only thing that ever has." Wouldn't this seem to suggest that repeal is possible? Doesn't it continue to sound a call to action to people for whom the status quo is not a destination, but a point of departure for a journey towards a more just future?

We all know the inspirational words that President John F. Kennedy spoke in his inaugural speech: "Ask not what your country can do for you. Ask what you can do for your country." Wouldn't this seem to tell us that we have an obligation to do what we can if it needs to be done?

Burnham, Mead, Kennedy, and others were not just visionaries. They were extremely practical people working in the real world to fix very concrete problems. I am sure that each of them was told by their associates and friends (not to mention their adversaries and critics) that they were being unrealistic. And yet, they accomplished great things, just as America has achieved greatness when it has risen to a righteous challenge. There is no reason to believe that the days when America could triumph over adversity are over.

Repeal of the Second Amendment only seems impossible because it hasn't been done yet. Once we have done it, people will start to ask what took us so long. Hopefully, our success will serve to encourage people that there are other worthwhile changes that can be made in our world, if only people will have the courage to try, and if only they will be confident enough to ignore the people who say what cannot be done.

Ward boss Mathias "Paddy" Bauler, a key figure in the political machine in Chicago from the 1930s to the 1960s, is still famous in that town for responding to a call for change by saying, "Chicago ain't ready for reform." The question we need to ask is whether America is ready for reform.[283]

I propose repealing the Second Amendment not as a dream, but as a necessity. I urge people to join in the effort with the zeal of someone called to a mission. This will not be an easy task; worthwhile tasks seldom are. It will call for dedication, sacrifice, patience, and impatience. Most of all, it will require faith.

In order to repeal the Second Amendment, we will have to come to grips with the violence that underlies the way the US presents itself to the world. We will also have to examine the attitudes that Americans have towards violence in general.

Repeal of the Second Amendment should not be seen merely as a way to enable greater regulation of the use and ownership of firearms by civilians. It has far greater implications, and therefore faces opposition from a broader range of opponents. Repealing the Second Amendment will impact the way we conduct foreign policy, which may incite powerful interests to oppose it. It will also change the way we view a lot of our domestic problems.

Everyone will benefit from this effort. Those who help to make it happen will have the joy of working in selfless devotion to their fellow humans. Those who live to see the ultimate success of repeal will have the extra benefit of knowing they caused a momentous, historical change in our world.

The movement has already begun. There's a train a-comin'. Get on board.

Appendix

Second Amendment

A well regulated Militia, being necessary to the security of a free State, the right of the people to keep and bear Arms, shall not be infringed.

Proposed Repeal Amendment

Section 1. The second article of amendment to the Constitution of the United States is hereby repealed.

Section 2. The Congress and the several States shall have concurrent power to regulate and ban the sale, possession, manufacture, use, import, export, and commerce in weapons of all kinds, including firearms and ammunition. No compensation will be due to any person whose property interests are affected by government action pursuant to this Section.

Notes

1 “Gabrielle Giffords Fires Gun for First Time Since 2011 Shooting.” *New York Daily News,* July 2, 2013.

2 Hemenway, David. *Private Guns, Public Health.* Ann Arbor: University of Michigan Press, 2004.

3 Violence Policy Center. www.vpc.org

4 Leventhal, John M., Gaither, Julie R., and Sege, Robert. “Hospitalizations Due to Firearm Injuries in Children and Adolescents.” *Pediatrics,* January 27, 2014. Accessed January 27, 2014. http://pediatrics.aappublications.org/content/early/2014/01/22/peds.2013-1809.full.pdf

5 “Medical examiner rules James Brady's death a homicide.” *The Washington Post,* August 8, 2014. Accessed September 1, 2014, http://www.washingtonpost.com/local/crime/james-bradys-death-ruled-homicide-by-dc-medical-examiner/2014/08/08/686de224-1f41-11e4-82f9-2cd6fa8da5c4_story.html

6 “Again, school shooting terror -- but a relieved outcome.” *USA Today,* August 20, 2013.

7 “Texas gun owners re-enact Charlie Hebdo massacre.” *KTVT,* January 14, 1025. Accessed January 19, 2015 http://kxan.com/2015/01/14/texas-gun-owners-re-enact-charlie-hebdo-massacre/

8 “If I Only Had a Gun.” *ABC News 20/20,* April 10, 2009, narrated by Diane Sawyer, accessed January 19, 2015. http://abcnews.go.com/2020/video/defend-gun-7312540

9 “U.S. expands airstrikes against Islamic State militants in northern Iraq.” *The Washington Post,* August 8, 2014. Accessed September 1, 2014. http://www.washingtonpost.com/world/middle_east/us-airstrikes-target-islamic-state-militants-in-northern-iraq/2014/08/08/a7a659d8-1efd-11e4-ae54-0cfe1f974f8a_story.html

10 Amnesty International, www.AmnestyUSA.org

11 “Stand Your Ground: SC judge grants immunity to man who mistakenly killed a bystander.” *HeraldOnline,* October 9, 2013.

12 Barr, Daniel P. *A Colony Sprung from Hell: Pittsburgh and the Struggle for Authority on the Western Pennsylvania Frontier, 1744-1794.* Kent, Ohio: Kent State University Press, 2014.

13 Hemenway, David. *Private Guns, Public Health.* Ann Arbor: University of Michigan Press, 2004.

14 ‘Boy in Shooting 'Unzipped' Special Purse Gun Pocket.” *ABC News,* December 31, 2014. Accessed January 13, 2015. http://abcnews.go.com/US/wireStory/year-accidentally-kills-mother-wal-mart-27918926

15 “Mom carries loaded gun in diaper bag into Philadelphia school, police say.” *Los Angeles Times,* January 11, 2013. Accessed December 12, 2013. http://articles.latimes.com/2013/jan/11/nation/la-na-nn-guns-school-20130111

16 “Man killed in apparent accidental shooting while hunting.” *TheIndyChannel,* August 18, 2013.

17 “Joliet Man Killed in Deer Hunting Accident.” *Joliet Patch,* October 24, 2013.

18 “‘Bigfoot hunt’ ends in Shooting, Arrests.” *Fox News,* November 4, 2013.

19 “Suicide Bigger Threat for Police than Criminal.” *New York Times,* April 8, 2008.
Army Times, September 12, 2012.

20 “Prosecutors: Man shoots friends, 1 fatally, over beer money.” *Chicago Tribune,* August 20, 2013.

21 Wintemute, Garen J. “The Choice of Weapons in Firearm Suicides.”

American Journal of Public Health, 78 No. 7, 1988. p. 824-826. "State-wide gun ownership tied to suicide deaths." *Chicago Tribune,* September 27, 2013.

22 "Can Faith Moderate US Gun Culture? Studies Link Religion to Lower Devotion to Firearms." David Briggs, *Huffington Post,* November 14, 2014, accessed November 14, 2014

23 "Richard Slotkin, interviewed on Moyer and Company." December 13, 2013. Accessed December14, 2013. www.billmoyers.com

24 Thompson, Chuck. *Better Off Without 'Em: A Northern Manifesto for Southern Secession.* New York: Simon & Schuster, 2012.

25 "CEO Pay 1,795-to-1 Multiple of Wages Skirts U.S. Law." April 30, 2013. Bloomberg.com

26 LaPierre, Wayne. Speech to the *Conservative Political Action Conference,* March 6, 2014. Accessed March 9, 2014. http://home.nra.org/pdf/waynelapierre_140306.pdf

27 "Why Gun-Rights Backers Win While Other Conservative Causes Lose." *The Atlantic,* April 29, 2014.

28 "10 Pro-Gun Myths Shot Down." *Mother Jones,* January 13, 2013.

29 "From_my_cold,_dead_hands," Wikipedia. Accessed September 2, 2014. http://en.wikipedia.org/wiki/From_my_cold,_dead_hands

30 "Why Sport Hunting is Cruel and Unnecessary." *People for the Ethical Treatment of Animals.* www.PETA.org

31 "Study: More Guns Lead to More Suicides." *Think Progress,* November 14, 2013.

32 Cook & Ludwig. "The Effects of Gun Prevalence on Burglary: Deterrence v. Inducement." *National Bureau of Economic Research,* May, 2002.

33 Dolan & Doyle. "Violence Risk Prediction: Clinical and actuarial measures and the role of the Psychopathy Checklist." *British Journal of Psychiatry,* October, 2000.

34 "Aurora Theater Shooting Prompts New Colorado Mental Health Law." *Huffington Post,* May 16, 2013.

35 "Gunman and 12 Victims Killed in Shooting at D.C. Navy Yard." *New York Times,* September 16, 2013. "Washington Navy Yard Shooting." Wikipedia. Accessed April 4, 2015. http://en.wikipedia.org/wiki/Washington_Navy_Yard_shooting

36 "CNN Poll: No change on gun law opinions after Arizona shootings." *CNN,* January 17, 2011. Accessed April 4, 2015. http://politicalticker.blogs.cnn.com/2011/01/17/cnn-poll-no-change-on-gun-law-opinions-after-arizona-shootings/ Quinnipiac University Poll, October 2, 2013. Accessed April 4, 2015. http://www.quinnipiac.edu/news-and-events/quinnipiac-university-poll/national/release-detail?ReleaseID=1959

37 "Repeal of Missouri's Background Check Law Associated With Increase in State's Murders." *Johns Hopkins Bloomberg School of Public Health,* February 17, 2014.

38 "Mayor Michael Bloomberg says 40 percent of guns are sold without a background check." *Tampa Bay Times Politifact,* July 25, 2012. www.politifact.com

39 FBI National Instant Criminal Background Check System (NICS). www.FBI.gov

40 Noyes, Dan. "Hot Guns: How Criminals Get Guns." *PBS Frontline.*

41 "Felon Seeks Firearm, No Strings Attached – How Dangerous People Evade Background Checks and Buy Illegal Guns Online." *Mayors Against Illegal Guns.* September, 2013. Accessed April 4, 2015. http://everytown.org/article/felon-seeks-firearm/

42 "Tragedy as Teenager Mistakes his Little Brother, 12, for Intruder and

Shoots him Dead in Florida Home." *Daily Mail,* March 23, 2013.

43 "Retired Cop Fatally Shoots Own Son, After Mistaking Him For Burglar." *CBS Chicago,* October 9, 2012.

44 "Virginia sheriff's deputy shoots daughter sneaking in house, crashes car en route to hospital: police." *New York Daily News,* August 14, 2014. Accessed September 1, 2104. http://www.nydailynews.com/news/national/va-officer-shoots-daughter-crashes-car-en-route-hospital-police-article-1.1904362

45 "Disabled children killed in Elmhurst murder-suicide." *Daily Herald,* August 31, 2014. Accessed September 1, 2014. http://www.dailyherald.com/article/20140831/news/140839796/

46 "Retired cop drops gun, shoots self at Des Plaines school." *Chicago Tribune,* April 16, 2013.

47 "Two injured in accidental shooting at Bridgeport gun range." June 6, 2013. My4News.com

48 "Man Shot By Instructor During Fairfield County Concealed Carry Class." August 12, 2013. 10TV.com

49 "NYPD: 9 shooting bystander victims hit by police gunfire." *Associated Press,* August 25, 2012.

50 "Cops Shoot Two Bystanders on Broadway." *New York Post,* September 15, 2013.

51 "Your Brain in a Shootout: Guns, Fear and Flawed Instincts." *Time,* January 16, 2013.

52 http://www.projectchildsafe.org/

53 "Florida's largest gun dealer bans gun rentals in wake of suicides." *Orlando Sentinel,* January 10, 2014.

54 Ferdman, Roberto A. "The racial divide in America's gun deaths." *The Washington Post, Wonkblog,* September 19, 2014.
Kalesan & Vasan, et al. "State-specific, racial and ethnic heterogeneity in trends of firearm-related fatality rates in the USA from 2000 to 2010." *BMJ Open,* Vol. 4, Issue 9, August 14, 2014.

55 Lepore, Jill. "Battleground America – One Nation, Under the Gun." *The New Yorker,* April 23, 2012.

56 Reeve, Elspeth. "The Rise of the Female Gun Nut is a Lie," *The Atlantic Wire,* April 11, 2013.

57 Healy, Melissa. "Study takes new look at gun access and risk of homicide, suicide." *LA Times,* January 20, 2014.
Anglemyer, et al. "The Accessibility of Firearms and Risk for Suicide and Homicide Victimization Among Household Members." *Annals of Internal Medicine* 160.2, January 21, 2014.

58 Norton, Michael I. and Sommers, Samuel R. "Whites See Racism as a Zero-Sum Game That They Are Now Losing." *Perspectives on Psychological Science* 6.3, May, 2011.

59 Kimmel, Michael. *Angry White Men: American Masculinity at the End of an Era.* New York: Nation Books, 2013.

60 Whites, O'Brien, Forrest, Lynott, Daly. "Racism, Gun Ownership and Gun Control: Biased Attitudes in U.S." *PlosOne,* October 31, 2013.

61 King Jr., Dr. Martin Luther. *Where Do We Go From Here: Chaos of Community?* Boston: Beacon Press, 1968.

62 Frank, Thomas. *What's The Matter With Kansas?* New York: Henry Holt & Company, 2004.

63 Wood, Gordon S. *The American Revolution.* New York: Modern Library, 2002. p. 99-106.

64 Rakove, Jack N. *Original Meanings: Politics and Ideas in the Making of the Constitution.* New York: Alfred A. Knopf, Inc., 1996. p. 119.

65 Barr, Daniel P. *A Colony Sprung from Hell: Pittsburgh and the Struggle for Authority*

on the Western Pennsylvania Frontier, 1744-1794. Kent, Ohio: Kent State University Press, 2014.

66 LaPierre, Wayne. Address to NRA annual convention, Official NRA transcript, April 26, 2014. Accessed 4-28-2014. http://home.nra.org/pdf/waynelapierre_140426.pdf

67 Kotlowitz, Alex. *There Are No Children Here*. New York: Anchor Books, 1991.

68 Venkatesh, Sudhir. *Gang Leader for a Day*. New York: Penguin Press, 2008.

69 "Views of Gun Control – A Detailed Demographic Breakdown." *Pew Research*, January 13, 2011.

70 "The demographics and politics of gun-owning households." *Pew Research*, July 15, 2014. Accessed September 1, 2014. http://www.pewresearch.org/fact-tank/2014/07/15/the-demographics-and-politics-of-gun-owning-households/

71 Johnson, Nicholas J. "Firearms Policy and the Black Community: An Assessment of the Modern Orthodoxy." *Connecticut Law Review*, Vol. 45, July 2013.

72 "U.S. Minorities Less Confident in Police, Small Business." *Gallup*, June 20, 2013.

73 "Minority Gun Owners Face Balancing Act, Weighing Isolation and Stigma of Violence." *New York Times*, June 14, 2014. Accessed September 1, 2014. http://www.nytimes.com/2014/06/15/us/minority-gun-owners-face-balancing-act-weighing-isolation-and-stigma-of-violence.html

74 Johnson, Nicholas. *Negroes and the Gun: The Black Tradition of Arms*. Amherst, NY: Prometheus Books, 2014. p. 110.

75 Johnson, Nicholas. *Negroes and the Gun: The Black Tradition of Arms*. Amherst, NY: Prometheus Books, 2014. p. 103.

76 "Views of Gun Control – A Detailed Demographic Breakdown." *Pew Research*, January 13, 2011.

77 Hout, Fischer, Chaves. "More Americans Have No Religious Preference." *Institute for the Study of Societal Issues*, March, 2013.

78 "In U.S., 77% Identify as Christian." *Gallup*, December 24, 2012.

79 "Gun Issue Divides Religious Community." *CNN*, January 12, 2013.

80 The Holy Bible, King James Version. Matthew 21: 12.

81 The Holy Bible, King James Version. Luke 22: 35-38.

82 Eisen, Robert, *The Peace and Violence of Judaism*. New York: Oxford University Press, 2011.

83 "Views of Gun Control – A Detailed Demographic Breakdown." *Pew Research*, January 13, 2011.

84 "Views of Gun Control – A Detailed Demographic Breakdown." *Pew Research*, January 13, 2011.

85 "U.S. Defense Spending vs. Global Defense Spending." *The Center for Arms Control and Non-Proliferation*, April 24, 2013.

86 "U.S. Has World's Highest Incarceration Rate." *Population Reference Bureau*, August, 2012.

87 "Police forces pick up surplus military supplies." *USA Today*, June 17, 2014. Accessed September 2, 2014. http://www.usatoday.com/story/news/nation/2014/06/15/local-law-enforcement-agencies-surplus-military-equipment/10286485/

88 "Police in Ferguson ignite debate about military tactics." *USA Today*, August 19, 2014. Accessed September 2, 2014. http://www.usatoday.com/story/news/nation/2014/08/14/ferguson-militarized-police/14064675/

89 "Poll: Most Approve of Spanking Kids." *ABC News*, November 8, 2008. Accessed December 16, 2013. http://abcnews.go.com/US/story?id=90406

90 "France Warns Its Tourists About Chicago's West Side, Far South Side."

Chicago Tribune, November 18, 2013. Accessed September 11, 2014. http://articles.chicagotribune.com/2013-11-18/news/chi-france-warns-its-tourists-about-chicagos-west-side-far-south-side-20131118_1_choose-chicago-far-south-side-france
United Kingdom Foreign Travel Advice. Accessed September 11, 2014. https://www.gov.uk/foreign-travel-advice/usa/safety-and-security

91 Bushman, Jamieson, Weitz, and Romer. "Gun Violence Trends in Movies." *Pediatrics,* November 11, 2013.

92 Bushman, Brad. "Do Violent Video Games Play a Role in Shootings?" *CNN,* September 18, 2013. Accessed September 11, 2014. http://www.cnn.com/2013/09/18/opinion/bushman-video-games/index.html

93 Sedensky, Stephen J., III. "Report of the State's Attorney for the Judicial District of Danbury on the Shootings at Sandy Hook Elementary School and 36 Yogananda Street, Newtown, Connecticut on December 14, 2012." *Office of the State's Attorney, Judicial District of Danbury.* November 25, 2013. Accessed April 4, 2015.
http://www.ct.gov/csao/lib/csao/Sandy_Hook_Final_Report.pdf

94 "25 Years Later, How 'Top Gun' Made America Love War." *Washington Post,* August 26, 2011.
""Top Gun' Boosting Service Sign-ups." *Los Angeles Times,* July 5, 1986.

95 "Heller: Banning, restricting shooter video games is 'virtual gun control.'" *Human Events,* October 14, 2013. (article featured on NRA website)

96 Crickett Firearms. www.Crickett.com

97 "Texas Gun Range to Host Birthday Parties for Children." *Good Morning America,* June 8, 2012.

98 "Family of instructor killed by 9-year-old with Uzi speaks." *CBS News,* August 29, 2014. Accessed September 2, 2014. http://www.cbsnews.com/news/family-of-instructor-killed-by-9-year-old-with-uzi-speaks/

99 "Families Shoot Easter Eggs at Local Gun Range." *NBC Charlotte, NC,* March 29, 2013,

100 "Four dead in Elmhurst Murder-Suicide." *CBS Chicago,* August 30, 2014. Accessed September 2, 2014. http://chicago.cbslocal.com/2014/08/30/elmhurst-police-several-family-members-found-dead/

101 Chopra, Deepak. *Peace Is the Way.* New York: Three Rivers Press, 2005.

102 "Moving Forward On Guns, Without Congress." *MSNBC,* October 26, 2013.

103 *Consumer Product Safety Commission.* www.CPSC.gov

104 58 USCode 5841 et seq

105 www.OSHA.gov

106 "The Health Consequences of Smoking—50 Years of Progress, A Report of the Surgeon General." U.S. Department of Health and Human Services, 2014. Accessed April 4, 2015.
http://www.surgeongeneral.gov/library/reports/50-years-of-progress/exec-summary.pdf
"380,000 U.S. Deaths Yearly Due to Smoking." *UPI,* June 11, 2012. Accessed April 4, 2015.
http://www.upi.com/Health_News/2012/06/11/380000-US-deaths-yearly-due-to-smoking/83531339472759/

107 "Gun Deaths Outpace Motor Vehicle Deaths in 10 States in 2009." Violence Policy Center, May, 2012. Accessed April 4, 2015.
http://vpc.org/studies/gunsvscars.pdf

108 Mothers Against Drunk Drivers. www.MADD.org

109 International Residential Code Sec. R309.1

110 *Consumer Product Safety Commission.* www.CPSC.gov
111 "Design Safety Standards for Handguns Policy Summary." *Law Center to Prevent Gun Violence,* May 12, 2012.
112 "NJ's 2002 smart-gun law could take effect soon, limit supply." *The Record,* October 14, 2013.
113 "California store's sale of smart guns prompts furious backlash." *Washington Post,* March 6, 2014.
114 "GOA Announces Boycott of Clinton & Wesson – Sell-out worse than originally reported." *Gun Owners of America,* September 29, 2008.
115 Atwood, James. *America and its Guns: A Theological Expose.* Eugene, OR: Wipf & Stock, 2012.
116 "Death tallies belie true impact of kids' gun injuries." *USA Today,* October 14, 2013. Citing study published in *Pediatrics,* November, 2013.
117 Protection of Lawful Commerce in Arms Act. 15 USC 7901. Public Law 109-92. Signed October 26, 2005.
118 Lemaire, J., "The Cost of Firearm Deaths in the United States: Reduced Life Expectancies and Increased Insurance Costs." *Journal of Risk and Insurance,* 2005.
119 Malinowski, W. Zachary and Milkovits, Amanda. "The cost of a bullet: Price of gun violence takes widespread toll in Rhode Island." *Providence Journal,* October 12, 2013.
120 "Two Studies Document a Rise in Gun Wounds, Homicides." *Family Practice News,* 2013.
121 Cook, Philip J. and Ludwig, Jens. *Gun Violence: The Real Costs.* New York: Oxford University Press, 2002.
122 Ozanne-Smith, Ashby, and Stahakis. "Firearm Related Deaths: The Impact of Regulatory Reform." *Injury Prevention,* 2004.
123 deSouza, Macinko, Alencar, Malta, deMorales, Otaliba. "Reductions in Firearm-Related Mortality and Hospitalization in Brazil After Gun Control." *Health Affairs,* 2002.
124 Hemenway, David. *Private Guns, Public Health.* Ann Arbor: University of Michigan Press, 2004.
125 "Gun Ownership and Firearm-related Deaths." *American Journal of Medicine,* October, 2013.
126 "Remarks by the President at the Memorial Service for Victims of the Navy Yard Shooting." September 22, 2013. www.WhiteHouse.gov
127 "Colorado Lawmakers Ousted in Recall Vote over Gun Law." *New York Times,* September 11, 2013.
128 *District of Columbia v. Heller,* 554 U.S. 570 (2008).
129 "Guns & Ammo column backing Illinois gun law brings vitriolic backlash, costs writer his job." *Chicago Sun-Times,* November 8, 2013.
130 Rynne, Terrence J. *Gandhi and Jesus: The Saving Power of Nonviolence.* Maryknoll, NY: Orvis Books, 2008.
131 Yoder, John Howard. *What Would You Do? A Serious Answer to a Standard Question.* Scottdale, PA: Herald Press, 1992.
132 Wright, James D. and Rossi, Peter H. *Armed and Considered Dangerous,* 2nd ed. New Brunswick, NJ: Transaction Publishers, 2008.
133 "Home Burglary Prevention Tips," Nationwide.com
"Burglary Prevention Checklist." Farmers.com
"Home Burglary Prevention Tips." State Farm.com
134 "Gun Ownership and Firearm-related Deaths." *American Journal of Medicine,* October, 2013.
135 "The Impact of Right to Carry Laws and the NRC Report: The Latest Lessons for the Empirical Evaluation of Law and Policy." Aneja, Donohue, and Zhang, Stanford Law School, September 4, 2014
136 "Two Studies Document a Rise in Gun Wounds, Homicides." *Family Practice*

News, September 20, 2013.
137 Sugarman, Josh. *Every Handgun Is Aimed at You: The Case for Banning Handguns.* New York: The New Press, 2002.
138 Atwood, James. *America and its Guns: A Theological Expose.* Eugene, OR: Wipf & Stock, 2012.
139 Donohue, John J. "The Impact of Concealed-Carry Laws." *Evaluating Gun Policy—Effects on Crime and Violence,* Ludwig, Jens, ed. Brookings Institution, 2003.
140 "Gun advocates credit new concealed carry laws for sharp drop in Chicago murder rate." *Washington Times,* April 5, 2014.
141 Simpson, Colton and Pearlman, Ann. *Inside the Crips.* New York: St. Martin's Press, 2005.
Rodriguez, Luis J. *Always Running,* New York: Touchstone Books, 2005.
Hagedorn, John M. *A World of Gangs.* Minneapolis: University of Minnesota Press, 2008.
142 Amar, Akhil Reed. *America's Constitution, A Biography.* New York: Random House, 2005.
143 "Con Job: Tea Party Mobilizing to Rewrite Constitution." *Institute for Research and Education on Human Rights*, April 24, 2014.
144 *Citizens United v. FEC,* 558 US 310 (2010).
145 Nichols, John. "America's Most Dynamic (Yet Under-Covered) Movement: Overturning 'Citizens United.'" *The Nation,* July 5, 2013.
Move To Amend. https://MoveToAmend.org
146 Levin, Mark R. *The Liberty Amendments: Restoring the American Republic.* New York: Threshold Editions, 2013.
147 "Give Me Amendments or Give Me Death." December 10, 2013. Accessed December 18, 2013. Salon.com
148 Vile, John R. *Encyclopedia of Constitutional Amendments,* 3d ed. Santa Barbara, CA: ABC-CLIO, 2010.
149 Horne, Gerald. *The Counter-Revolution of 1776: Salve Resistance and the Origins of the United States of America.* New York: New York University Press, 2014.
150 "Measures Proposed to Amend the Constitution." United States Senate website. Accessed April 4, 2015.
www.senate.gov/pagelayout/reference/three_column_table/measures_proposed_to_amend_constitution.htm
151 "Bill Text: 102nd Congress (1991-1992). H.J.RES.438.IH." Library of Congress. http://thomas.loc.gov/cgi-bin/query/z?c102:H.J.RES.438:
152 "Repeal the Second Amendment." *The Dispatch,* March 20, 1991.
153 Burger, Warren. Interview by Charlayne Hunter-Gault. *MacNeil/Lehrer NewsHour,* December 16, 1991. Lexis News Library, Transcript #4226. Accessed May 27, 2014.
154 Greene, Bob. "A Gun-free Nation – Just Think About It." *Chicago Tribune,* August 23, 1993.
155 "Repeal the Second Amendment." April 18, 2007. Salon.com
156 Beauchamp, Zack. "Ban the Second Amendment." *The Week*, February 20, 2014. Accessed February 21, 2014.
http://theweek.com/article/index/256692/ban-the-second-amendment
157 "Ditch the Second Amendment." *Brookings Institution,* March 19, 2007.
158 Real Clear Politics, November 6, 2011
http://www.realclearpolitics.com/video/2011/11/06/msnbc_and_huffington_posts_wagner_get_rid_of_second_amendment.html accessed January 22, 2015.

159 "Let's Repeal the Second Amendment." *Vanity Fair,* January 3, 2013.
160 "Texas A&M Law Prof Says It's Time to Repeal Second Amendment." *Daily Caller,* November 16, 2013.
161 "America." *The National Catholic Review,* February 13, 2013.
162 Villareal, Timothy. *Tyrranydissolution.wordpess.com.* Accessed June 2, 2014. http://tyrannydissolution.wordpress.com/
163 Stevens, John Paul. *Six Amendments: How and Why We Should Change the Constitution.* New York: Little Brown, 2014.
164 "Common sense calls for repeal of Second Amendment." *Seattle Times,* April 30, 2014.
165 "It's Time to Repeal the 2d Amendment." *San Jose Inside,* May 30, 2014.
166 "Something's Wrong With the Bill of Rights." *Valley News,* June 8, 2014.
167 Goldstein, Allan. "Repeal the Second Amendment." *OpEdNews,* July 1, 2014. Accessed September 4, 2014. http://www.opednews.com/articles/1/Repeal-the-Second-Amendmen-by-Allan-Goldstein-Constitutional-Amendments_Guns_Murder_NRA-140701-557.html
168 "Stop the insanity: Ban guns." *Tallahassee Democrat,* November 23, 2014.
169 "I was wrong about the Second Amendment: Why my view of guns totally changed." by Philip Gulley, November 13, 2014. Salon.com Accessed November 13, 2014.
170 "Repeal the Stupid Second Amendment." *Common Dreams,* December 26, 2014.
171 Henry, Bob. "Let's rethink Second Amendment 'rights.'" *Desert Sun,* February 13, 2015.
172 Thrasher, Jamar. "A modest proposal—how about we ban all civilian gun ownership?" *PennLive,* March 23, 2015.
173 "Gunned Down: The Power of the NRA" PBS Frontline, January 6, 2015.
174 Carlson, Andrew. *The Antiquated Right: An Argument for Repeal of the Second Amendment.* New York: Peter Lang Publishing, 2002.
175 Bowen, Catherine Drinker. *Miracle at Philadelphia.* Boston: Back Bay Books, 1966.
176 Maier, Pauline. *Ratification: The People Debate the Constitution 1787-1788.* New York: Simon & Schuster, 2010.
177 Palmer, Kris E., ed. *Constitutional Amendments, 1789 to the Present.* Detroit, MI: Gale Group, 2000.
178 Smith-Rosenberg, Carroll. *This Violent Empire: The Birth of an American National Identity.* Chapel Hill, NC: University of North Carolina Press, 2010.
179 *District of Columbia v. Heller,* 554 U.S. 570 (2008).
180 *U.S. v. Miller,* 307 U.S. 174 (1939).
181 *McDonald v. Chicago,* 561 U.S. 3025 (2010).
182 *Lujan v. Defenders of Wildlife,* 504 U.S. 555 (1992).
183 *U.S. v. Richardson,* 418 U.S. 166 (1974).
184 *Moore and Shepard v. Illinois,* 7th Cir. Ct. of Appeals (December 2012).
185 *NOW v. Idaho,* 459 U.S. 809 (1982).
186 *Coleman v. Miller,* 307 U.S. 433 (1939).
187 Pollock v. Farmers' Loan and Trust Company, 157 US 429 (1895).
188 16th Amendment to the U.S. Constitution. "The Congress shall have power to lay and collect taxes on incomes, from whatever source derived, without apportionment among the several States, and without regard to any census or enumeration."
189 Jenkins, William. "Concealed Carry in Illinois: A New Look at an Old Question." Created for the Illinois Firearm Public Awareness Task Force, 2012.
190 Amar, Akhil Reed. *America's Constitution, A Biography.* New York: Random House, 2005.

191 *The Constitutions of the Several Independent States of America.* Published by order of Congress, MDCCLXXXII.

192 Nelson, Eric. *The Hebrew Republic: Jewish Sources and the Transformation of European Political Thought.* Cambridge: Harvard University Press, 2010.

193 Wills, Garry. "To Keep and Bear Arms." *New York Review of Books,* September 21, 1995.

194 *D.C. v. Heller,* 554 U.S. 570 (2008).

195 Horne, Gerald. *The Counter-Revolution of 1776: Salve Resistance and the Origins of the United States of America.* New York: New York University Press, 2014.

196 Winkler, Adam. *Gun Fight: The Battle Over the Right to Bear Arms in America.* New York: W.W. Norton, 2011.

197 Bogus, Carl T. "The Hidden History of the Second Amendment." *University of California at Davis Law Review* 31 (1998).

198 Horne, Gerald. *The Counter-Revolution of 1776: Salve Resistance and the Origins of the United States of America.* New York: New York University Press, 2014.

199 Waldstreicher, David. *Slavery's Constitution: From Revolution to Ratification.* New York: Hill and Wang, 2009.

200 Hartmann, Thom. "The Second Amendment was Ratified to Preserve Slavery." *Truthout,* January 15, 2013.

201 DeConde, Alexander. *Gun Violence in America: The Struggle for Control.* Boston: Northeastern University Press, 2001.

202 Saunt, Claudio. *West of the Revolution: An Uncommon History of 1776.* New York: W.W. Norton & Co., 2014.

203 Barr, Daniel P. *A Colony Sprung from Hell: Pittsburgh and the Struggle for Authority on the Western Pennsylvania Frontier, 1744-1794.* Kent, Ohio: Kent State University Press, 2014.

204 Constitution, Article I, Section 8.

205 Carr, J. Revell. *Seeds of Discontent: The Deep Roots of the American Revolution 1650-1750.* New York: Walker & Company, 2008.

206 Holton, Woody. *Unruly Americans and the Origins of the Constitution.* New York: Hill and Wang, 2007.

207 Barr, Daniel P. *A Colony Sprung from Hell: Pittsburgh and the Struggle for Authority on the Western Pennsylvania Frontier, 1744-1794.* Kent, Ohio: Kent State University Press, 2014.

208 Wills, Garry. "To Keep and Bear Arms." *New York Review of Books,* September 21, 1995.

209 Resolution of Congress, September 29, 1789.

210 Bowen, Catherine Drinker. *Miracle at Philadelphia.* Boston: Back Bay Books, 1966.

211 *U.S. v. Timothy Joe Emerson,* 46 F.Supp.2d 598 (1999).
Gales and Seaton's History, Amendments to the Constitution, June to September 1789, Library of Congress.
http://www.loc.gov/rr/program/bib/ourdocs/billofrights.html

212 Bowling, Kenneth R. "A Tub to the Whale: The Founding Fathers and Adoption of the Federal Bill of Rights." *Journal of the Republic,* 8, Fall, 1988. p. 223-251.

213 *The Constitutions of the Several Independent States of America.* Published by order of Congress, MDCCLXXXII.

214 Dumbauld, Edward. *The Bill of Rights and What It Means Today.* Westport, CT: Greenwood Press, 1957.

215 Bowling, Kenneth R. "A Tub to the Whale: The Founding Fathers and Adoption of the Federal Bill of Rights." *Journal of the Republic,* 8, Fall, 1988. p. 223-251.

216 Maier, Pauline. *Ratification: The People Debate the Constitution 1787-1788.* New York: Simon & Schuster, 2010. p. 446.

217 Cogan, Neil H. *The Complete Bill of Rights.* New York: Oxford University Press, 1997. p. 169-204.
218 Posner, Richard A. "In Defense of Looseness." *The New Republic,* August 27, 2008.
219 Lepore, Jill. "Battleground America – One Nation, Under the Gun." *The New Yorker,* April 23, 2012.
220 *Schenck v. U.S.,* 249 U.S. 47 (1919).
221 Greene, Bob. "To Be Suddenly Free From the Fear." *Chicago Tribune,* September 27, 1993.
222 "Text: President Bush Addresses the Nation." *The Washington Post,* September 20, 2001. http://www.washingtonpost.com/wp-srv/nation/specials/attacked/transcripts/bushaddress_092001.html
223 Burns, Ken and Novick, Lynn. *Prohibition.* PBS, 2011.
224 Rostker, Bernard T. et al. "Evaluation of the New York City Police Department Firearm Training and Firearm-Discharge Review Process." *RAND Center on Quality Policing,* 2008.
225 Charter of the United Nations, Chapter VII, Article 51.
226 *Wesberry v. Sanders,* 376 U.S. 1 (1964).
Reynolds v. Sims, 377 U.S. 533 (1964).
227 *De Jonge v. Oregon,* 299 U.S. 353 (1937).
228 *Chicago, B & Q Railroad v. City of Chicago,* 166 U.S. 226 (1897).
229 Kimmel, Michael. *Angry White Men: American Masculinity at the End of an Era.* New York: Nation Books, 2013.
230 Breen, T.H. *American Insurgents, American Patriots.* New York: Hill and Wang, 2010.
231 Pincus, Steve. *1688: The First Modern Revolution.* New Haven, CT: Yale University Press, 2009.
232 Pinker, Steven. *The Better Angels of our Nature: Why Violence Has Declined.* New York: Viking Penguin, 2011.
233 Touze, Adam. *The Wages of Destruction: The Making and Breaking of the Nazi Economy.* New York: Penguin, 2006.
234 Temes, Peter S. *The Just War.* Chicago: Ivan R. Dee, 2003.
235 Short, Philip. *Mao: A life.* New York: Henry Holt and Company, 1999.
236 Gandhi, M.K. *Non-Violent Resistance.* New York: Schocken Books, 1951.
237 Josephus, Flavius. *The Wars of the Jews,* Book II.
238 Nagler, Michael N. *Is There No Other Way? The Search for a Non-Violent Future.* Berkeley, CA: Berkeley Hill Books, 2001.
239 Ackerman, Peter and Duvall, Jack. *A Force More Powerful.* New York: PALGRAVE, 2000.
240 "Why Won't We Talk about Violence and Masculinity in America?" *Ms Magazine,* December 17, 2012.
241 Gray, Emma. "Bushmaster Rifle Ad Reminds Us to Ask More about Masculinity and Gun Violence." *Huffington Post,* December 17, 2012.
242 Bork, Robert H. *Slouching Towards Gomorrah.* New York: Regan Books, 1996.
243 *At Issue: Concealed Weapons.* Detroit, MI: Gale Publishing, 2011.
244 Winkler, Adam. *Gun Fight: The Battle Over the Right to Bear Arms in America.* New York: W.W. Norton & Co., 2011.
245 "How the NRA and its Allies Helped Spread a Radical Gun Law Nationwide." *Mother Jones,* June 7, 2012.
246 FBI Uniform Crime Reports.
247 Blaine, Charley and Sauter, Michael B. "The Most Dangerous States in America." *24/7 Wall Street,* October 4, 2013.
248 Wilson, Ward. "5 Myths about Nuclear Weapons." *Publishers Weekly,* January 18, 2013. Accessed December 19, 2013. http://www.publishersweekly.com/pw/by-topic/industry-news/tip-sheet/article/55552-5-myths-about-nuclear-weapons.html

249 Gilbert, G.M. *Nuremberg Diary.* New York: Farrar, Straus, 1947.

250 "40 Armed Gun Advocates Intimidate Mothers Against Gun Violence in a Restaurant Parking Lot." *Think Progress,* November 12, 2013.

251 Putnam, Robert D. *Bowling Alone: The Collapse and Revival of American Community.* New York: Simon & Schuster, 2000.

252 Feldman, Richard. *Ricochet: Confessions of a Gun Lobbyist.* Hoboken, NJ: John Wiley & Sons, 2008.

253 Friess, Steve. "How the NRA Built a Massive Secret Database of Gun Owners." *BuzzFeed,* August 20, 2013.

254 Gerney, Arkadi and Parsons, Chelsea. "License to Kill: How Lax Concealed Carry Laws Can Combine with Stand Your Ground Laws to Produce Deadly Results." *Center for American Progress,* September 2013.

255 Vedantam, Shankar and Schultz, David. "'Stand Your Ground' Linked to Increase in Homicides." *National Public Radio,* January 2, 2012.

256 "Standing your ground? Black woman shot in head seeking help in white neighborhood." *Salon,* November 6, 2013.

257 "How the NRA and its Allies Helped Spread a Radical Gun Law Nationwide." *Mother Jones,* June 7, 2012.

258 "Obama to Thousands of Young Climate Activists: Push Me." *The Nation,* April 18, 2011.

259 "Hold Him to his Progressive Pledges—Make Obama Do It." *Counterpunch,* November 14, 2012.

260 "Clinton Signs Brady Bill, Urges More Gun Controls." *Los Angeles Times,* December 1, 1993.

261 Naylor, Brian. "Key Player In '94 Assault Weapons Ban: 'It's Going to Be Much More Difficult' Now." *National Public Radio,* January 18, 2013. Accessed April 4, 2015. http://www.npr.org/blogs/itsallpolitics/2013/01/29/169551103/banning-assault-weapons-now-much-more-difficult-than-94-aides-say

262 "President Clinton Announces New Crime Bill Grants to Put Police Officers on the Beat." *U.S. Department of Justice News Release,* October 12, 1994.

263 Nagler, Michael N. *Is There No Other Way? The Search for a Non-Violent Future.* Berkeley, CA: Berkeley Hill Books, 2001.

264 "Opinions Collide at Gun Control Forum." *Northbrook Patch,* January 21, 2013.

265 Lee, Esther Yu-Hsi. "40 Armed Gun Advocates Intimidate Mothers Against Gun Violence in a Restaurant Parking Lot." *Think Progress,* November 10, 2013. Accessed December 19, 2013. http://thinkprogress.org/justice/2013/11/10/2921121/dallas-gun-advocates-protest-restaurant-gun-control-advocates/

266 Executive Director's Message, *Illinois State Rifle Association Thursday Bulletin,* February 6, 2014. http://campaign.r20.constantcontact.com/render?llr=86exi4bab&v=001C8QXJYUMj5dYclZmxTgN-JR0-sL7NsPIZ2yXDo6q7QB_PvFSWD10yPDCUer-r4b8Y3HWAIH1FLtton_NCkIjGo2ZQQFzeTUSTMib0wj7JHCwJXIDl7KdedZNNjxny1O_lcdAQAABANbEMY0TMLZyqXdfbxb02GdzDnTEPqzksSxf4p_ux4Ni7ZdKXX0MQyI__kdk9SVu6j_FLQatmOMLktXKcXq3hAT5QAtOcmvM8VyC6BtQe7KceNhx8BFOo_-b. Accessed February 8, 2014

267 "Iowa grants permits for blind residents to carry guns in public." *Des Moines Register,* September 8, 2013.

268 "Firearms and Ammunition Industry Economic Impact Report 2012." *National Shooting Sports Foundation.*

269 Jeffreys-Jones, Rhodri. *The CIA and American Democracy.* New Haven, CT: Yale University Press, 1989.

270 United Nations Office for Disarmament Affairs. www.UN.org
271 Sánchez, Óscar Arias. "Don't Arm Thy Neighbor." *New York Times,* October 23, 2013.
272 Zeskind, Leonard. "A Nation Dispossessed: The Tea Party Movement and Race." *Critical Sociology,* 38 (2011). p. 495.
273 Flatow, Nicole. "Why Cops Pull The Trigger." *Think Progress,* December 23, 2013.
274 "Former Police Chief: Repeal the Second Amendment." *The Blaze,* December 18, 2012.
275 "Repeal the Second Amendment – We the People Petition http://wh.gov/Rord." *Ground Report.* http://groundreport.com/repeal-the-second-amendment-we-the-people-petition-httpwh-govrord/
276 Okrent, Daniel. *Last Call: The Rise and Fall of Prohibition.* New York: Scribner, 2010.
277 "The Telling Tale of the Twenty-Seventh Amendment: A Sleeping Amendment Concerning Congressional Compensation Is Later Revived." 2002. Findlaw.com
278 "Men, Married, Southerners Most Likely to be Gun Owners." *Gallup,* February 1, 2013.
279 Woodard, Colin. "Up In Arms." *Tufts University Alumni Magazine,* 2013.
280 "More Older Texans are Packing Heat." *Star-Telegram,* September 16, 2013.
281 "General Social Survey Final Report: Trends in Gun Ownership in the United States 1972-2014." *NORC at the University of Chicago,* March 2015.
282 Federalist 40 & 78 (1788).
283 "Chicago Politics in the Grand Style of 'Paddy' Bauler," *Chicago Tribune,* September 11, 1988.

45810798R00141

Made in the USA
Lexington, KY
11 October 2015